Date Due

DEMOCRATIZING MEXICO

DEMOCRATIZING MEXICO

*Public Opinion
and Electoral Choices*

JORGE I. DOMÍNGUEZ
JAMES A. McCANN

THE JOHNS HOPKINS UNIVERSITY PRESS
BALTIMORE AND LONDON

Written under the auspices of the Center for International Affairs, Harvard University.

The Johns Hopkins University Press
2715 North Charles Street
Baltimore, Maryland 21218-4319
The Johns Hopkins Press Ltd., London

Library of Congress Cataloging-in-Publication Data will be found
at the end of this book.
A catalog record for this book is available from the British Library.

ISBN 0-8018-5146-7

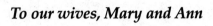

To our wives, Mary and Ann

CONTENTS

FIGURES

TABLES

PREFACE

"The commitment to democracy, understood in terms of its liberal procedures and its social content, is the essence of the doctrinal continuity and the efficacy of action of the Mexican political system."[1] These words of Carlos Salinas de Gortari were rushed to press on October 8, 1987, just as Mexicans were learning that he had been chosen as the long-ruling Institutional Revolutionary Party's candidate for president in the July 1988 elections. Though surely a piece of hyperbole, Salinas's statement poses issues that are indeed central for Mexico and for its people.

Is there a commitment to democracy in Mexico? Are Mexicans democrats? Are democracy's liberal procedures—above all, free and fair elections—part of the essence of Mexican politics? What is the significance of the social and economic content of issues and attitudes for the political behavior of Mexicans? Are Mexicans ideologues? What are the factors that help to explain how and why Mexicans vote? How do the answers to these questions shed light on Mexico's 1994 presidential election? These are the subjects of this book.

In our research and writing we have incurred many debts. We thank Richard W. Burkholder, vice president, the Gallup Organization, and Ian M. Reider, president, IMOP/Gallup México, for allowing us to use three of their polls. We also thank Austin Hoyt, WGBH-TV, Boston, for making available to us the transcripts of hours of interviews with Mexican public figures. Mary Klette, director for elections and polling of NBC News, and Mexico's Televisión Azteca made available to us the results of the 1994 nationwide election exit poll. Domínguez is grateful for the longstanding support of Harvard University's Center for International Affairs and government department; his field research in Mexico was made possible by two Fulbright Distinguished Lecturer grants in 1983 and 1988, and by the hospitality of the Centro de Estudios Internacionales, El Colegio de México, directed respectively by Blanca Torres and Soledad Loaeza. The writing of the first full draft was completed while Domínguez served as visiting senior fellow at the Inter-American Dialogue, thanks to Dialogue president Peter Hakim's generosity. McCann is grateful to Purdue University's political science department for research support and, especially, for an assigned research leave during the spring of 1994.

We have published a very preliminary study of Mexico's 1988 presidential election; some of that material also appears in chapter 4. See "Whither the PRI? Explaining Voter Defection in the 1988 Mexican Presidential Election," *Electoral Studies* 11:2 (1992): 207–22. A preliminary version of some of the arguments and part of the evidence for chapters 4 and 5 has been published as "Shaping Mexico's Electoral Arena: The Construction of Partisan Cleavages in the 1988 and 1991 National Elections," *American Political Science Review* 89, no. 1 (1995): 1–15; we are grateful to Jeffry Frieden, G. Bingham Powell, Jennifer Widner, and Ashutosh Varshney for their comments on earlier drafts of this article, which have also benefited the writing of chapters 4 and 5 (we are, of course, solely responsible for all errors).

ABBREVIATIONS

IFE	Federal Elections Institute
NAFTA	North American Free Trade Agreement
PAN	National Action Party
PARM	Authentic Party of the Mexican Revolution
PCM	Mexican Communist Party
PDM	Mexican Democratic Party
PEM	Mexican Ecologist Party
PEMEX	Mexican Petroleum Company
PFCRN	Frente Cardenista National Renovation Party
PMS	Mexican Socialist Party
PNR	National Revolutionary Party
PPS	People's Socialist Party
PRD	Party of the Democratic Revolution
PRI	Institutional Revolutionary Party
PRM	Party of the Mexican Revolution
PRONASOL	National Solidarity Program
PRT	Revolutionary Workers' Party
PST	Socialist Workers' Party
PSUM	Mexican Unified Socialist Party
PT	Workers' Party
PVEM	Mexican Green Ecologist Party
TELEVISA	largest private television network

DEMOCRATIZING MEXICO

1 ✛ CHALLENGES TO MEXICO'S DEMOCRATIZATION

The young woman stood up to speak.[1] "I'm really nervous," she blurted out. Seated at her left was Carlos Salinas de Gortari, the presidential candidate of Mexico's long-governing Institutional Revolutionary Party (PRI). The 1988 national elections were only a month away. In his campaign Salinas had barnstormed the country and had come even to this very poor neighborhood, called El Arbolito, on the outskirts of the town of Pachuca in the rural state of Hidalgo, to mobilize support in this closely contested election. The crowd was happy and enthusiastic.

Dressed in a simple skirt and blouse, the woman spoke of the town's joy and pride that Salinas was visiting El Arbolito. She focused on one of the community's key problems. They had very little drinking water, she said, adding that they could go for several days without any drinking water at all: "And so, my neighbors and I turn to you, because we think you are like a god. And, like god, we want you to give us drinking water."

Carlos Salinas de Gortari is a cartoonist's dream come true. Short, thin, and with big ears, in 1988 he sported a large mustache and was already mostly bald. After listening to various speeches at the rally at El Arbolito, Salinas rose to respond, bringing his unimposing frame to the podium. He referred to the requests that he had heard, working his way rhetorically to address the woman's plea for water. He paused for effect and then asserted, "El Arbolito demands water. El Arbolito shall have water." Like the pre-Columbian Tláloc, Salinas had become the god of rain.

In a subsequent interview Salinas was asked about his impersonation of Tláloc.[2] He laughed, noting that the interviewer had forgotten that he, Salinas, had once been a researcher.[3] This time too, he said, he had done his homework. Before the rally at El Arbolito he had learned that a water project had already been approved for that area. "I know how much it will cost, how long it will take, how much they will have to pay. Oh yes, I know the project." Tláloc, alas, had had technical assistance.

THE "GOD PROBLEM," THE RULING PARTY, AND DEMOCRACY IN MEXICO

On the eve of the 1988 national elections, Mexico's political regime was not "democratic."[4] By *democracy* we understand a political regime where rulers are chosen in free and fair elections, held at regular intervals, in the context of guaranteed civil and political rights. Democracy requires a responsible government, that is, the accountability of the executive, administrative, and coercive arms of the state to the elected representatives, as well as universal suffrage and the nonproscription of parties. In a democracy, elections are competitive, and it is presumed that political change occurs only in accordance with rules and precedents.[5]

Mexico's political system has long been highly centralized.[6] At its apex the president has combined the godlike majesty of the office and the impressive technical resources of the national government. Common citizens believe it appropriate to petition the president to help with community and, sometimes, personal needs. During a presidential campaign the candidate himself connects myth, technical skill, and societal demands.

Presidents and prime ministers in democratic regimes typically receive deference and public esteem, but the godlike public role of the Mexican presidency has exceeded those standards. Recent Mexican presidents have exhibited quite varied personal traits, but they have all sought to emphasize the majesty of the presidency. Even the most venal have exhibited regal behavior in the performance of their official roles.[7] A central concern of this book (chapters 4 and 5) is to assess how the public views the president and the candidates for the presidency, seeking to understand how presidential gods help to ensure the continued rule of the governing party.

Ordinarily, the machinery of politics—the ruling party and the government officials charged with managing political affairs on the public payroll—mediates between state and society, between office holder and citizen. Mexico's political leaders have often governed wisely and well, but to maintain their political control they have also resorted regularly to electoral fraud and abuse of power. In this book we examine whether individuals choose to identify with this political machine and how the problem of electoral fraud affects electoral outcomes (chapters 4–6).

The ruling party (PRI) dates its history to 1929, when the military chieftains and regional bosses who survived the Mexican revolution created the National Revolutionary Party (PNR)[8] to put an end to two decades of often-brutal civil war. Since then the PRI and its partisan predecessors had never acknowledged the loss of a presidential election and had always controlled both houses of Congress. Until 1982 the official party had always filled no fewer than 80 percent of the seats in the Chamber of Deputies; going into the 1988 national elections, the PRI still filled 72 percent of the seats in this chamber. Until 1988 the PRI had controlled all the seats in the Senate. Until 1989 no opposition party member had ever been acknowledged as having won a gubernatorial election. This combination of factors made democracy in Mexico problematic at best.[9]

The July 1988 national elections were a political earthquake, given that history. The main actors were the three principal presidential candidates. Carlos Salinas de Gortari was the PRI's candidate; he claimed barely over one-half of the votes cast. The oldest established opposition party was the National Action Party (PAN); usually positioned to the right of the PRI, favoring less government intervention in the economy than the PRI typically had over the years, for the 1988 elections it nominated Manuel Clouthier, an entrepreneur. By the official count, Clouthier got 17 percent of the votes cast. In the months before the election a new political force emerged to the left of the PRI; its leaders objected strongly to the measures adopted by President Miguel de la Madrid (1982–88), with PRI support, to reduce the government's role in the economy and to free up market forces. The left was led by Cuauhtémoc Cárdenas, a former PRI-backed governor of the state of Michoacán, and son of one of Mexico's most revered presidents, Lázaro Cárdenas (1934–40).

The official count in the 1988 elections gave Cárdenas 32 percent of the votes cast, but he and his supporters claimed that Salinas and the PRI had stolen the election; Cárdenas and his supporters staged massive public protests in the weeks that followed the election. The PAN and Clouthier too sharply contested the results of an election they also perceived to have been fraudulent. Although Salinas was installed as president, the combined opposition parties commanded 48 percent of the seats in the Chamber of Deputies, the highest proportion ever in Mexican history.

In the 1991 nationwide congressional elections, these three blocs remained. The Cardenistas divided, however. Cárdenas continued to lead the party he had founded after the 1988 elections, called the Party of the Democratic Revolution (PRD), but the other parties that had supported him in 1988 contested the 1991 elections on their own. (Chapters 4 and 5 focus directly on the 1988 and 1991 elections, respectively.) Contrary to the expectations of many that the PRI would continue to weaken, the ruling party rebounded in the 1991 elections, winning 64 percent of the seats in the Chamber of Deputies; Carlos Salinas had become an immensely popular president who seemed to have single-handedly turned Mexico's economic fortunes around. The era of one-party government had seemed to end in 1988 only to be reborn, phoenixlike, in 1991.

In the 1994 election the PRI could claim, for the first time, that it had won a contested presidential election in a "free enough" election, despite many remaining inequities in the electoral process. Heading the PRI ticket, Ernesto Zedillo was elected president of Mexico, with just under 49 percent of the votes officially tabulated. The PAN's candidate, Diego Fernández de Cevallos, came in second, with nearly 26 percent of the official count. Cuauhtémoc Cárdenas received almost 17 percent of the formal results. Six smaller parties received about 6 percent of the votes, and not quite 3 percent of the ballots were annulled. Thanks mainly to constitutional and electoral law changes mandating a modified form of proportional representation in allocating seats in Congress, the combined opposition captured 40 percent of the seats in the Chamber of Deputies and one-quarter of the Senate seats. The era when one party could lord it over the nation was certainly over, but the PRI's rebirth was consolidated for several more years. Mexico had taken important strides along the path of democratization, but a full transition to democracy was not yet complete.

THE SCHOLARSHIP ON DEMOCRATIZATION AND PUBLIC OPINION

In the definition of democracy given earlier, two factors stand out: contestation and participation.[10] Curiously, the scholarly literature on democratization rarely discusses the likelihood of the spread of political participation and assumes that the emergence of contestation does not have to be explained. For example, Samuel Huntington's magisterial study of democratization between the 1970s and the 1990s expresses no doubt that there exists contestation between government and opposition, and even within the governing coalition; moreover, his principal concern about participation is not how it emerges but whether it needs to be contained in order to consolidate democracy.[11] Similarly, in their path-breaking study of transitions from authoritarian rule in Latin America, Guillermo O'Donnell and Philippe Schmitter do not question that elites will divide to contest each other or that political participation will occur once repressive controls are loosened.[12]

Both contestation and participation must be explained, however, not just assumed. Party contestation and citizen participation in elections require some combination of political leadership and organizational skill to mobilize the voters as well as voter decisions to support specific parties. Party contestation may be weak, but an election may still be called democratic if citizens choose freely to support one party far more than they do any of the others.[13] Democratization may be delayed if insurgent opposition parties committed to regime change are unable to mobilize new blocs of voters effectively; Mexico's 1988 and 1991 elections (chapters 4 and 5) demonstrate aspects of this problem, that is, opposition politicians missed their chance to mobilize the strong opposition tendencies evident in public opinion.

Electoral contestation may be vitiated, even when it is potentially vigorous, by the behavior of opposition politicians and the effects of electoral laws.[14] A large bloc of voters may be ready to support a particular electoral option, but their votes may be "wasted" if the electoral law allocates seats in Congress according to a single-member plurality-victory electoral law—also known as "winner take all"—and if the politicians whom such a bloc would back divide into competing parties that fight for the same bloc of voters; Mexico's 1991 election (chapter 5) is a good illustration of the latter problem.

Electoral contestation, moreover, must rest on "something." For the most part there are four kinds of "something": party allegiance, issue commitments, performance assessments, and affiliation with organizations representing socioeconomic cleavages. Where voters change their allegiance from election to election, where views on policy issues and on the government's economic (and other) performance have little impact on the electorate, and where socioeconomic cleavages insufficiently divide the electorate, electoral contestation is likely to be quite weak—even if other traits of a democratic regime exist—and the consolidation of a democratic regime is likely to be impaired.[15]

To be sure, contestation in many historical settings has led to civil war and repression. In order to avoid such disasters, "the development and maintenance of democracy," Larry Diamond and Juan Linz have argued, "is greatly facilitated by values and behavioral dispositions (particularly at the elite level) of compromise, flexibility, tolerance, conciliation, moderation, and restraint."[16] Seymour Martin Lipset has emphasized a similar point, though he has anchored it in the recognition of specific citizen rights. "Democracy requires," in his view, "the acceptance by the citizenry and political elites of principles underlying freedom of speech, media, assembly, religion, of the rights of opposition parties, of the rule of law, of human rights, and the like."[17]

There is a lively scholarly debate on whether there are prerequisites for the establishment and consolidation of democracy. For example, Karl has argued that the search for preconditions for democracy is "futile"; instead, she suggests, the study of democratic transitions ought to focus on elite "strategic interactions," which "help to determine whether political democracy will emerge and survive."[18] One often mentioned prerequisite is political culture or, more specifically, democratic norms. In a related vein, Muller and Seligson have shown that interpersonal trust is unrelated to changes in a country's level of democracy; thus such attitudes could not be a major cause of democracy.[19]

We agree with the position sketched by Diamond and Linz: "Historically, the choice of democracy by political elites clearly preceded . . . the presence of democratic values among the general public or other elites." On the other hand, they also argue, "democratic culture helps to maintain" democracy. Thus the relationship between political attitudes and structures is "reciprocal."[20] This view was articulated much earlier by Gabriel Almond and Sidney Verba in their work on the civic culture in five countries (including Mexico): "It is quite clear that political culture is treated as both an independent and a dependent variable, as causing structure and as being caused by it."[21] Where the values typically found in democracies are strong and manage to spread among the people, democracy's eventual emergence and, especially, its consolidation are more likely. In chapter 2 we argue that the emergence and consolidation of democracy in Mexico are facilitated by the shift in the public's values but that such values by themselves have not caused democracy to emerge in the Mexican political system.

Just as scholars of democratization have tended to ignore the study of how contestation and participation come to be, so too, for the most part, scholars who have sought to explain the emergence of contestation and the early evolution of democratic norms and political participation have been unable to examine public opinion directly. The benchmark comparative study of the emergence of contestation in Western Europe by Seymour Martin Lipset and Stein Rokkan, for example, focused on time periods before the development of public-opinion polling.[22] The comprehensive study of the conditions for the emergence and consolidation of democracy in Latin America by Diamond and Linz was similarly unable to make much use of research on public opinion, and it tended to focus on long-term factors rather than on moments of transition, as we do in this book.[23] Most of the research on political participation based on public-opinion polling, moreover, has occurred in countries with consolidated democracies in Western Europe and North America, or it has focused on topics other than democratizing transitions.[24] For the most part the same is true with regard to research on political participation in Latin American countries.[25]

We seek, therefore, to wed two scholarly partners: the scholarship on democratization, and the scholarship on the emergence of contestation and democratic norms and the spread of political participation. We do so in Mexico at a moment of undoubted transition, namely, the 1988 and 1991 national elections (the 1994 election is addressed in a long Epilogue), with reference to preceding attitudinal evidence for comparative purposes. We ask whether the bases for democracy have emerged in Mexican public opinion, that is, whether there are strong and stable bases for contestation and participation. We are conscious that this research does not exhaust the discussion of democratization in Mexico—the role of the state, the parties, and the behavior of elites matter greatly as well—but we believe equally firmly that no discussion of democracy can ignore the beliefs and behavior of the nation's citizens. Our principal method, though not our only one, is the analysis of public-opinion surveys conducted in Mexico from the 1950s to the 1990s. The questions we have used are listed in appendix 1; a more technical description of the surveys and a discussion of the political contexts in which they were taken are presented in appendix 2.

THE ARGUMENT OF THIS BOOK

For democratization to occur, citizens must participate in elections, and they must divide in their assessments about those who should rule them and about what should be the broad direction of governance. These criteria do not cover all that matters for democratization, but the process cannot occur in the absence of such bases in public opinion. This is a study about public opinion in Mexico at a time of political transition in the late 1980s and early 1990s, when the longstanding monopoly of the ruling party cracked for the first time ever, even though the party retained its control of the government.

Our starting point is to ask whether Mexicans are democrats. A possible explanation for Mexico's long experience with authoritarian rule is that its citizens may demand it. In England in the seventeenth century, Thomas Hobbes argued in *The Leviathan* that citizens in the midst of prolonged and brutal war, and severe uncertainty about the prospects for political stability, should choose order, even authoritarian order, above all else. Heirs to one of the world's most violent revolutions, Mexicans too might prefer authoritarian order.

We cannot assess, of course, whether a *Leviathan*-like "social contract" might have appealed to war-ravaged Mexico in the late 1920s, but as recently as the late 1950s there was some good evidence of mass public support for aspects of authoritarianism in Mexican politics. Between the late 1950s and the late 1980s, however, democratic politics became possible, as we show in chapter 2.

Despite some residual evidence of authoritarian beliefs, for the most part, by the late 1980s Mexicans were much more likely to be interested in politics, to be attentive to political campaigns, and to discuss politics freely. The Mexican electorate, moreover, was just as politicized as were the electorates of many democracies in Europe and the United States. As time passed, Mexicans became less likely to prefer strong leaders to reliance on the rule of law; by the 1980s they did not favor the participation of undemocratic institutions in political life, while they strongly favored the internal democratization of the ruling party's presidential nomination practices.

Mexico had also developed a national electorate. In their attitudes toward the values that serve as the cornerstone for the construction of democracy, Mexicans showed a narrowing over time in serious differences in terms of education and gender. Mexicans of all demographic types were ready for a more democratic polity.

The persistence of authoritarian practices in Mexican politics, therefore, is best explained in terms of existing state institutions, policies, and leadership choices, not in terms of the preferences of Mexican citizens. The prospects for democratic participation were good. By the late 1980s Mexicans were ready to give Thomas Hobbes a decent burial.

What, then, were the foundations for democratic contestation in Mexican public opinion? The comments above suggest that differences in attachments to democratic values do not serve as a basis for contestation. Mexican public opinion does not divide between a party of democrats and a party of tyrant-lovers. There are democrats and, alas, authoritarians across the Mexican political party spectrum. To put it more bluntly, yes, there are democrats in the PRI, and there are opposition party supporters who hold authoritarian values. That is why these variables do not explain voter preferences.

An alternative basis for contestation in the 1980s may have been the diverse views that Mexicans held on economic matters. We explore this question in chapter 3. We seek to know whether Mexicans hold coherent views on economic matters and whether these views are consistent across different issues. Do Mexicans who favor freer trade also favor foreign investment, for example? Do Mexicans of different social classes hold different views on economic matters? In short, we analyze the extent of issue polarization and of issue consistency in order to understand the possible foundations for contestation.

By the late 1980s, we argue, Mexicans were polarized in their assessment of various economic policies adopted by their government in response to the severe economic crisis that had afflicted them for most of that decade. Mexicans also showed consistency across issues. And yet while the level of issue polarization was high, the level of issue consistency was not. Attitudes toward some issues, such as the privatization of state enterprises, were not well related to other issues that are ordinarily considered to be part of the same economic package (e.g., freer trade, foreign investment).

Even among economic issues that were related to each other in the public's view, the strength of association was modest.

Nor was there analytical consistency as various kinds of people approached the issues. Education, social class, and level of political interest, for example, were not consistent explanations from one issue to the next. The level of economic-issue consistency among Mexicans on the eve of the 1988 presidential election remained below the comparable level for the United States in the 1950s—a time in U.S. history not marked by intense ideological combat in the mass public.

During Mexico's 1988 presidential election, anyone who listened to the presidential candidates or who followed the campaign in the mass media surely must have felt that the election was intensely ideological. And yet Mexican public attitudes provided a weak basis for such a campaign. Mexicans were indeed divided over the issues but not "cumulatively" so; that is, their views on one issue did not control their views toward other, even apparently closely related issues.

Just as the persistence of authoritarian practices in Mexico should not be blamed on its citizens, so too the ideological thunderstorm of the 1988 election should not be blamed on public beliefs. Politicians chose to frame their message ideologically even though the Mexican public did not demand consistent, cross-issue ideologies.

The findings in chapter 3 set the stage for the related findings in chapters 4 (on the 1988 elections) and 5 (on the 1991 elections), namely, that views on policy issues and on retrospective and prospective assessments of the nation's and one's own economic conditions are only marginally related to voter intentions. That is, attitudes toward economic matters were not the principal source of political contestation in the mass public. Supporters of freer trade, for example, could be found backing different presidential candidates; many of those who held pessimistic expectations about Mexico's economic future were found to be still supporting the governing party. For the most part issue cleavages did not markedly overlap with candidate and party coalitions. As we explain in chapters 4 and 5, the weak explanatory utility of attitudes on policy issues is not surprising in comparative perspective, but the weak explanatory utility of retrospective and prospective economic assessments is unusual. In chapters 4 and 5, therefore, we refine the analysis.

We show that general expectations about the economy's future performance matter little in explaining voter intentions, but that general expectations about the economy's future performance if a party other than the PRI were to win power is one of the strongest explanations for voter attitudes.

It is the explicit combination of prospective partisan with prospective economic expectations that provides a powerful explanation for the views of voters.

In chapters 4 and 5 we also turn to a consideration of the possible foundation for political contestation in socioeconomic cleavages. We find that these were neither very important nor very consistent explanations for the party preferences of voters. Two items do seem fairly important. Religious secularism helps to explain support for Cárdenas and the PRD, though religious fidelity is unrelated to support for the PAN, despite the common assumption that the PAN was a confessional party. Second, in the 1991 elections territorial bases for cleavage became more evident, with the PAN stronger in the north, the PRD in Mexico City, and the other small opposition parties also in Mexico City and in southern Mexico.

Somewhat to our surprise, therefore, many of the "somethings" that are expected to provide the bases in mass public opinion for political contestation in democratic politics did not provide such a basis in Mexico. Attitudes toward democratic values, toward policies, toward general assessments of past or future economic performance, and, for the most part, social attachments did not explain well or consistently why voters supported one party versus another in election after election.

Instead, we argue also in chapters 4 and 5, partisan, institutional, and candidate assessments provide the stronger bases for the divisions in Mexican mass public opinion, and therefore for political contestation. PRI voters were likely to be loyal to the PRI in election after election, just as supporters of opposition parties were likely to be loyal to the opposition across elections. But partisan expectations were also important. In both 1988 and 1991, voters who believed that the PRI would get stronger and voters who believed that the economy would suffer if a party other than the PRI were to gain power were much more likely to support the PRI and much less likely to support the opposition. Also in both elections, the greater the approval for the incumbent president, the greater the likelihood of voting PRI. A core political division existed between the PRI and the opposition parties. That was the principal basis for political contestation as Mexico lurched toward democratic politics.

It follows from the preceding analysis that we believe that Mexico did not experience an electoral realignment in the late 1980s and early 1990s, nor do we believe that Mexican voters shunned the parties on election day (e.g., no dealignment).[26]

Such a lack of realignment in turn calls attention to important though somewhat different organizational explanations for the outcomes of the

1988 and 1991 elections. In 1988 the principal effect of the entry of Cardenismo was to reshuffle the voters among existing parties, not to mobilize the previously unmobilized or to shift the underlying partisan allegiance of demographic or economic groups or sectors. The new opposition failed organizationally to activate a new portion of the electorate, while the long-existing PAN opposition failed to develop a refurbished organizational capacity.

In 1991 the main organizational story was the fragmentation of Cárdenas's 1988 coalition into various parties that fought each other and that lost electoral support. The divisions of the opposition, and especially the divisions on the left, virtually assured PRI victories even among the voters who were most ready to respond to opposition appeals. For the most part these divisions between the parties of the left were not substantive; most voters for the small left-wing parties made their decision quite late in the campaign. Opinion alignments as they affected voter choice were fairly stable from 1988 to 1991. A large pool of potential left-wing voters awaited the organizational reconstruction of Cardenismo.

The left's 1991 election campaign was based on expectations that lower-class Mexicans did not share the economic optimism of wealthier Mexicans and that a large pool of voters agreed with the left on the issues to oppose the Salinas government. Both assumptions were inaccurate; the electoral campaign failed as a result.

After decades of single-party rule and well-founded suspicions about the conduct of their rulers and the fairness of their elections, Mexican citizens approached national elections by focusing on the fate of the party that had long governed them. First and foremost they asked themselves, Am I for or against the "party of the state" and its leader? Many voters asked themselves no other questions; they backed the PRI. A significant proportion of Mexican voters were ready to change the governing party, however; for them, a much more ideologically competitive election lurked beneath the partisan, institutional, and candidate traits that for the most part shaped the voting decision.

We argue, consequently, that the attitudes of Mexican voters are best understood in terms of a two-step model. Voters decide, first, on their view of the ruling party. For those open to the possibility of being governed by another party, but only for them, there is a second step. They support an opposition party, and they choose among such parties motivated by policy preferences and social cleavage attachments (though more in 1988 than in 1991). There were important differences among the opposition parties. The prospects for democratic contestation were quite good among those voters who made it past the first voting decision (Keep or change the governing party?) to vote for the opposition and, in that second step, to express their political views more fully responding to ideology and social attachments.

As we modeled the full complexity of Mexican voting behavior, we were struck by the importance of a large minority of sophisticated strategic voters in the opposition. These anti-PRI Mexicans wanted to defeat the governing party so much that they suppressed their ideological preferences in order to back the party most likely to beat the PRI, even when such a party espoused views with which they disagreed. Such strategic opposition voters were in evidence both in 1988 and in 1991. In 1988, for example, many voters with right-wing predispositions voted for Cárdenas; in 1991 many voters with left-wing predispositions voted for PAN candidates.

Scholars of Mexican elections must wonder, of course, about the distortions that fraud may introduce into the election results and even about the fear some ordinary citizens may have about answering survey questions. We deal with the latter question in some detail in our assessment of the surveys on which this book rests (appendix 2); thanks to the care of the polltakers and the safeguards introduced into the survey, we believe that the evidence is valid and reliable. In chapter 6 we assess the substantive significance of electoral fraud.

Mexican elections have long been marred by fraud; so too were the elections we study here. By the late 1980s the novelty was the existence of a much stronger and better-organized civic and partisan opposition to protest the electoral fraud. Our data are not suited to document the actual incidence of fraud, but our findings shed light on the effect of fraud in Mexican public opinion in anticipation of the 1991 elections.

For the most part, in 1991 Mexicans worried more about economic and social issues than about corruption and electoral fraud.[27] Nonetheless, the perception of electoral fraud was widespread, and it lowered the likelihood of voting turnout. Fraud-fearing nonvoters were disproportionately likely to support the opposition, thereby distorting the election results. Opposition campaigns against fraud, however justified, backfired because one result was that many opposition backers believed the allegations that there would be fraud; they were more likely to stay away from the voting booth on election day.

The "geography" of fraud turned out to be especially important. The PRI was most likely to commit fraud against the opposition where the opposition was strongest, typically in urban areas. Because opposition and other election observers were concentrated in such areas, this pattern of fraud backfired on the PRI because it was "seen," increasing thereby the perception that fraud was widespread in the entire election. Despite the incidence of fraud, however, we do not believe that the final outcomes of the most hotly contested gubernatorial elections in August 1991 were altered by fraud.

The Salinas presidency took various steps to address these concerns about fraud. One of its well-meaning strategies was counterproductive, however. Beginning in 1991 Salinas and PRI party president Luis Donaldo Colosio overturned several PRI electoral "victories" to accommodate opposition and public protests about election fraud; the practice of overturning election results would continue in subsequent years. Some of those PRI election victories had been real, while others had been the result of fraud. The decision to overturn state and local election results through presidential intervention rendered such elections nondecisive; after many elections, back-room bargaining and public protests were the means to determine the final outcome. As a result, Mexican politics became less stable while the credibility of elections or the nation's democratization did not advance.

By late 1993 Salinas and PRI presidential candidate Luis Donaldo Colosio—assassinated in March 1994—turned to electoral reforms that sought to increase the fairness and transparency of the process. Such electoral changes were accelerated substantially as one response to the insurgency launched in the southernmost state of Chiapas in January 1994. Colosio's successor as the PRI presidential candidate, Ernesto Zedillo, also endorsed the process of electoral reform. These reforms rendered the 1994 election much fairer than previous ones, though much unfairness persisted during the electoral process and many irregularities, mostly at the local level, still occurred on election day. In the Epilogue we assess how our earlier analysis informs the study of themes in the 1994 election; in particular we consider the impressive though still insufficient steps taken toward democratization in preparation for that election.

In this book, therefore, we seek to understand the attitudes of Mexican citizens toward politics and to shed light on voter behavior through a detailed analysis of the results of several nationwide public-opinion polls. Our study is set in the context of Mexico's profound economic crisis, which lasted from 1982 until the beginning of the 1990s; in the remainder of this chapter we provide additional information about contemporary Mexican politics in order to make this context clearer.

THE INSTITUTIONAL BASES FOR MEXICO'S AUTHORITARIAN POLITICAL REGIME

From 1934 through 1940 Mexico was governed by its most radical president of the twentieth century. During his term of office President Lázaro Cárdenas carried out an extensive and important agrarian reform and expropriated all foreign-owned petroleum firms, among other measures. He also reorganized the National Revolutionary Party (PNR) into "sectors," three of which have survived to this day (one each for labor and peasants, and a third called the "popular" sector—a catchall for various middle-class organizations). The new party was called the Party of the Mexican Revolution (PRM). In the 1940s the Mexican political system settled into less radical and more stable patterns. In 1946 the ruling party changed its name again, this time to become the Institutional Revolutionary Party, to signal its shift of focus, purpose, and methods. The authoritarian features of these institutions were observed by many scholars. In 1959 Robert Scott published *Mexican Government in Transition;* it became an instant classic in the analysis of Mexican politics. It was Scott's intention to demonstrate Mexico's gradual democratization. Consider, nonetheless, several of his conclusions:

1. "Even those citizens who have adjusted successfully to the conditions inherent in Western life do not have deeply ingrained in their consciousness . . . that solid core of shared values and respect for the other individual per se that seems so important an ingredient in the formation of a democratic syndrome."
2. "Strategically located functional interest associations such as the government bureaucrats union or certain other labor groups enjoy unusually advantageous positions in the political process."
3. "Neither the internal nominating procedures of the official party nor the elections themselves are entirely free."[28]
4. "Even today it would be hard to overstate the amount of political power the president wields . . . [who is] director of an increasingly powerful government bureaucracy that arbitrates among the reasonably well adjusted functional interest associations which submit themselves to the discipline of the emerging governmental system."[29]

Scott argued, despite his own preferences, that Mexicans were not democrats. In turn, this made it much easier for a powerful presidency to manage an increasingly competent bureaucracy,[30] to lord it over intermediary associations, which lost their autonomy, and to rig elections, which lost both their decisiveness and their legitimating effect. The PRI and its network of labor, peasant, and other organizations managed this system. (In chapter 2 we analyze whether Mexicans in the late 1980s and early 1990s were democrats, in order to ascertain whether the beliefs of citizens or the institutions sustained by the regime's elites better explain the persistence of authoritarian practices.)

The strongly presidentialist character of Mexican politics has been one of its most distinctive and enduring features; it explains the regime's most authoritarian features as well as the high stakes of presidential elections.[31] In practice, presidents have chosen their own successors as well as most state governors, members of Congress, judges, heads of state enterprises, and government officials down to midlevel bureaucrats; presidents can arbitrarily remove state governors, PRI legislators, and labor union leaders who oppose them or perform poorly on the job.[32] The constitutional prohibition of the reelection of members of Congress prevents the development of a cadre of experienced and powerful legislators who might challenge the executive branch, or at least monitor it effectively.[33] This pronounced presidentialism—reproduced as executive dominance at the state and local levels—enforces discipline and loyalty.

A key political means to extend the reach of the presidency has been the ruling party, whose distinctness from the state has at times been difficult to discern. The PRI has long nurtured this blurring of the boundaries between party and state; the colors and configuration of the national flag and those of the party logo are identical. Not until the 1994 presidential election did Mexico begin to acquire legislation and means of enforcement to curb government financing of PRI election activities (and even in 1994 such constraints were modest). Government officials have routinely used the power of their offices to support the PRI. The close connections between the government and the privately owned mass media have also given a marked advantage in media, especially television, coverage to the PRI and its candidates, even in the 1994 presidential election.[34]

Presidents de la Madrid and Salinas had to work harder than their predecessors to strengthen the PRI in order to build support for their economic programs, which at first had scant popularity, and to retain power for their governing teams during the processes of major economic and political change in the 1980s and 1990s.[35]

Since the 1930s, as noted above, the PRI's internal structure has been "sectoral"; that is, the party has been constituted through the affiliation of organizations grouped in its labor, peasant, and "popular" sectors. In this fashion the PRI has coopted and controlled the organizations that otherwise might have represented the autonomous interests of society and economy. Moreover, because of the state's central role in the economy (discussed in the next section), even business federations rarely challenge the government or the PRI; they have preferred to work informally to advance their goals.

Over the years the government and the PRI have also combined to commit electoral fraud with impunity. As Craig and Cornelius have noted, the

PRI-government agents have stuffed ballot boxes, intimidated opposition candidates, disqualified opposition poll watchers, relocated voting places at the last minute, manipulated voter registration lists, issued multiple voting credentials to PRI supporters, manipulated voting tallies, and even nullified adverse electoral outcomes.[36] (This repeated electoral fraud has also made official electoral results understandably suspect, leading us to make relatively little use of them in this book.) As noted earlier, on the eve of the 1988 national elections the PRI held every state governorship as well as every seat in the federal Senate and 72 percent of the seats in the federal Chamber of Deputies. (By law, one-quarter of the seats in the chamber were guaranteed to opposition parties, allocated through a national proportional-representation formula; opposition parties had won only 3 percent of the chamber's seats on their own in single-member districts.)

The pattern of organizational cooptation described above was also apparent in the PRI's relations with two of the three small opposition political parties represented in the Chamber of Deputies since the 1963 electoral reform law guaranteed them some seats. Beginning with the 1958 presidential elections, the People's Socialist Party (PPS) and the Authentic Party of the Mexican Revolution (PARM) routinely endorsed the PRI candidates in every presidential election (up to 1988) in exchange for patronage and some local offices. Thus even a part of the formal opposition seemed more apparent than real. In 1988 the decision of the leaders of these two parties to break their long-lasting alliance with the PRI opened the way for Cárdenas's presidential candidacy.

The 1977 electoral reform law eased the requirements for registering political parties to enable them to run candidates for office. As a result, in the 1979 congressional elections the Mexican Communist Party (PCM), the Mexican Democratic Party (PDM), and the Socialist Workers' Party (PST) also qualified for opposition proportional-representation seats in the Chamber of Deputies. Each of these parties was very small. The PDM represented Roman Catholic voters in some regions. The PST learned to behave as the PPS and the PARM typically had, namely, at times joining the PRI in political alliances in exchange for patronage; in 1988 the PST changed its name to the Frente Cardenista National Renovation Party (PFCRN) and joined with the PARM and the PPS in breaking with the PRI to support Cuauhtémoc Cárdenas for president. In the early 1980s the PCM aligned with other even smaller political parties of the left to found the Mexican Unified Socialist Party (PSUM). In time for the 1988 election the PSUM made other alliances to become the Mexican Socialist Party (PMS); it too backed Cárdenas.[37] After the 1988 election the PMS merged into the new party that Cárdenas founded, the Party of the Democratic Revolution (PRD).

In brief, through the decades only the PAN had provided a clear opposition to the PRI. Beginning in the late 1970s a legalized communist party also opposed government policies in straightforward fashion. But the existence of political parties like the PPS, the PARM, and the PST served in practice to make all opposition parties suspect as "fronts" for the PRI—ruses to make it appear that the Mexican political system was more democratic. Fraudulent elections and fraudulent opposition parties made it more difficult for Mexico to make a clean break in a transit from authoritarianism to democracy.

These manifold antidemocratic practices could only be curtailed or stopped once opposition parties—and nonpartisan organizations within civil society—became better organized and more autonomous from the PRI; this began to happen only in the second half of the 1980s. In 1988 Mexico's political regime was stunned by a political earthquake: the appearance of a powerful organized opposition to contest the presidential elections (on which chapters 4 and 5 focus much attention).

MEXICO'S POLITICAL REGIME IN PERIL

On December 1, 1988, President Miguel de la Madrid strode into Mexico's Chamber of Deputies for the last formal act of his six-year presidency, namely, to turn over power to his successor, Carlos Salinas de Gortari. As de la Madrid approached the podium, pandemonium seemed to break out.[38] The PRI members of Congress applauded and cheered. Some members of Congress from the parties of the opposition booed loudly; there were many cries of "fraud," referring to the fraud allegedly committed during the previous July 6 presidential elections to secure Salinas's election. After a few minutes most members of Congress who had supported the candidacy of Cuauhtémoc Cárdenas—former governor of Michoacán, and once a prominent PRI member—walked out of the chamber. Most members of Congress from the opposition National Action Party (PAN) stood with their backs to the podium or held up signs that said "FRAUDE." The hall became calm again, allowing de la Madrid to make his final remarks and Salinas to take the presidential oath and to make his acceptance speech.

This description is, however, only one level of "truth." A second level of truth was conveyed to the public at large through Mexican radio and television broadcasts. The cameras and microphones remained fixed firmly on the podium. Most Mexican citizens did not see or hear the protest in Congress. At most they saw a slightly nervous president waiting longer than usual for his moment to begin speaking. The Mexican mass media, private as well as state-owned, conveyed an image of unity and orderliness on a solemn occasion.[39]

A third level of truth became evident only after these events had concluded. A private agreement had been reached between Salinas representatives, led by Manuel Camacho—whom Salinas had just appointed to serve as mayor of Mexico City—and those of the opposition parties to permit but also to contain the protest.[40] Opposition members would be free to say what they wished prior to de la Madrid's arrival and could stage a brief protest evident only to those present in the chamber. The members from the left-wing parties would walk out, while the members from the PAN could stay provided that their protest was silent—and invisible on television.

Each of these levels signals aspects of Mexico's remarkable political system at a moment of crisis. Never before the 1988 elections had 48 percent of the seats in the Chamber of Deputies gone to the opposition parties (the prior high had been 28 percent of the deputies in 1985). Not since the 1940 presidential elections had the presidency itself been so sharply contested, and not since the outbreak of the Mexican revolution had a major presidential candidate refused to accept the official results.

Days after the July 6, 1988, election, Cuauhtémoc Cárdenas challenged the results at a huge mass meeting in the Zócalo, the main square in downtown Mexico City: "If the government ratifies its election results, it will be in effect a coup d'etat for the purpose of installing a usurper government."[41] The large crowd of Mexican citizens who joined Cárdenas in this civic protest howled their outrage at the election outcome.

And yet even at their hour of peril, ruling elites showed their power and their skill. They did install Salinas as president. They did control the transmission of sound and images to the Mexican people even over the privately owned television network TELEVISA. And they reached the first of many subsequent pacts to enable Salinas to govern Mexico. The political regime had been weakened, but its ruling elites still held impressive powers. As we shall see, in 1988 Mexican citizens understood the many faces of power in Mexico. Just as they sharply criticized the government's economic performance, many citizens continued to believe that those who had governed Mexico for so long were still the best suited to continue governing it. This paradox in citizen assessments of the political regime will recur throughout this book.

Mexico's political regime was in peril, to be sure, from much more than the possibility of electoral fraud in 1988. In August 1982 the world's international "debt crisis" was born in Mexico. Within a short span of time the Mexican government ran out of cash to meet its international financial obligations. It could not continue to service its international debt, and it sought a major rescheduling of its international financial obligations. The international financial community, in turn, expected Mexico to adjust economically to its new circumstances and to adopt an appropriate economic stabilization program in order to become solvent once again. Mexico did so, but with severe costs to its standard of living.

Mexico's gross domestic product per capita (in 1988 constant dollars) fell each and every year of Miguel de la Madrid's six-year presidential term, from $2,192 in 1982 to $1,920 in 1988—a cumulative drop of 12.4 percent.[42] Both the magnitude and the persistence of the drop, as we shall see, caused profound public pessimism about the prospects for economic recovery.

This economic decline hit workers hard, and workers had long been one of the key constituencies of the official party—and one of the pillars of state authority.[43] Setting an index of average annual "real" wages (i.e., adjusted for inflation) in manufacturing to equal 100 in 1980, such wages plummeted from 104.4 in 1982 to 71.3 in 1988. That is, real average manufacturing wages dropped by about one-third in this six-year period. Not surprisingly, those who were less well organized than workers in manufacturing lost out even more. The real minimum wage in Mexico City fell drastically. Setting this index also to equal 100 in 1980, real minimum wages dropped to 92.7 in 1982 and to 54.2 in 1988, a drop of 41.5 percent. All citizens were hurt by the acceleration of inflation. In the late 1970s and early 1980s Mexico's annual consumer price index (CPI) rose just below 30 percent. In 1982, inflation jumped by nearly 100 percent. The CPI decelerated to an annual rate of just below 60 percent in 1984, whereupon it accelerated again to reach a peak of nearly 160 percent in 1987.[44] These economic results deepened pessimism and fostered frustration. They are the background to the 1988 presidential election.

THE REDESIGN OF ECONOMIC POLICY

To stem Mexico's economic decline, President Miguel de la Madrid made two key economic policy decisions. One was not to declare a unilateral debt payments moratorium and instead to continue to service the international debt and to negotiate its rescheduling with Mexico's creditors. The other was to shift away from the long-reigning policies of industrialization by means of import substitution and of reliance on a heavy state involvement in the economy toward a market-oriented strategy, a reduction of the state's impact on the economy, and export promotion.

Large-scale import-substitution industrialization began in Mexico in the early 1940s. The government reshaped the economy to foster domestic manufacturing by substituting for imports. As a consequence, the government had become a leading actor in the economy. Such a strategy rendered domestic industry less efficient and less competitive internationally, however. When the price of petroleum, Mexico's principal export, dropped in the early 1980s at the same time that international debt service payments rose suddenly, the search for a more competitive and diversified export profile became urgent.

In the 1970s and early 1980s Presidents Luis Echeverría (1970–76) and José López Portillo (1976–82) turned to state enterprises as an engine for economic growth and distribution. Government-owned and operated firms spread throughout the economy; the largest was in petroleum (PEMEX), founded in 1938 with the expropriation of foreign-owned oil firms by President Lázaro Cárdenas. The discovery of vast petroleum reserves in the mid-1970s financed the growth of government spending and of state enterprises. By 1982, however, nearly all state enterprises except PEMEX were unprofitable, deepening the economic crisis of the government as the international debt crisis struck and petroleum prices fell.

Miguel de la Madrid thus faced a plunging economy in the wake of falling world petroleum prices, skyrocketing international interest rates, a huge government deficit as well as the government's insolvency in debt service payments, and an inefficient and costly state enterprise apparatus. President de la Madrid at first imposed severe cutbacks on government spending, cut subsidies on a wide array of goods and services, and renegotiated the foreign debt. These policies proved insufficient. As Peter Gourevitch has argued with regard to other countries and historical moments, severe economic crises in the end generally lead to far-reaching changes in economic policy.[45] That too proved to be Mexico's experience, especially in the second half of de la Madrid's presidency. In 1985 the Mexican government began to dismantle the trade protectionist apparatus; in 1986 Mexico joined the General Agreement on Tariffs and Trade (an option President López Portillo had explicitly rejected in 1980 because he thought that petroleum would suffice to open the gates of world trade for all Mexican exports).[46] The government's program to privatize state enterprises, begun in 1983, picked up speed. The rules for foreign investment were liberalized.[47]

Carlos Salinas de Gortari had served as de la Madrid's secretary for budget and planning; de la Madrid chose him as the PRI's candidate to continue the economic reform program. The Salinas administration accelerated and widened the shift in economic policy. It reached a comprehensive international debt settlement with Mexico's creditors. It erased the budget deficit by means of expenditure cuts and more efficient tax collections. It privatized a great many state enterprises, including the airlines, the telephone system, the banks, many firms producing capital goods, and so forth. It reformed the Constitution to permit private individual ownership of the collective rural entities known as *ejidos*, which had long symbolized the radicalism of the Mexican revolution. The Salinas administration removed many barriers to direct foreign investment and sought to promote such investment. It greatly liberalized international trade and took the lead in launching the North American Free Trade Agreement with the United States and Canada, which went into effect on January 1, 1994. It also left an overvalued peso, however; the failure to adjust economic policy early in 1994 helped to trigger a financial panic in December 1994 and a new economic recession in 1995.

Of special interest to us are the results of such programs prior to the 1991 national elections. Gross domestic product per capita (in constant 1980 prices) grew 1.4 percent in 1989, 2.5 percent in 1990, and 1.7 percent in 1991. Given the marked decline in the preceding years, these growth rates were too modest to restore the standard of living of most Mexicans; on the eve of the August 1991 elections, Mexico's gross domestic product per capita was still below the level it had achieved ten years earlier.

The deceleration of inflation was a more impressive accomplishment. The consumer price index dropped each year from its high of 159.2 percent in 1987 to 18.9 percent in 1991. Real average wages in manufacturing recovered. As noted above, this index (with 1980 = 100) had reached 71.3 in 1988, but it rose steadily to 84.7 in 1991. The minimum wage in Mexico City, however, failed to recover. Its index (with 1980 = 100) continued to drop each year, from 54.2 in 1988 to 43.6 in 1991.[48]

By the time of Mexico's 1991 nationwide elections, many though not all citizens had benefited from the recovery, but there remained significant differences of opinion over the proper course of the nation's future economic policies. As we shall see, changes adopted after 1988 in the electoral system did not assure the opposition that elections would be free and fair. Fears about fraud remained. Above all, partisanship remained markedly vibrant in Mexico for the 1991 elections.

The run-up to the 1994 election, in contrast, would be more problematic. Gross domestic product per capita (in constant 1980 prices) inched forward by 0.9 percent in 1992, fell 1.2 percent in 1993, and rose 1.3 percent in 1994. The inflation rate continued to decelerate; the consumer price index dropped to 8 percent in 1993—the first year of single-digit annual inflation in a generation. Equally impressive was the jump in real average wages in manufacturing. With 1980 set to equal 100, this index jumped from 84.7 in 1991 to 99.4 in 1994; nonetheless, this also meant that industrial workers had yet to recover the salary level of fourteen years earlier. Finally, the urban minimum wage in real terms continued to slide; in 1993 it stood at 41.6 percent of its 1980 level.[49] For the most part these were not propitious circumstances for the PRI to launch its election campaign. Most Mexicans had already given it credit for inflation containment. In 1994 they wanted economic growth—a growth that proved elusive still.

2 ❖ NORMS OF MEXICAN CITIZENSHIP: ARE MEXICANS "DEMOCRATS?"

Are Mexicans "democrats?" There is a long tradition of scholarship that has sought to address this question—a question that remains unanswerable to some extent and that can be addressed only in part through survey research. To understand the nature of the Mexican political system and the circumstances that foster or hinder democratic politics, one must look at political, economic, and social structures and institutions (see chapter 1), in addition to studying opinions. One should not take an exclusively national perspective, but should also study local communities and their traditions.[1] Nonetheless, the beliefs of citizens in the aggregate do matter to an understanding of the history of a political system and the prospects for change. If political institutions were to open up more than they have, would Mexican citizens be ready for democracy?

In this chapter we focus on certain "minimal" standards for democratic politics. First, we ponder the level of interest, attention, and involvement that Mexicans display with regard to politics. An apathetic public would permit routine authoritarian rule. An interested, attentive, and involved public might suffer from, but not contribute to, authoritarian rule. This first concern should help us to determine whether the extant authoritarian practices in Mexico, sketched in the previous chapter, are better explained by the structures of the political regime or by the beliefs of Mexicans.

We turn, second, to assessing the dimensions of national pride and its complex relationship to democratic politics. National pride can serve as a ruler's weapon to stifle the opposition, but it can also enhance a nation's coherence by means of support for those aspects of politics and society that might foster democratization.

Finally, we discuss the attitudes toward specific political objects that, in various settings, have been associated with the prospects for democracy. Do Mexicans prefer "strong leaders" as their governors, do they call for clerical participation in politics or military participation in the general tasks of government, and do they approve of authoritarian practices within the long-governing party, the Institutional Revolutionary Party (PRI)? In subsequent chapters we focus on agreements and disagreement among Mexicans over issues and candidates. But in this chapter we seek to set a baseline.

We argue that democratic politics is indeed possible in Mexico. The remaining authoritarian features in Mexican politics (see chapter 1) are best explained with reference to factors other than the beliefs of Mexican citizens. Despite some ambiguous responses and some residual problems, Mexicans are ready for a more democratic polity. By the late 1980s and early 1990s, moreover, the attitudes of Mexican citizens toward politics had become much more "nationalized" than in the past; that is, on important questions the differences that have existed among Mexicans by education, gender, region, or social class had attenuated.

This finding, in turn, bears on the scholarship on democratization. Although the values of Mexican citizens became more consistent with the practice of democratic politics, the structures of the Mexican political system changed much less. A change in public norms does not democratize a political regime in the absence of other strategic actions by political elites.[2] On the other hand, the public's demand for democratization increased markedly during the 1980s and 1990s and put pressure on elites to speed up the pace of democratization. The demand for greater democracy was a central concern of the opposition parties in the 1988, 1991, and 1994 elections. The democratization of public values makes it more likely that the political regime would some day become more democratic.

THE SCHOLARLY LITERATURE

In a lecture delivered in 1960, Mexico's distinguished historian, the late Daniel Cosío Villegas, focused on "the situation of the government in Mexican society." He argued that the government's "political power is almost unlimited" and vested in specific leaders: "the President in all the Republic; . . . the governors in their respective States as regards local matters; and . . . the municipal authorities in their respective jurisdictions as regards the minor matters that they manage." He wondered about the "basis" for this concentration of power in a few very strong leaders. He argued that it stemmed "in part [from] the laws themselves, since the federal Constitution gives the executive very broad powers, and the local constitutions also give very broad powers to the governors of the States," but also "in part [from] the fact that when legal power does not suffice . . . the law is simply ignored." Cosío Villegas observed that in "a real democracy" one corrective for this use and abuse of power was the role of the courts, and another was a "public opinion" that "denounces the abuse and compels the authority to correct it." In Mexico, he noted with sadness, "these two checks function sporadically and ineffectively."[3] In this book we focus on public opinion; in subsequent chapters we return to the special role of the presidency in Mexican politics.

The year before Cosío Villegas's lecture, Gabriel Almond and Sidney Verba surveyed the opinions of Mexicans who lived in communities larger than ten thousand. In their path-breaking book *The Civic Culture* they characterized Mexican politics as follows:

> What have been most striking in the Mexican pattern of political culture are the imbalances and inconsistencies. Mexico is lowest of all five countries [the United States, the United Kingdom, West Germany, Italy, and Mexico] in the frequency with which impact and significance are attributed to government and in its citizens' expectation of equal and considerate treatment at the hands of the bureaucracy and police. At the same time, the frequency with which Mexicans express pride in their political system is considerably higher than that of the Germans or Italians.

And, in a passage that foreshadows this book's opening story, they record that "the objects of this pride tend predominantly to be the Mexican Revolution and the presidency." They go on to note that "what sense of participation there is appears to be relatively independent of a sense of satisfaction with governmental output."[4]

In this chapter we compare responses to questions first asked in 1959 with the responses to identical questions repeated nationwide by the Gallup poll in Mexico in 1986, 1988, and 1991. We also make use of the fine survey conducted by Dr. Miguel Basáñez in 1983. Our purpose is to assess the trends in the responses to key questions that shed light on the citizenry's normative orientations toward politics as well as to consider the attitudinal outcome as of the early 1990s. In particular, is there greater support for democratic practices since 1959, and are there variations beyond those noted by Almond and Verba?

Research by other scholars on the political attitudes of Mexicans has focused on various topics, some of which are pertinent for this study. We refer only to those studies that also employed opinion survey research. We now turn to the specific research issues that inform our study.

Education and Gender

In addition to the explicit cross-national aspects of their research design, Almond and Verba focused on some intracountry sources of variation.

They found that educational attainment had the most important demographic effect on political attitudes. Among other findings, the better-educated person felt freer to discuss politics with a wider range of people, was more likely to follow politics and to pay attention to election campaigns, was more likely to feel capable of influencing the government, and was more likely to believe that other people are trustworthy and helpful. Almond and Verba also found that gender made a difference in political attitudes, though this varied by country and by level of education. In Mexico women were much less likely to discuss politics, to follow political campaigns, to be aware of and participate in politics, or to feel that they could influence government and politics. In contrast, Almond and Verba found that social class did not matter much once education was considered on its own terms, in part because educational differences captured the effects of class differences. They also found that church attendance did not matter much. Their analysis did not focus at all on subnational regional variations.[5]

The Demographic Underpinnings of Political Participation

In their extensive sociological investigation in 1982 of the values held by Mexicans on various topics, Alberto Hernández Medina, Luis Narro Rodríguez, and their associates focused part of their attention on certain political values. Although they found that only about 4 percent of Mexicans reported themselves as politically active, an additional 43 percent considered themselves interested though not active in politics. Consistent with Almond and Verba's findings, women were much less likely to be interested or to participate in politics; university graduates as well as individuals of higher socioeconomic status were much more likely to be interested and to participate in politics than those who had not completed primary schooling or whose socioeconomic status was lower. Age did not make a difference in the likelihood of interest or participation.[6] More general sociological research by Mexican scholars suggests as well that education and gender help to shape important values held by Mexicans on a wide array of topics.[7]

Democracy's Meanings and Social-Class Variation

In their study of politics in the city of Jalapa (Veracruz state) in 1966, Richard Fagen and William Tuohy found that Jalapeños across social classes were nearly unanimous in their support for democracy as the best form of government, for the election of public officials by majority vote, and for according an equal chance to every citizen to influence government policy. It was only when Fagen and Tuohy asked beyond what they called these "platitudinous formulations" about the rights of minorities, opposition groups, women, and illiterates to free expression and the franchise that they found a much lower acceptance of democratic practices. Thus their findings revealed greater complexity in public opinion. Unlike Almond and Verba, but like Hernández Medina and Narro Rodríguez, Fagen and Tuohy found that social class made a difference. The lower classes were more supportive of reform-oriented economic programs but at the same time were less supportive of democratic political practices as identified by Fagen and Tuohy.[8] This last observation is generally consistent with the broader cross-national argument made years earlier by Seymour Martin Lipset about what he called "working-class authoritarianism."[9]

Democracy's Likelihood and the Leader-Law Relationship

Another aspect of this complex picture was explored in 1969 by Rafael Segovia in his fine study of the political socialization of Mexican schoolchildren. Segovia found ample evidence of authoritarian attitudes among these children, though he also noted that the likelihood of democratic orientations increased markedly as levels of education increased—an observation consistent with that of Almond and Verba and Hernández Medina and Narro Rodríguez. Segovia found that the image of the president of the republic was more associated with his maintenance of public order than with his representativeness of public opinion; the president is most admired for his capacity to command, for his strength far more than for his benevolence. Moreover, as Cosío Villegas might also have expected, in the view of the schoolchildren Segovia reported (in French) that the law "c'est le fait du prince."[10]

Authoritarianism and Problem Solving?

In his comprehensive study of the migrant poor in Mexico City in 1970, Cornelius found that there was "a positive relationship between authoritarianism (defined here as a preference for strong, autocratic leadership and a low level of tolerance for minority opinions) and political participation." Those migrants who were participants in a broad array of endeavors were especially likely to exhibit such tendencies. Cornelius hypothesized that this could derive from the action of local bosses or *caciques* who spent a good deal of time in political mobilization. Cornelius also suggested, however, that support for these local bosses could be a rational way for urban migrant poor people to solve some of their community's problems: "Demonstrated performance in securing benefits for the community is particularly important," he noted, as a way to explain how bosses retained support.[11]

Economic Stakes

Henry Landsberger and Bobby M. Gierisch studied various aspects of peasant participation in one of Mexico's most important agricultural regions, La Laguna, in the northern states of Durango and Coahuila. Levels of participation were found to have been quite high, but they were not explained by value systems: "Neither modern values, nor modernizing experience, nor even parental socialization in any direct sense, seem to predict the individual's propensity to participate. What does so is above all the size of the individual's economic stake. . . . The less the stake, the less the propensity to participate." The second best explanation was the by now familiar level of education, including mass media involvement.[12]

A Democratic Political Culture, Gender, Education, and Social Class

In 1978–79 John Booth and Mitchell Seligson studied the political attitudes of middle-class and working-class Mexicans in seven cities, focusing on support for widespread political participation and for the right to dissent. They found rather strong and consistent democratic, libertarian support for all but one of the eleven items measured. They also found that in all but one case, workers were on the liberal democratic side of the spectrum, though they were less supportive of those practices than were middle-class Mexicans. In this sense, though social class made a difference, there was no basis for speaking of working-class authoritarianism. Women were less supportive of democratic liberties than men; the difference was statistically significant but not large. Education played its familiar, key role, dwarfing the effect of social class (which by itself was not statistically significant).[13]

In brief, pertinent scholarly work has focused generally on an assessment of authoritarian or democratic values. Our review of such related scholarship suggests that support for authoritarianism may have weakened between the 1960s and the early 1980s, perhaps to the point where majority support would exist for democratic values. Education remained an important source of explanation for variance in support for or opposition to authoritarian values; gender seemed to matter as well. Some studies suggest that economic stakes and instrumental motivations may explain the range of variation in support for authoritarian values. Religiosity did not seem to explain authoritarian propensities. There was no consensus on whether social class was a helpful explanation for such variance.[14]

Unlike these studies more closely related to the analysis of political culture, Miguel Basáñez's studies of electoral behavior in the 1980s suggest that both regionalism and social class are important explanations of voter attitudes. The differences by region, albeit noteworthy, are more modest than the differences among occupational categories.[15]

Table 2-1.   Political Interest, Campaign Attentiveness, and Sources of
Political Information (percent)

	1986	1988	1991
Political interest			
Great	11	16	12
Some	24	23	21
Little	35	32	34
None	30	29	33
Attention given to the current political campaign			
Great	—	30	25
Some	—	19	19
Little	—	35	39
None		15	17
Media used to obtain political information			
Television	—	92	—
Radio	—	75	—
Newspapers/magazines	—	54	—
International newspapers	—	3	—
Cable	—	1	—

Source: *New York Times* Mexico survey, 1986; IMOP S.A. (Gallup) polls, May 1988 and July 1991.

Note: N = 1,899 (weighted, 1986), 2,960 (1988), and 3,053 (1991).

DESCRIBING THE PATTERN OF BELIEFS

Political Interest, Attentiveness, and Talkativeness

Significant portions of the Mexican electorate express an interest in politics and in political campaigns. As evident in table 2-1, about two-fifths of the electorate express some to great interest in politics during a presidential election year (1988); this proportion is nearly identical to that found by Hernández Medina and Narro Rodríguez for the 1982 presidential elections. During the 1988 presidential campaign, nearly half of the electorate gave some to great attention to the campaign.

More surprising is the relative constancy of political interest and attentiveness. When there was no national election (1986), 35 percent of the electorate expressed some or great political interest. When there was a national election for Congress but not for the presidency (1991), 33 percent expressed a comparable level of political interest. And when there was a national election for both the presidency and Congress (1988), the level of interest rose but only to 39 percent. In short, not fewer than one-third of

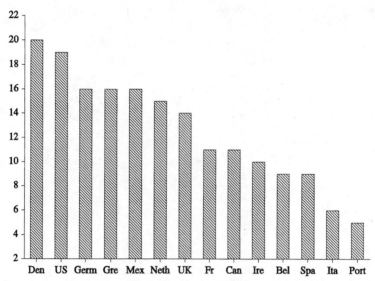

Figure 2-1. Mexican Political Interest, in Comparative Perspective (percentage expressing great interest)

Source: Euro-Barometer Study, no. 31, March–April 1989 (data made available through the Inter-University Consortium for Political and Social Research, ICPSR study no. 9322); United States General Social Survey, 1972–91 (National Opinion Research Center of the University of Chicago, data made available through ICPSR study no. 9710); Canadian National Election Study, 1988 (originally collected by the Institute for Social Research, under the direction of Richard Johnston et al., data made available through ICPSR study no. 9386); IMOP S.A. (Gallup) poll in Mexico, May 1988.

Note: Euro-Barometer smallest country N = 991. In the U.S. General Social Survey, the item on political interest appears in 1987; N = 353. Canadian National Election Study N = 3,609. IMOP S.A. N = 2,960.

Mexicans express political interest at any time, with that proportion rising only during a presidential campaign and then just slightly. So too with attention to a current political campaign. During the 1988 presidential campaign, 49 percent paid some to great attention to it; during the 1991 congressional election, the comparable statistic was 44 percent. Clearly, short-term electoral stimuli have little impact on the level of political interest or of campaign attentiveness, which appear to be both relatively high and constant.

In the late 1980s the level of political interest expressed by Mexicans was similar to that expressed by citizens of several advanced industrial democracies. Figure 2-1 presents data for Mexico's 1988 presidential election—the percentage of those expressing "great" interest in politics—along with data for West European democracies for 1989 and for the United States during the 1988 presidential election.[16] As the evidence reported in figure 2-1 shows, the level of political interest expressed in Mexico in 1988 was comparable to levels of political interest in Germany and Greece; it was exceeded but only slightly by levels of political interest in Denmark and the United States. The level of political interest was higher in Mexico than in the Netherlands, the United Kingdom, France, Canada, Ireland, Belgium, Spain, Italy, and Portugal.

Returning to table 2-1, nearly all Mexicans obtain political information from television, which underscores the influence of the country's only important television network, TELEVISA. Only 8 percent of Mexicans claimed not to use television to obtain political information. To be sure, the fact that Mexicans obtain much of their political information from television makes them similar to citizens in advanced industrial democracies (as compared with the United States, for example; in the 1988 General Social Survey only 3 percent of U.S. respondents claimed never to watch television). What is strikingly different in the case of Mexico, however, is the disproportionate reliance on television as the medium of choice to obtain information. Whereas only 5 percent of U.S. respondents to the General Social Survey claimed never to read newspapers, 46 percent of Mexican respondents claimed never to do so.[17]

What has happened to the level of attentiveness to political campaigns over time? Unfortunately, we cannot answer with precision because the 1959 *Civic Culture* survey was conducted at a time when there was no nationwide campaign under way in Mexico. Nonetheless, the evidence in table 2-2 suggests a significant jump in the level of attentiveness between 1959 and the two more recent surveys. Given the discussion, above, about what appeared to be relatively high and constant levels of political interest from the mid-1980s to the early 1990s—a level of interest that held up even in 1986, when there was no national election—the difference between 1959, on the one hand, and 1988 and 1991, on the other, can be plausibly attributed to change over time, rather than to the accidents of campaign timing.

The most important finding is the evidence on the trend toward the nationalization of Mexican politics from the late 1950s to the early 1990s. In 1959 there was very wide regional variance in attentiveness to political campaigns. Such attentiveness was rather high in the Federal District and quite low in northern Mexico. By 1988 and 1991 those differences had narrowed. The north remained less attentive to campaigns than the rest of the country, but other regional differences were modest. Curiously, central Mexico outside of the Federal District scored at the top in both 1988 and 1991, though these differences are small.

Table 2-2.   Changes in Attentiveness to Political Campaigns (percentage expressing great interest)

	1959	1988	1991
Whole sample	15	30	25
Region			
North	9	28	21
Central	12	33	29
South	19	29	23
Federal District	24	30	25
Education			
Secondary or less	13	27	23
Preparatory	25	27	24
University	24	40	29
Age			
18–25	10	24	21
26–35	16	31	26
36–50	19	33	26
51+	14	36	26
Gender			
Female	11	27	24
Male	22	33	25
Class			
Upper	23	32	23
Lower/middle	14	29	25
Church attendance			
Weekly	13	28	27
Less than weekly	20	32	23

Source: Mexican component of the *Civic Culture* study; IMOP S.A. (Gallup) polls, May 1988 and July 1991.

Note: N = 1,295 (weighted, 1959), 2,960 (1988), and 3,053 (1991).

As we have indicated, Almond and Verba had reported that education was an important explanation for differences in attentiveness to political campaigns and in other issues. We concur with their findings for 1959. The differences between those with a secondary education or less and those with a preparatory education had disappeared by 1988 and 1991, however. In 1988 those with a university education followed the campaign with much greater intensity than other Mexicans, but by 1991 the university-educated had reverted to their earlier level of attentiveness. In 1991, education helped to explain attentiveness to campaigns, but to a lesser extent than in 1959.

Almond and Verba had also called attention to gender differences, as had Hernández Medina and Narro Rodríguez and Booth and Seligson. The evidence in table 2-2 suggests the gradual disappearance of the gender gap. Once again we concur with Almond and Verba's findings for 1959. Booth and Seligson's research in the late 1970s had indicated that gender made some but not a major difference in explaining political attitudes; linked to the finding in table 2-2 for 1988, the Booth and Seligson observation serves as an intermediate link in this long behavioral chain. By the 1991 congressional election, gender differences did not seem to explain variance in attentiveness to the campaign at all.

In 1959 there was a large social-class difference in attentiveness to political campaigns. That finding is consistent with Fagen and Tuohy's 1966 study in Jalapa. Hernández Medina and Narro Rodríguez also found that social class helped to explain variance in political interest in 1982, though the differences were modest. Basáñez reports that social class mattered in shaping electoral preferences in elections during the 1980s. The evidence in table 2-2 indicates, however, that social-class differences in campaign attentiveness were quite minor in 1988 and 1991.

Religiosity, measured by church attendance, was also an important factor in 1959, but its significance seemed to have weakened by 1988 and 1991. In 1991, moreover, weekly churchgoers were more attentive to the campaign, reversing the findings for previous years. And except for the lower campaign attentiveness of voters between the ages of eighteen and twenty-five—typical of first-time voters in most countries—age has never made much difference in explaining campaign attentiveness.

We turn now to consider the relationship among these variables when they are included in the same multivariate summary regression equation (table 2-3). In each case we seek to "predict" interest in political campaigns by means of the demographic factors first reported in table 2-2. With some exceptions the results of this more comprehensive analysis are consistent with the discussion above.

Regionalism, education, and gender are statistically significant explanations for interest in political campaigns in all three surveys, but their importance lessened from the late 1950s to the early 1990s. In 1959, regional differences clearly demarcated different geographic political environments, but by the late 1980s and early 1990s residence in the Federal District no longer separated its citizens from the rest of the country on this dimension (e.g., the regression coefficient for the Federal District was no longer statistically significant). Education was a consistently important factor, but it had become less important by the late 1980s and early 1990s (the coefficient for education was cut in half between 1959 and the later surveys). The pattern

Table 2-3.   Predicting Interest in Campaigns: A Multivariate Model

	1959	1988	1991
North	-.11 (.05) *	-.07 (.03) *	-.09 (.03) **
South	.05 (.06)	-.06 (.04)	.05 (.03)
Federal District	.21 (.05) **	-.06 (.04)	.05 (.03)
Education	.16 (.05) **	.09 (.02) **	.08 (.02) **
Age	-.17 (.10)	.27 (.07) **	.03 (.06)
Female	-.29 (.04) **	-.08 (.02) **	-.06 (.02) **
Class	.11 (.03) **	.06 (.02) **	-.02 (.02)
Religiosity	-.08 (.04) *	-.03 (.02)	.09 (.02) **
Constant term	1.76 (.15) **	1.96 (.07) **	1.82 (.06) **
Adjusted R^2	.11	.03	.02

Source: Mexican component of the Civic Culture study; IMOP S.A. (Gallup) polls, May 1988 and July 1991.

Note: The coefficients above are unstandardized linear regression estimates. Standard errors appear in parentheses. N = 1,206 (weighted, 1959), 2,926 (1988), and 2,956 (1991). The scaling of each variable is consistent across samples.

* = $p < .05$.   ** = $p < .01$.

for gender is the same as for education, namely, important throughout but markedly less so by the late 1980s and early 1990s. (This finding contradicts the inference drawn from table 2-2 simply because the multiple statistical controls present in table 2-3 allow us to see the enduring though declining importance of gender as an explanatory variable.)

Consistent with the previous discussion, the importance of social class as an explanatory factor for interest in campaigns weakened steadily over time until it became insignificant in 1991. Age mattered only in the 1988 election but is otherwise insignificant. The finding for religiosity in table 2-3 is somewhat different from the inference drawn from table 2-2. The importance of religiosity did weaken from the late 1950s to the late 1980s, but in the early 1990s it appears to have become significant again, though this time because churchgoers had become more interested in campaigns.

In conclusion, by the early 1990s the Mexican political system had become more homogeneous in terms of the political interests of its citizens. Whereas in 1959 there were marked regional, educational, gender, social-class, and religious differences, by 1988 and 1991 nearly all of these differences had weakened. In 1991 there was still a regional gap, albeit a modest one, between the north and the center. The differences in education and gender still mattered but had narrowed greatly; social class had become statistically insignificant. Only religiosity had become more important as churchgoer interest in campaigns rose. Mexico had indeed changed politically during one-third of a century. Its people had become more interested in political campaigns, and the demographic differences in their level of interest had generally narrowed (the proportion of the total variance in political interest explained by these combined demographic factors dropped from 11 percent in 1959 to 2 percent in 1991, as measured by the adjusted R^2). Mexicans had shifted to become one people, and a more politically attentive one in the process.

If Mexicans had become more attentive to political campaigns, and more uniformly so, had they also begun to talk more openly about their political views? The data in table 2-4 suggest that the answer is yes. In 1959, 19 percent of Mexicans talked freely about politics with anyone; in 1991 that statistic had risen to 27 percent. The likelihood of speaking freely about politics with everyone had risen for women and for men, for each of the country's regions, for each of the educational, religious, and social-class categories, and for each age group. Such a consistent pattern of increase is remarkable.

There is, however, greater complexity to this pattern of change. In 1959 the Federal District's citizens were the most reluctant to discuss politics with anyone. The proportion of Federal District citizens willing to engage in that kind of discussion had more than doubled by 1991, when the district led the country. Similarly, in 1959 the most highly educated were the most reluctant to discuss politics with anyone. By 1991 the willingness of the most highly educated to talk politics with anyone had more than doubled. It is as if the "best-informed" Mexicans in 1959 might have known that it could be imprudent to talk about politics with anyone; such reluctance had declined markedly by the early 1990s.

Unlike our findings with regard to political interest and attentiveness to political campaigns, the differences among categories of citizens in their willingness to discuss politics with anyone had not narrowed between 1959 and 1991, but they were not wide in either year. For example, the gap between the Federal District and other parts of central Mexico in the willingness to discuss politics with anyone was about the same in 1959 as in 1991 (though the gap had widened a bit, and the rank order had been reversed). Similarly, the gap between educational categories remained fairly similar (though widening and with the rank order also being reversed). Differences by gender and church attendance were quite narrow in both years, but the gender gap widened slightly while the religious gap disappeared altogether. Differences among age groups also disappeared, but they had also been modest. The only category where the gap narrowed appreciably was social class.

Finally, there also developed a wider political stratification between 1959

Table 2-4. Willingness to Discuss Politics (percent)

	Talk Freely about Politics with Anyone		Never Talk about Politics	
	1959	1991	1959	1991
Whole sample	19	27	21	20
Region				
North	20	25	23	18
Central	20	23	20	24
South	20	30	23	18
Federal District	14	32	19	21
Education				
Secondary or less	20	24	22	24
Preparatory	15	33	11	18
University	14	32	11	12
Age				
18–25	22	29	17	19
26–35	14	28	19	19
36–50	20	25	18	21
51+	20	28	29	24
Gender				
Female	18	25	25	23
Male	20	29	13	28
Class				
Upper	14	25	13	16
Lower/middle	20	28	22	21
Church attendance				
Weekly	19	27	22	21
Less than weekly	17	27	18	20

Source: Mexican component of the *Civic Culture* study; IMOP S.A. (Gallup) poll, July 1991.

Note: N = 1,295 (weighted, 1959) and 3,053 (1991).

and 1991, namely, the proportion of Mexicans who never talk about politics remained unchanged, while the proportion who talk quite freely about politics increased. Among these politically uncommunicative Mexicans, there was a trend toward somewhat greater uniformity from 1959 to 1991. Differences narrowed among age groups, educational, social-class, and re-ligious categories, and between men and women; they widened only slightly between regions. This greater homogeneity among the politically uncommunicative, and the unchanged demographic variance among the politically talkative, indicates that the differences that widened between the late 1950s and early 1990s were *political,* not sociological. For reasons that we observe but cannot explain, Mexicans differed more in 1991 than in 1959 in their willingness to talk about politics; these differences are not well related to demographic factors.

In short, Mexicans have become more willing to discuss politics. Mexicans from all walks of life have become more politically talkative. The best-informed Mexicans—those who reside in the Federal District or have a university education—have become much less politically suspicious. The likelihood of discussing politics is not well explained by sociological categories; that is, poorer or less well educated Mexicans are not markedly less likely to discuss politics than those with greater resources. Thus the greater gap among Mexicans in 1991 in terms of their willingness to discuss politics is itself an eminently political phenomenon—one that we deem favorable for the future of democratic politics.

National Pride

What, then, of national pride in Mexico? Despite the country's severe economic difficulties in the 1980s, Mexicans expressed a very high pride in Mexico in both 1988 and 1991. (In each case Mexicans were asked whether they agreed with the statement, "I am very proud of my country." Table 2-5 reports those who agreed or strongly agreed with that statement.) The increase in pride between those two dates was also marked, perhaps reflecting the Mexican economy's modest recovery during those years. This increase in pride between 1988 and 1991 is evident for all regions, for all educational, social-class, and religious categories, for all age groups, and for both men and women. This uniform increase in national pride is extraordinary.

In 1988 there were some demographic differences in the likelihood of expressing pride in Mexico. Residents of the Federal District and the university-educated were less likely to express pride in Mexico. Younger Mexicans were also somewhat less likely to express such pride. The differences by gender, social class, and religiosity did not matter. By 1991, however, all such differences had disappeared. There was, alas, "national unity" concerning national pride.

In the 1989 Euro-Barometer study, few countries in the European Community had a measure of citizen pride as high as Mexico's in 1988, and none of the largest European countries did. For example, only 65 percent of West Germans said that they were "extremely" or "moderately" proud to be German; the comparable statistics were 78 percent for France and 81 percent for the United Kingdom.[18]

We turn, then, to a related question, namely, an examination of pride in

Table 2-5.   Pride in Mexico (percentage expressing pride)

	1988	1991
Whole sample	89	96
Region		
North	88	97
Central	92	96
South	92	96
Federal District	84	94
Education		
Secondary or less	91	96
Preparatory	87	96
University	83	94
Age		
18–25	86	95
26–35	89	96
36–50	91	96
51+	91	96
Gender		
Female	89	96
Male	88	96
Class		
Upper	91	95
Lower/middle	88	96
Church attendance		
Weekly	91	97
Less than weekly	87	95

Source: IMOP S.A. (Gallup) polls, May 1988 and July 1991.

Note: N = 2,960 (1988) and 3,053 (1991).

political attributes. The evidence in table 2-6 shows the extent to which the source of pride was specifically political (the state, the Constitution, democracy, or equality in Mexico). These views surfaced in response to similar open-ended questions that were asked in both 1959 and 1991. Whereas in 1959, 28 percent of Mexicans expressed pride in such political attributes, that statistic had risen to 35 percent in 1991.

This increase in pride in the Mexican political system was especially noteworthy in northern Mexico and among women and upper-class respondents, but increased political pride was manifest for all age groups and all social-class and religious categories. There was a slight drop among preparatory school–educated Mexicans and among residents of the Federal

Table 2-6. Pride in the Mexican Political System
            (percentage expressing pride)

	1959	1991
Whole sample	28	35
Region		
North	23	38
Central	31	39
South	26	34
Federal District	32	28
Education		
Secondary or less	27	33
Preparatory	39	36
University	38	41
Age		
18–25	26	32
26–35	26	34
36–50	33	37
51+	28	37
Gender		
Female	23	33
Male	38	37
Class		
Upper	34	48
Lower/middle	28	33
Church attendance		
Weekly	29	37
Less than weekly	27	33

Source: Mexican component of the *Civic Culture* study;
IMOP S.A. (Gallup) poll, July 1991.
    Note: N = 1,295 (weighted, 1959) and 3,053 (1991).

District, and basically no change among men, but there was increased political pride in all other regions of Mexico and in the two other educational categories.

No doubt the legitimacy of Mexico's political system was sharply contested in 1988, and to a lesser degree in 1991, but there is also no doubt that a significant proportion of Mexicans volunteered that they were proud of Mexico's political institutions, practices, and outcomes. Such feelings of political pride or the more expansive national pride were not themselves hostile to democratic politics, for Mexicans chose to name constitutional government and democracy among the reasons for their pride. Nonetheless, the specific content of the views of Mexicans about democratic institutions and practices needs to be assessed; to that we now turn.

Political Leaders, Institutions, and Practices

In 1959 Almond and Verba asked Mexicans whether they agreed with the statement, "A few strong leaders would do more for Mexico than all the laws and talk." That question was repeated in the 1988 and 1991 surveys; the results are presented in table 2-7. The evidence in table 2-7 shows that a majority of Mexicans agreed with such a statement even in 1991, but that there had been a substantial decline in agreement with that statement since 1959 and even some decline since 1988. Over time, Mexicans have become more attached to the rule of law, though there remains considerable room for improvement.

From 1959 to 1988, with one important exception, and again from 1988 to 1991, the preference for strong leaders declined for each of the categories in table 2-7; that is, with the passing of years such preference for strong leaders fell for both men and women, all age groups and regions, all religious and social-class categories, and all educational categories—except for university-educated Mexicans. There has been a stunning increase in the likelihood that university-educated Mexicans would prefer strong leaders in 1988, and even in 1991, as compared with 1959.

In 1959 by far the single best explanation for variance in the preference for strong leaders was education; the university-educated were much less likely to express such preferences. The other important factor was region, with citizens from northern Mexico being less likely to prefer such strong leaders than residents of the Federal District. Younger Mexicans were also less likely to prefer strong leaders. Gender, social class, and religiosity hardly mattered.

By 1988, region had become the single most important explanation, with the north still remaining the region least likely to prefer strong leaders. Education still mattered some, but much less than in 1959, as an explanation for variance in the preference for strong leaders. Some modest differences had appeared in terms of gender and religiosity, but social class continued to be unimportant. Age had an interesting role. The "over age 51" group in 1988 and in 1991 refers, of course, to the "below age 25" group in 1959. In all three surveys these citizens consistently showed the lowest preference for strong leaders. Their formative political socialization experiences endured over three decades.

By 1991, age, gender, social-class, and religious differences explained none of the variance in the preference for strong leaders. Education's explanatory importance continued to decline. Region had become the only

Table 2-7. "A Few Strong Leaders Would Do More for Mexico Than
All the Laws and Talk" (percentage agreeing)

	1959	1988	1991
Whole sample	67	59	54
Region			
North	62	53	49
Central	68	61	60
South	68	61	51
Federal District	72	64	56
Education			
Secondary or less	69	61	55
Preparatory	65	58	54
University	38	57	51
Age			
18–25	63	59	55
26–35	66	62	53
36–50	70	60	55
51+	69	55	53
Gender			
Female	67	62	55
Male	67	57	54
Class			
Upper	66	59	54
Lower/middle	67	60	54
Church attendance			
Weekly	69	62	55
Less than weekly	66	57	53

Source: Mexican component of the Civic Culture study; IMOP S.A.
(Gallup) polls, May 1988 and July 1991.

Note: N = 1,295 (weighted, 1959), 2,960 (1988), and 3,053 (1991).

important explanation, but it was important in a new way. Whereas the
preference for strong leaders had declined markedly over time in the north,
the south, and the Federal District, it had declined much less in other parts
of central Mexico, which had become for the first time the region with the
strongest support for such strong leaders.

As in the case of our analysis of interest in political campaigns, we want
also to assess the roots of Mexican authoritarianism by means of a multivariate model. We do so in table 2-8. Its results are clear and quite consistent
with the preceding analysis.

Education was the most important factor explaining the variance in au-

Table 2-8.   The Roots of Mexican Authoritarianism: A Multivariate
              Model

	1959	1988	1991
North	−.39 (.18) *	−.63 (.12) **	−.47 (.11) **
South	−.02 (.23)	−.33 (.12) **	−.36 (.13) **
Federal District	.32 (.20)	−.11 (.12)	−.28 (.11) *
Education	−.62 (.16) **	−.17 (.06) **	−.09 (.05)
Age	.08 (.04) *	−.02 (.02)	.01 (.02)
Female	.19 (.15)	.26 (.08) **	.11 (.08)
Class	.16 (.12)	−.01 (.06)	−.09 (.06)
Religiosity	.04 (.15)	.13 (.06) *	.02 (.07)
Constant term	1.13 (.52) **	.81 (.23) **	.73 (.22) **

Source: Mexican component of the Civic Culture study; IMOP S.A.
(Gallup) polls, May 1988 and July 1991.

Note: The coefficients above are maximum likelihood logit estimates.
For each year, the dependent variable was coded 1 if respondents preferred "strong leaders" over "all the laws and talk" and 0 otherwise.
Standard errors appear in parentheses. Initially the LLF equaled −768.7
(1959), −1,875.7 (1988), and −1,924.9 (1991); at convergence the LLF equaled
−597.2 (1959), −1,723.4 (1988), and −1,874.3 (1991). The model correctly
predicted 76.2 percent (1959), 65.3 percent (1988), and 57.1 percent (1991)
of the cases. $N = 1,109$ (weighted, 1959), 2,706 (1988), and 2,777 (1991). The
scaling of each variable is consistent across samples.
    $* = p < .05.$ $** = p < .01.$

thoritarian attitudes in 1959, but its importance had declined markedly by
1988—the regression coefficient is much smaller—and by 1991 it had become statistically insignificant. Age was statistically significant just in 1959,
and gender and religiosity just in 1988; they do not contribute to the explanation over time. Regionalism rose in importance from 1959 to 1988, and
by 1991 it was the only factor that helped to explain variance in authoritarian attitudes.

Because education was so important as an explanation for authoritarian
attitudes in the late 1950s, we focus on it more directly in table 2-9. For
table 2-9 we have computed the hypothetical expected probabilities of preferring "a few strong leaders" over "all the laws and talk." These probabilities are derived from the equations in table 2-8; in table 2-9 the expected
probabilities calculation controls for all the other variables included in
table 2-8 so that only education varies and thus its effect can be seen most
plainly.

Consistent with the previous discussion, education made a marked difference in 1959, less difference in 1988, and hardly any difference in 1991.

Table 2-9. Educational Levels and Expected Probabilities of Preferring "A Few Strong Leaders" over "All the Laws and Talk"

	1959	1988	1991
University	.51	.59	.55
Secondary	.66	.64	.57
Less than secondary	.78	.67	.59

Note: These probabilities were derived from the equations in table 2–8, where all independent variables except education have been set to their mean values.

But this more refined analysis permits us to reflect upon an important analytical point. The probability that a Mexican with limited education would prefer strong leaders fell from 78 percent in 1959 to 59 percent in 1991 once all other statistical controls apply. In the same vein and following the same calculation, the probability that Mexicans with intermediate levels of education would prefer strong leaders fell from 66 percent in 1959 to 57 percent in 1991. Consistent with our inference from table 2-7, the probability that university-educated Mexicans would prefer strong leaders did rise from 1959 to 1988 while it fell back in 1991, but once the full panoply of statistical controls is applied, the increase over time in the likelihood of such preferences by university-educated Mexicans turns out to be quite modest and therefore much less alarming.

Returning to the arguments in an earlier section, we can also affirm with confidence that these data provide no support for a "working-class authoritarianism" argument. Social class was never a useful predictor of attitudes toward strong leaders, and education—a close proxy for social class—came to matter less and less as an explanatory factor.

On the other hand, we cannot quite gauge what the preference for strong leaders means in the late 1980s and early 1990s. In 1959, education was the overriding explanation for variance in leadership preferences. An argument about "political culture" might have sufficed. In more recent years arguments about education, or even about regional subcultures, are much less persuasive. Those who might claim, for example, that the north is the cradle of a democratic Mexico would be unable to explain why the differences in 1991 between northern and southern respondents are so modest, given that the south does not have the reputation for democratic political practices. It is possible, but we cannot prove it, that the preference for strong leaders in the late 1980s and early 1990s might respond to the perceived need for such leaders to rescue Mexico from the economic and political crises of those times. If so, then the reason for the remaining high preference for strong leaders could be instrumental—the tough-minded

Table 2-10. Attitudes toward the State's Autonomy (percent)

	Believe the Church Should Not Participate in Politics	Believe the Military Should Not Participate in Government
Whole sample	66	44
Education		
Secondary or less	60	38
Preparatory	69	50
University	74	53
Age		
18–25	68	45
26–35	68	46
36–50	62	45
51+	65	40
Gender		
Female	59	39
Male	69	47
Monthly income (pesos)		
Less than 10,000	61	40
10,000–40,000	69	46
40,000–80,000	72	51
More than 80,000	72	59
Employment		
Government worker	73	47
Nongovernment worker	66	45
Unemployed	59	42

Source: Miguel Basáñez poll, March 1983.
Note: N = 7,051.

problem-solving leader of whom Wayne Cornelius has written. We leave this hypothesis as speculation for further research.

Beyond the preference for a strong leader, we were interested in the views of Mexicans about the proper political role of institutions that are themselves not internally democratic. Table 2-10 records the responses to two questions asked in 1983, namely, should the Roman Catholic church participate in politics, and should the military participate in government? These questions address in part the need for a democratic political system to retain its autonomy from institutions that are not internally democratic. Thus we move here from abstract democratic norms to the more practical question of the state's autonomy.

In the Mexican context, these questions may evoke memories of a highly conflictive national history. Armies fought each other during Mexico's revolution earlier in the twentieth century. Warlords shaped Mexican politics at least into the 1930s. One aspect of Mexico's civil wars was a religious conflict, which in the late 1920s was the central factor in the so-called Cristero war. This specific Mexican context may help to explain the different responses to the questions about clerical and military involvement in politics. Just as important, the questions address quite different themes. The church is a part of civil society, not of the government; we seek to understand what Mexicans believe about the appropriateness of church engagement in politics. The military is a part of the state; we seek to understand what Mexicans believe about the appropriateness of a generalized military involvement in the government.

In 1983 two-thirds of Mexicans opposed participation in politics by the Roman Catholic church. Fewer than one-tenth of Mexicans favored church participation in politics. Church-state relations have remained quite controversial in contemporary Mexico, even though the church does not threaten Mexico's established political institutions.[19] Even though the military is an arm of the state, fewer than half of all Mexicans support its participation in the general tasks of the government. Only about one-fifth of all Mexicans actually favored military participation in the government generally. As Alain Rouquié has put it, "Few Armies in the [American] continent appear to be less politically involved."[20] The overall proportions in Mexican attitudes toward church and military participation in politics and government changed little during the remainder of the 1980s.[21]

Opposition to church participation in politics was strongest among the university-educated and the wealthiest Mexicans as well as among men and government workers. Indeed, only age seemed not to matter much as an explanation. Opposition to military participation in government was also substantial; it was strongest among the university-educated and among the wealthiest Mexicans as among men, but age and occupation did not make a difference.

In short, education, social class, and gender were not helpful in understanding variation in the preferences for strong leaders in the 1980s, but they help to explain the varying levels of opposition to clerical and military involvement in politics and government respectively. The dimensions of democratization in Mexico differ, therefore, depending on whether one considers norms or practices, leadership styles or institutional roles.

Finally, we look at the extent of authoritarian or democratic preferences within the context of the PRI. Table 2-11 reports the results of a practical question: How should the PRI's presidential nominee be chosen? The selec-

Table 2-11.   How Should the PRI Choose Its Presidential Nominee?
(percent)

	Primary Elections	Party Conventions	Presidential Prerogative
Whole sample	60	24	4
Region			
North	63	18	4
Central	65	20	3
South	57	32	2
Federal District	56	26	6
Education			
Secondary or less	62	21	5
Preparatory	60	26	3
University	57	30	3
Age			
18–25	62	24	4
26–35	61	25	3
36–50	59	24	4
51+	59	21	4
Gender			
Female	59	23	4
Male	62	25	3
Class			
Upper	53	33	4
Lower/middle	62	22	3
Church attendance			
Weekly	60	23	3
Less than weekly	60	24	4

Source: IMOP S.A. (Gallup) poll, May 1988.
Note: N = 2,960.

tion of the PRI's candidate formally rests with PRI institutions, but in effect the party's candidate has been chosen by the outgoing president, who consults informally but retains the decisive power.[22] This informal but effective presidential prerogative in choosing the next president has been the operative norm of Mexican politics for decades. In 1988 only 4 percent of Mexicans supported it.

In 1988, Mexicans strongly supported changing the way in which PRI presidential candidates were nominated; most Mexicans preferred primary elections to party conventions. This lopsided preference is evident throughout all the categories listed in table 2-11, but there are some differences in the intensity of such preferences. The preference for party conventions is strongest among upper-class Mexicans and among the university-educated, who may believe that they might have greater influence on a party convention than on the results of a primary election. (Support for a party convention is also strong in southern Mexico.) In contrast, gender, religion, and age seem to explain little about the variance with regard to such preferences.

CONCLUSION

The attitudes of Mexican citizens have changed in important and consistent ways since the late 1950s. By the early 1990s Mexicans had become much more likely to be interested in politics, to be attentive to political campaigns, and to discuss politics freely. The rising level of politicization of the electorate is still high when Mexico is compared with advanced industrial democracies. It remains high both in years when Mexico holds national elections and when it does not.

Not everything had changed, however. As in the late 1950s, Mexicans in the early 1990s are extraordinarily proud of their homeland. The level of national pride Mexicans exhibited in an economic recession year (1988) continued to exceed that found in West European countries when their economies were growing (1989). The pride of Mexicans was focused on the nation's political institutions to a considerable degree. This pride was not hostile to democratic institutions, however. In the 1950s as in the 1990s, pride is connected to certain democratic political practices. As time has passed, Mexicans have also become less likely to prefer reliance on strong leaders over reliance on the rule of law; they do not favor the participation of nondemocratic institutions in political life; and they strongly favor the internal democratization of the ruling party's presidential nomination practices.

Our findings agree with those of other scholars, whose work was reviewed earlier in this chapter, who suggest that the trend over time in the attitudes of Mexican citizens has been favorable to the possibilities of democratic politics. The residues of authoritarian practices in Mexican politics are best explained in terms of existing institutions and policies (see chapter 1), not the preferences of Mexican citizens.[23] Especially noteworthy is the fact that the most highly educated Mexicans have become less suspicious of and less alienated from politics.

We have confirmed a number of the demographic differences noted by other scholars and summarized earlier in this chapter. Nonetheless, our findings suggest that Mexican politics has become more nationalized. The differences among demographic categories, such as education or gender, that had concerned Almond and Verba and other scholars have in general narrowed over time. The point is not that Almond and Verba or the others were incorrect in their analysis; they were not. The point is that Mexico has changed, and that its citizens are ready for a more democratic polity.

Explaining Attitude Changes

Why did the political attitudes of Mexicans change between the 1950s and the 1980s, even though the institutions of the political regime did not? Our answer to this important question is less certain and more speculative; four explanations emerge from our data.

One part of the answer is the spread of elementary education. In 1960, just after the Almond and Verba survey, over 40 percent of Mexican adults did not know how to read and write; on the eve of the 1988 presidential election, that proportion had dropped below 10 percent. As recently as 1970 the median schooling level of the population age twelve and older was 3.5 years; by 1990 the median schooling level for that population had risen to 6.4 years.[24] The narrowing of the education gap in the attitudes of Mexicans can be attributed to a significant degree to the virtual elimination of illiteracy and to the upgrading of the population's educational levels. Educationally, Mexicans became more alike with the passing of time.

A second factor, evident also in the surveys, is the relative insignificance of church attendance as an explanation for democratic attitudes. Roman Catholics and secular citizens have comparable commitments to democracy. As Samuel Huntington has argued most explicitly, the "third wave" of democratization has been especially noteworthy among Catholic countries, and it is attributable to some extent to the important worldwide changes that have occurred since the 1960s within the Roman Catholic church.[25]

Third, Roman Catholic aggiornamento has permitted the wider incorporation of women into social life outside the home, thereby reducing the role of gender as an explanation for differences in political attitudes. A contributing factor to the narrowing of the attitudinal differences between men and women is exposure to cosmopolitan international influences, particularly television programs and films from the United States, which are quite pervasive in Mexico.[26]

Finally, recall a point we made in the previous chapter, namely, the potential reciprocity between attitudes and political processes. Even though the nation's governing institutions have remained closed for the most part to the opposition, Mexican politics in the 1990s had become much more competitive than in the 1950s. The very fact of such increased competition may help to explain why Mexicans have become more interested in politics, more willing to participate, and less dependent on a few strong leaders for solving problems. As E. E. Schattsneider first argued about the United States in the 1950s, party competition can be "contagious." As parties take sides on issues and battle each other, citizens are drawn into the electoral arena; their predispositions to engage in democratic politics change as a consequence.[27] And as Mexicans have become more democratic in their values, they have placed further pressures on governing elites to reform political processes even more (on this point, see the discussion of the 1994 election in the Epilogue).

Mexico in Comparative Perspective

In the early 1990s Mexico was much less democratic than the attitudes of its citizens might lead us to expect. This observation supports the argument of those who stress that the construction of a democratic political regime requires, above all, a change in elite strategies and behavior.[28] From the 1950s to the 1980s a change in the mass public in the direction of democratic values did not bring about a democratic regime.

Scott Mainwaring has noted one consequence of the scholarly focus on elite behavior, however: the "dismissal of the importance of a normative commitment to democracy" as a subject for research and reflection. This has had two regrettable consequences. First, it ignores the ample evidence that the construction of democratic political regimes in contemporary Latin America has certainly involved "people who have devoted much of their lives to the democratic cause." Second, Mainwaring has also observed that "a society in which there is limited support for democracy does not bode very well for this form of government."[29] The likelihood of the consolidation of democracy increases if there is mass support for it (see also chapter 1).

Mexico's slow process of democratization in the 1980s cannot be understood without reference to the change in public attitudes. Mexicans began to demand democracy. These demands were localized at first, as in the state of Chihuahua in widespread protest against fraud in the 1986 gubernatorial elections,[30] but they soon spread. These mass-based national demands for democracy are evident in what Soledad Loaeza has labeled "the call to the voting booth"[31]—the belief, growing in the late 1980s and in the 1990s, that elections ought to be fair and decisive. In this chapter we have documented the increasing support for democratic practices during the 1980s; such growing support accounts well for the content and significance of the campaigns of opposition parties in the 1988 presidential election (see chapter

4). The perception of substantial fraud committed during and just after that election (see chapter 6) brought forth what some have called a "civic insurrection."[32]

These demands for greater democracy through fair elections resurfaced loudly during the 1994 presidential elections and are one part of the explanation for the important reforms in electoral procedures that were adopted during the months prior to the 1994 election (see Epilogue). These societal demands explain as well the belated but nonetheless effective blossoming in the early 1990s of organizations in civil society concerned with the defense of human rights—and in particular, organizations (such as the Civic Alliance) concerned with the defense of the fairness of the electoral process.

Consequently, prior to a transition to a fully democratic political regime, the demand for democracy has been more long-lasting in Mexico—in part because the transition has been slow and prolonged—than in other cases of democratization.[33] The Mexican transition toward democracy resembles the slow-moving mass-based experience of democratization in Poland more than it does other Latin American cases. Mexican citizens have pressured elites to democratize the political regime and in so doing have become actors on the nation's public stage. The changed attitudes and behavior of Mexicans have induced elites to change their own strategies and behavior.

Most optimistically, the shift in the matrix of political attitudes makes it more likely that a democratic political regime could be consolidated in Mexico in the future. Economic growth may well help to consolidate the Mexican political system in the future, after Mexico recovers from the recession begun in 1995, but comparative studies show, as Ronald Inglehart has put it, "that economic development per se does not necessarily lead to democracy."[34] Whether economic growth consolidates an authoritarian or a democratic regime is strongly affected by political attitudes. Where democratic norms have come to prevail, as is increasingly the case in Mexico, the likelihood of democratic consolidation rises.[35]

3 ❖ IDEOLOGY, ISSUE PREFERENCES, AND APPREHENSION: PUBLIC OPINION DURING THE 1988 PRESIDENTIAL ELECTION

Are Mexicans "ideologues?" Do they hold consistent views across different issues? Do those who favor continued payments on the foreign debt also favor the privatization of state enterprises? Do Mexicans with a university education hold views on various issues that point in the same direction as their social-class origins and their levels of political interest? Are the views of Mexicans sharply polarized across issues? If the views of Mexicans were to be both consistent across issues and sharply polarized over these issues—consistent free-market advocates versus consistent statist advocates—political life in Mexico might become especially difficult to manage. In this chapter we propose to explore the extent of polarization among Mexicans over various issues, and the extent to which they hold ideologically consistent views across issues.

There is reason to suppose that Mexicans may have been more polarized in the late 1980s than in previous years because of the combined effect of greater economic hardship (discussed in chapter 1) and, as we shall see, major shifts in the economic policies of Mexico's national government. The hardship raised the salience of economic issues, while the change in policies was likely to draw diverse attitudinal responses and to help some Mexicans more than others. Moreover, both the governing party and the opposition fostered issue consistency in their political campaigns and statements, as did many academics and journalists.

In their path-breaking study *The Changing American Voter,* Nie, Verba, and Petrocik found that U.S. voters in the 1950s were not sharply polarized ideologically or in terms of demographic categories and that there was little consistency across issues. On the other hand, the effect of the sharp political conflicts in the United States in the 1960s was to sharpen ideological polarization and to raise issue consistency.[1] That is, jolting events can transform a nonideological, issue-inconsistent electorate into one that is much more ideological and consistent. Could something like this have happened in Mexico under the economic shocks of the 1980s in time for the 1988 presidential elections, when sharply polarized visions of Mexico were presented to the electorate for their choice?

In this chapter we argue that Mexicans were indeed deeply divided in their attitudes toward economic and other specific issues by the time of the 1988 presidential election. This polarization ran through various demographic categories of citizens. On certain issues important demographic, social-class, and regional sources of division could be readily identified. There were also statistically significant associations in individual attitudes across an array of economic issues, denoting issue consistency.

On the other hand, we did not find consistent relationships across issues among the demographic variables. University education, for example, pointed in the same analytical direction as such variables as social class or political interest in some instances but not in others. Moreover, the level of consistency across issues was modest (though statistically significant), much lower than one might expect from the way in which economic issues were debated in Mexico. Mexicans who favored "market solutions" in some instances opposed them in others.

Because Mexicans were not highly consistent in their views across economic issues, and because education, social class, and other variables also did not point analytically in similar directions across issues, the fact that Mexicans were polarized over most issues had little impact on the nation's governability. The Mexican government could construct different coalitions for support for different issues. Nonetheless, in 1988 Mexicans were united on their general pessimism about the circumstances of Mexico's economy and about its prospects, even though many Mexicans also believed that their personal financial circumstances were good and that the national economic trend was toward recovery.

THE RISE OF "NEW" ISSUES IN MEXICO IN THE 1980s

Under economic shock, in the mid-1980s the government led by President Miguel de la Madrid opened up a new era in Mexican economic policy. The government systematically took measures to open up the Mexican economy to the forces of the international market while also seeking to make the domestic economy less dependent on highly intrusive regulatory policies and on state ownership of productive firms.

This double economic change—in actual circumstances and in government policy—created a new environment for political issues. There were two kinds of "new" or renewed issues. Some were quite specific: Do you favor facilitating imports? Even if questions about foreign trade are nearly timeless, Mexico's changed economic circumstances in the mid-1980s gave these age-old issues an entirely new, more pressing meaning. But there was also a new "super issue": How did Mexicans feel about the sum total of changes that affected the nation's economy and the country more generally? Was Mexico moving in the right direction?

There is no consensus among Mexican analysts on how to assess President Miguel de la Madrid's presidential term (1982–88). Consider the views of two very able analysts. According to Luis Rubio, "In the end, the great merit of Miguel de la Madrid's administration was to make possible an historic break [with past Mexican economic policy] and to create new opportunities for Mexican development thanks to his readiness to accept short-term costs for the sake of long-term objectives. . . . Mexico changed dramatically between 1982 and 1988."[2]

Alternatively, Adolfo Gilly has written about these same years:

> Restructuring the Mexican economy was the principal task pursued by the government of Miguel de la Madrid. . . . These years were marked by economic and social changes, a drop in wages and living standards for the poorest sectors of the population, and various cultural transformations. Until the middle of the presidential term, a profound inertia enveloped the people, who were surprised by the ruling party's apparent shift toward a policy of rigorous austerity on wages and social spending and growing encouragement of a new formal approach to the entry of the Mexican economy into the world market.[3]

Rubio and Gilly agree, nevertheless, that President Miguel de la Madrid's decisions were of momentous importance for Mexico, and that they were a break with past practices and with expectations that such practices would continue. Rubio and Gilly also agree that many people incurred important costs during the course of de la Madrid's presidency, but they differ on whether Mexico would reap longer-term gains. In chapter 1 we reviewed some of the evidence concerning economic hardship between 1982 and 1988 and in a general way noted the redesign of economic policies during President de la Madrid's term. To understand the division of opinion among Mexicans on various issues that we explore in this chapter, we now sketch some of the changes in economic policy in greater detail.[4]

Upon becoming president in December 1982, Miguel de la Madrid inherited Mexico's severe international debt crisis. As noted in chapter 1, he decided to continue to honor Mexico's international financial obligations by means of debt rescheduling. As Lorenzo Meyer has written, a great many groups in Mexico, ranging from the political left through the center, called for a moratorium on debt payments pending an economic recovery.[5] De la

Madrid was severely criticized for this decision throughout the duration of his presidential term; our data will reflect the division of opinion concerning the wisdom of this decision.

Even at the end of de la Madrid's presidential term, the verdict on the wisdom of his policies on the foreign debt was not yet entirely clear. On the one hand, the interest due on the foreign debt as a percentage of Mexican exports of goods and services had fallen impressively, from 47.6 percent in 1982 to 29.9 percent in 1988. On the other hand, the total disbursed external debt as a percentage of Mexican exports of goods and services remained unchanged: it was 337 percent in 1982 and 346 percent in 1988. And, of course, the Mexican economy had yet to recover fully from the earlier shocks.[6]

Because the debt crisis and the challenges of economic stabilization were so severe, President de la Madrid was able to focus on other fundamental economic issues only midway through his term. In 1984 and 1985 he made decisions that fundamentally reordered the course of Mexican economic history.

President de la Madrid liberalized the terms for the entry of foreign investment into Mexico on a case-by-case basis. In 1973, Mexico had codified its regulations on foreign investment, but it had also made them—and the associated laws and decrees pertaining to such investments—more restrictive, even if considerable discretion had always been exercised in the administration of these and other related rules.[7] Beginning in 1984 such regulations governing foreign investment were liberalized in order to stimulate its flow. Foreign investment projects required prior approval from Mexico's National Commission on Foreign Investment if they were unusually large or located in strategic sectors; in any event, all foreign investment projects had to be registered with the commission. President de la Madrid's government reduced sharply the margin for discretion that the commission could apply in deciding which projects to accept or reject.

As a result of these and other changes, about 90 percent of the projects presented to the commission between 1985 and 1988 were approved. Despite Mexico's deep economic recession in 1986—on top of its economic "crash" in 1982–83—the annual value of new foreign direct investments increased by a factor of 2.5 between 1984 and 1987. As much foreign direct investment flowed into Mexico between 1982 and 1988 as had ever gone into Mexico before de la Madrid's presidency.[8]

This considerable change in Mexico's longstanding rules and practices governing foreign investment became, therefore, a subject over which Mexican public opinion divided, as we shall see. Was it right to turn away from the legacy of decades of much closer regulation of foreign investment and from the occasional discouragement of some investment projects that the government had deemed ill advised for Mexico?

In February 1985 President de la Madrid announced that 237 state enterprises would be sold to private owners and that others would be liquidated.[9] He thus signaled an effort to begin to reverse the series of measures that had led over many years to the remarkable and sustained growth of the state's ownership and operation of firms directly involved in the production of goods and services.[10] Many of the firms to be privatized in 1985 had been owned by Mexico's private banks until the moment of their expropriation by President José López Portillo on September 1, 1982. This process of privatizing state enterprises would be consolidated during the Salinas presidency. Because the privatization of state enterprises signaled a reversal of longstanding policies of the Mexican state in its relationship to the economy, it also became an object of political contention, as we shall also see.

President de la Madrid also liberalized Mexican foreign trade policies. In April 1985 the United States and Mexico reached a trade agreement to address disputes that involved export subsidies and countervailing duties to negate such subsidies. In July 1985 the Mexican government took further unilateral steps to modify its trade policies; it announced a significant reduction in tariffs and a schedule to dismantle nontariff barriers. It also adopted an aggressive export-promoting exchange rate policy. In August 1986 Mexico at last joined the General Agreement on Tariffs and Trade (GATT); de la Madrid thereby reversed his predecessor's March 1980 decision, which had confirmed Mexico's longstanding nonparticipation in the GATT. In November 1987 the United States and Mexico signed a "framework agreement" to discuss bilateral trade issues in key sectors in order to liberalize such trade.

By the end of de la Madrid's presidency, 95 percent of Mexican tariff items no longer required import permits (such measures freed up 75 percent of the value of imports). Whereas some tariff rates were as high as 100 percent in 1982, all tariff rates had dropped to between zero and 40 percent by 1988. By the end of 1988 over 80 percent of U.S. imports into Mexico entered at a duty rate of between zero and 5 percent. The trade-weighted Mexican tariff for all products fell below 10 percent by the end of de la Madrid's presidency; that is, it was similar to the level of tariff protection in many developed countries.

In part as a result of these measures, from 1983 through the first half of 1988, Mexican imports from the United States doubled, and Mexican exports of nonpetroleum products to the United States more than doubled. Moreover, in 1988 alone, imports into Mexico from all sources jumped by

55 percent over the previous year.[11] No wonder, therefore, that the question of Mexico's import policy was salient among many Mexicans, and that it would sharply divide those Mexicans who benefited from those who suffered from the change in trade policies.

During de la Madrid's presidency there were serious disputes over each of these specific issues—debt, foreign investment, privatization, and trade. There was ample praise as well as sharp criticism of de la Madrid's effort to reorient Mexico toward a market economy in which the state played a smaller role in directly productive activities in order to integrate Mexico's economy more fully with the world market. The praise and the criticism were aimed as much at the overall program of economic reorientation—as the opening quotations from Rubio and Gilly make clear—as they were at any one of its components.

In order to compare attitudes toward these economic issues with attitudes toward noneconomic issues, we also consider views toward capital punishment. Between 1982 and 1988 the number of reported crimes committed in the Federal District of Mexico City rose by 63 percent. Comparable data do not exist for the entire country; however, between 1982 and 1987 the number of criminals indicted nationwide by Mexican courts rose 66.5 percent, while the number of criminals convicted by Mexican courts rose 43.9 percent.[12] Because of the severity of Mexico's economic recession, the real crime rate may well have increased during those years, posing more sharply the dilemma of how to respond to a crime wave. As is common in many countries in debates over the death penalty, Mexicans too differed in their views.

ISSUE POLARIZATION

Heir to a social revolution, contemporary Mexican politics has often been identified with "left-wing" political perspectives. In the preceding discussion we noted that Mexico had long had policies of substantial state intervention in the economy and of protection of the nation's economy from some of the forces of international trade and investment. Thus it may come as a surprise that so few Mexicans in 1986 identified themselves as leftists (table 3-1). More than half of Mexico's citizens thought of themselves as being ideologically located in the political center, but over one-third described themselves as being ideologically on the right. Fewer than one in ten Mexicans agreed to a self-placement on the political left.

Education helped to polarize Mexicans; the greater one's education, the more likely that one's views would be located at one or the other end of the spectrum. This observation calls for an important qualification of the views reported in the previous chapter. Education is somewhat more likely to in-

Table 3-1. Ideological Identification in 1986 (percent)

	Left	Center	Right
Whole sample	9	53	35
Education			
Secondary or less	8	56	34
Preparatory	11	52	36
University	14	45	39
Age			
18–29	9	53	37
30–49	10	54	34
50+	9	55	34
Gender			
Female	8	57	33
Male	11	50	37
Class			
Upper	7	61	30
Lower/middle	10	53	36
Church attendance			
Weekly	7	54	37
Less than weekly	11	53	34

Source: *New York Times* Mexico survey, 1986.
Note: N = 1,899 (weighted).

crease the sheer quantity of engagement in politics—greater attentiveness to political campaigns or greater willingness to discuss politics—but it need not lead to political moderation.

Because, as we saw in the previous chapter, there is an association between education and political interest, it should not be surprising that those who display greater political interest are also more polarized ideologically. Males and lower- to middle-class Mexicans are also somewhat more polarized ideologically, but age and religiosity do not matter much.

Although the Mexican political system "hugs" the political center, Mexicans in 1988 were divided over most issues—except payment of the foreign debt (see tables 3-2 through 3-6). In no case except debt payment was there a majority or plurality larger than 53 percent, and in no case except debt payment was there a minority smaller than 31 percent. The typical split in opinion had only about 10 percentage points between those holding one position and those holding the opposite position. Mexico's ideological consensus in 1986 ("center hugging") had not yielded an issue consensus by 1988. We turn to consider specific issues.

Table 3-2. Attitudes toward Capital Punishment (percent)

	Favor	Oppose
Whole sample	42	52
Region		
North	34	58
Central	40	53
South	45	48
Federal District	52	46
Education		
Secondary or less	38	55
Preparatory	45	51
University	51	45
Political interest		
Great	45	49
Some	43	53
None	40	52
Age		
18–29	44	52
30–49	41	52
50+	41	52
Gender		
Female	42	52
Male	43	52
Class		
Upper	51	45
Lower/middle	40	54
Church attendance		
Weekly	40	54
Less than weekly	44	50

Source: IMOP S.A. (Gallup) poll, May 1988.
Note: N = 2,960.

In 1988 a majority of Mexicans opposed capital punishment (table 3-2). Education, social class, and region were among the better predictors of attitudes toward capital punishment. A majority of university-educated and of upper-class Mexicans favored capital punishment, whereas a majority of the least well educated and of middle- and lower-class Mexicans opposed capital punishment. A comparably effective predictor of attitudes was region. A majority of residents of the Federal District favored capital punishment, whereas a strong majority of northern Mexicans opposed it. Age and gender made no difference at all in attitudes toward capital punishment,

Table 3-3. Attitudes toward Economic Investment by
Foreign Companies (percent)

	Favor	Oppose
Whole sample	53	31
Region		
North	62	25
Central	54	28
South	47	39
Federal District	49	36
Education		
Secondary or less	49	32
Preparatory	58	32
University	61	28
Political interest		
Great	60	30
Some	59	29
None	48	32
Age		
18–29	56	33
30–49	53	30
50+	48	31
Gender		
Female	50	30
Male	57	33
Class		
Upper	56	30
Lower/middle	53	32
Church attendance		
Weekly	52	32
Less than weekly	55	31

Source: IMOP S.A. (Gallup) poll, May 1988.
Note: N = 2,960.

while levels of political interest and religiosity had at best a minor impact. The better-off Mexicans who lived in the Federal District felt especially threatened by the crime wave in Mexico City in the mid-1980s and, perhaps as a result, became supporters of the death penalty.

Turning to economic issues, Mexicans strongly favored investment by foreign companies; this is one of the most lopsided distributions of opinion. The support for investment by foreign companies was broad as well as deep. Majorities or pluralities of Mexicans of all educational, social-class, and church-attendance categories, of all levels of political interest, and of all age groups and regions supported investment by foreign companies. No margin in favor of foreign investment was narrower than 8 percentage points.

In contrast to the comparable direction of education and social class in responses to the question about capital punishment, education and class do not have the same explanatory effect in the responses to the question on foreign investment. With regard to investment, education and political interest pointed in similar direction. Those with university education and those with substantial political interest were much more likely to support investment by foreign companies. On the other hand, social class, along with age, gender, and religiosity, made little difference in explaining variance in support for foreign investment. Not surprisingly, support for foreign investment was strongest in northern Mexico, where foreign-owned in-bond industries (*maquiladoras*) were most likely to operate and where jobs had been created as a result.

A majority of Mexicans also favored making the import of foreign goods a bit easier, but the division of opinion on this question was much narrower than on foreign investment. Nevertheless, by small majorities or small pluralities, Mexicans of all levels of political interest, all age groups, and all social-class and church-attendance categories, as well as both males and females, favored making importing easier. The same was true for Mexicans from all regions except the Federal District and Mexicans of all educational levels except the university-educated.

Education and region are the main explanations for variance in attitudes toward freer importing. University-educated Mexicans were evenly divided on whether to place stricter limits on imports; a slight majority of residents of the Federal District would impose such restrictions. The lesser "outward orientation" of Federal District respondents was also evident in the discussion of foreign investment, but with regard to the latter even Federal District respondents favored it by a wide margin. It is among those with more education that the difference in attitudes toward foreign investment and freer importing is especially marked. University-educated Mexicans favored investment by foreign companies by a margin larger than two to one, but they were narrowly divided in their views toward facilitating or restricting imports, leaning to restriction. (On the other hand, age, gender, social class, and church attendance explain no variance; levels of political interest have an ambiguous effect.)

Attitudes toward the payment of Mexico's foreign debt present yet another pattern of the distribution of opinion. On this issue Mexicans lined up overwhelmingly to one side: they favored continued payments on the foreign debt. Never fewer than two-thirds of respondents for all the cate-

Table 3-4.   Attitudes toward Foreign Imports (percent)

	Make Importing Easier	Place Stricter Limits
Whole sample	50	43
Region		
North	50	43
Central	54	36
South	49	44
Federal District	47	51
Education		
Secondary or less	50	40
Preparatory	52	46
University	48	50
Political interest		
Great	55	42
Some	49	46
None	51	38
Age		
18–29	50	40
30–49	50	42
50+	50	46
Gender		
Female	49	45
Male	51	42
Class		
Upper	51	45
Lower/middle	50	43
Church attendance		
Weekly	50	42
Less than weekly	49	45

Source: IMOP S.A. (Gallup) poll, May 1988.
Note: N = 2,960.

gories listed in table 3-5 favored continued payments on the foreign debt. There is near uniformity in the relative distribution of opinion per category. Consistent with other answers, the fewest "outward-oriented" responses, in this case continued debt payments, were found in the Federal District, but even there the margin in favor of continuing debt payments is larger than two to one. In no other category was the opinion gap as large as with regard to region, but even among regions this gap was small.

Table 3-5. Attitudes toward Mexico's Foreign Debt
(percent)

	Continue Paying	Stop Paying
Whole sample	70	24
Region		
North	69	24
Central	71	22
South	73	22
Federal District	66	30
Education		
Secondary or less	69	24
Preparatory	74	23
University	69	27
Political interest		
Great	68	27
Some	72	22
None	67	25
Age		
18–29	73	24
30–49	67	25
50+	70	24
Gender		
Female	70	24
Male	70	25
Class		
Upper	73	24
Lower/middle	69	24
Church attendance		
Weekly	70	24
Less than weekly	70	25

Source: IMOP S.A. (Gallup) poll, May 1988.
Note: N = 2,960.

Whereas the policies on foreign investment and freer imports dated from the second half of the de la Madrid presidency, the policy of honoring debt payments marked the beginning of his term. Clearly a consensus had been forged over continued debt payments in ways not evident in the responses to other issues.

Finally, we consider attitudes toward the privatization of state enterprises (table 3-6). Mexicans were evenly divided in their views about the

Table 3-6. Attitudes toward Government-Owned
Industries (percent)

	Sell to Private Companies	Maintain State Control
Whole sample	44	44
Region		
North	52	35
Central	33	52
South	40	48
Federal District	51	42
Education		
Secondary or less	37	47
Preparatory	49	45
University	60	37
Political interest		
Great	44	49
Some	46	46
None	44	39
Age		
18–29	43	48
30–49	45	41
50+	45	41
Gender		
Female	39	44
Male	49	45
Class		
Upper	58	34
Lower/middle	41	47
Church attendance		
Weekly	42	45
Less than weekly	47	43

Source: IMOP S.A. (Gallup) poll, May 1988.
Note: N = 2,960.

relative wisdom of such policies, but this tie masks the most strongly polarized pattern of responses to a given issue. University-educated and upperclass Mexicans strongly favored privatization, perhaps in part because they could benefit from it. Less well educated and lower- and middle-class Mexicans opposed privatization, though by lesser margins than their educational and social-class opposites favored it. Northern Mexicans strongly favored privatization, as did Federal District respondents, though by a lesser margin. Respondents from central Mexico outside the Federal District and, by a lesser margin, those from southern Mexico strongly opposed privatization. The regional differences might have been related to perceptions about the kinds of firms active in those particular regions. Private enterprises are more visible in the north, whereas state enterprises have often undertaken development or distributional projects in the south.

In comparison to these sharp differences, other differences were more modest, but they do exist. Males favored privatization, while females did not. The youngest Mexican adults opposed privatization, while older Mexicans favored it. The greater the level of political interest, the greater the opposition to privatization. Religiosity mattered the least of all the variables, with the more churchgoing opposing privatization slightly and the more secular favoring it slightly.

Mexicans tended to disagree rather more sharply over specific issues than over broad ideological concepts. Just as important, the attitudinal configuration is different for each of the specific issues. Focus, for example, on the attitudes of those with a university education. They favored the death penalty, foreign investment, continued debt payments, and privatization, but they were split on trade. In the responses to the death penalty, university education and upper social class were important explanatory factors pointing strongly in similar directions; higher political interest was a much less important explanation. In the responses to foreign investment, in contrast, university education and high political interest were important explanatory factors that pointed strongly in the same direction, but social class was much less important. In the responses to freeing imports, university education remained an important explanation, but social-class differences explained nothing while the analytical effect of varying levels of political interest was ambiguous. Finally, in the responses to privatization, university education, social class, and political interest were important explanations for variance, and they pointed in similar directions in the single most polarized set of responses. It is impossible to give a unified interpretation of the analytical significance and comparability of effect of the combination of university education, social class, and levels of political interest.

We have shown, therefore, the complexity of Mexican public opinion. Even on economic issues, attitudes did not cumulate consistently to a very high degree, even if they did so to some degree. Different kinds of Mexicans held different patterns of views as one turned from economic issue to economic issue. It was possible to favor foreign investment but to oppose freeing imports. Even on economic issues that seemed similar, Mexican public opinion was varied and multifaceted.

Table 3-7.   Consistency among Issue Positions

	Pro–Foreign Investment	Pro–Foreign Imports	Repay Foreign Debt	Sell State Industries
Pro–foreign imports	.32 **			
Repay foreign debt	.21 **	.14 **		
Sell state industries	.12 **	.03	−.04 *	
Reinstate capital punishment	−.02	.04 *	−.07 **	.10 **

Source: IMOP S.A. (Gallup) poll, May 1988.
Note: The coefficients above are maximum likelihood polychoric correlations.
$N = 2,262$.
$* = p < .05$. $** = p < .01$.

ISSUE CONSISTENCY

Did Mexicans display consistency in their approach across issues? Did they respond to questions along a pattern that would indicate that they held an ideology? Did Mexicans who favored freeing imports also favor foreign investment, foreign debt payments, and the privatization of state enterprises? Conversely, did Mexicans who would restrict imports also oppose investments by foreign companies, continued debt payments, and the selling off of state enterprises? And how did these economic issues relate to attitudes toward capital punishment?

In table 3-7 we present correlation estimates to assess the connection among attitudes toward five issues. Focusing at first just on the four economic issues, we can see that there was an economic ideology. Of the six correlations among the four economic issues, five are statistically significant, four of them strongly so. Moreover, attitudes on capital punishment also correlate with the economic attitudes; three of the four correlations between capital punishment and economic issues are statistically significant. Those who would reinstate capital punishment would also privatize state enterprises and favor freer trade, but they would not support continued payments on the foreign debt. The correlations between the economic issues and capital punishment are not strong, however.

We were especially interested in the relationship between education and political interest, on the one hand, and economic-issue consistency, on the other. Did education and political interest foster economic-issue consistency? Figures 3-1 and 3-2 present the results of our analysis. We have called "neoliberal" those who favor foreign investment, freer trade, the pri-

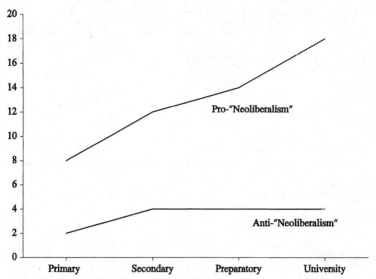

Figure 3-1. Consistency of Economic Policy Preferences, by Educational Level (percentage having consistent preferences)
Source: IMOP S.A. (Gallup) poll, May 1988.
Note: The "neoliberalism" measure is a composite of four items: attitudes toward foreign investment, foreign imports, Mexico's foreign debt, and state-controlled industries. Education is significantly correlated with consistently pro-"neoliberal" positions (tau = .10, χ^2 = 35.8, p < .001). N = 2,949.

vatization of state enterprises, and continued payment of the foreign debt. We have called "anti-neoliberal" those who take opposite views.

As evident from figure 3-1, there is a strong, statistically significant relationship between consistently neoliberal attitudes and level of education: the greater the level of education, the greater the level of consistent neoliberalism. As evident from figure 3-2, there is also a statistically significant relationship between consistently neoliberal attitudes and levels of political interest; in general, the greater the level of political interest, the greater the level of consistent neoliberalism. The relationship between neoliberalism and level of political interest is more complex than in the case of education, however, because those with the greatest political interest are somewhat less likely to be consistent neoliberals. The relationships between consistent anti-neoliberalism and either education or level of political interest are not statistically significant, however.

Therefore, the levels of education and political interest help to explain only one of the two possible economic ideological orientations, namely,

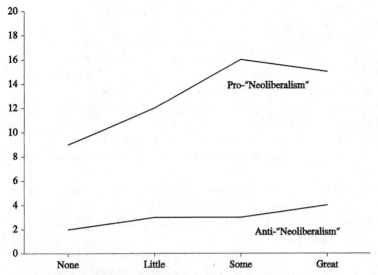

Figure 3-2. Consistency of Economic Policy Preferences, by Level of Political Interest (percentage having consistent preferences)

Source: IMOP S.A. (Gallup) poll, May 1988.

Note: The "neoliberalism" measure is a composite of four items: attitudes toward foreign investment, foreign imports, Mexico's foreign debt, and state-controlled industries. Political interest is significantly corelated with consistently pro-"neoliberal" positions (tau = .07, χ^2 = 19.0, p < .001). N = 2,939.

neoliberalism. The sources of anti-neoliberalism are much harder to pin down. To put the same point differently, education and political interest do not explain economic-issue consistency in general in Mexico, but they do explain one kind of economic-issue consistency, namely, neoliberalism. In the 1980s the Mexican government made a strong pitch to propagate an economic ideology favorable to open markets. Mexico's most politically interested and best-educated citizens clearly picked up on these official cues and were most likely to make the connections between attitudes toward the foreign debt, imports, foreign investment, and the selling off of state firms.

The information presented in figures 3-1 and 3-2 also allows us to estimate the overall level of economic-issue consistency in 1988. At its maximum, about 22 percent of university-educated Mexicans were consistent in their attitudes toward economic issues in 1988 (22 percent being the sum of consistent neoliberals and consistent anti-neoliberals in figure 3-1). The level of economic-issue consistency was typically lower for the less well educated and for the various levels of political interest. Should such a maximum of 22 percent of economic issue–consistent university-educated Mexicans be considered high or low?

Nie, Verba, and Petrocik calculated an index of issue consistency for the mass public—not just the university-educated—in the United States that did not just focus on economic issues; their index combined attitudes toward the size of government, welfare support for blacks, school racial integration, economic welfare, and foreign policy. The lowest level of U.S. mass public issue consistency, so measured, was 26 percent in both 1956 and 1960 (from 1964 to 1973, during the time of the Vietnam war and domestic racial conflict, U.S. issue consistency hovered between 39 and 44 percent).[13]

Therefore, even the most economic issue–consistent Mexicans—those with a university education—were much *less* consistent over a more narrowly defined set of economic issues during the presumably ideologically charged 1988 elections than were ordinary U.S. citizens even in one of the least ideological eras of U.S. history, namely, the 1950s.

We conclude, therefore, that there was issue consistency in Mexico that conformed to an economic ideology. Those who favored foreign investment did indeed favor increasing foreign imports, repaying the foreign debt, and selling off state enterprises to the private sector, for example. Issue consistency extended somewhat beyond the economic realm to include attitudes toward such issues as capital punishment. Moreover, issue consistency was greater among those who were more highly educated (as is also true in the United States).[14] The pattern of statistical significance, the size of the coefficients, and figure 3-1 support this inference.

On the other hand, these correlations about issue consistency were not very strong. The strongest correlation was between attitudes toward foreign investment and attitudes toward foreign imports: those who favored one were likely to favor the other, but even this linkage was much weaker than scholarly, journalistic, or political commentary had suggested in 1988. The privatization issue in particular seems not to belong to the same economic ideology. True enough, those who favored the selling off of state enterprises also favored foreign investment, but those who favored privatization did not necessarily favor freer imports. Moreover, there is the suggestion in the evidence that those who would stop payments on the foreign debt were somewhat more likely to favor privatization.

The support for the selling off of state enterprises is difficult to interpret because all relationships were weak. But there seemed to be a cluster of Mexicans who might be called "business nationalists." They favored a larger national private business sector and fewer state enterprises, but they did not necessarily favor letting imports in more easily and might oppose continued payments on the foreign debt. In this sense privatization might not be part of policies of economic liberalization such as those that would foster the free movement of traded goods and investments.

As might be expected from the trauma of Mexican politics and economics in the 1980s, there is evidence of issue consistency in Mexico, but it is striking—given the usual sharply contested, issue-consistent commentary reported earlier in this chapter—that the levels of issue consistency in the electorate were not higher, and that the privatization of state enterprises seemed unrelated or very weakly related to the other economic issues of which it is thought by some to be a part. Certainly the level of economic-issue consistency in Mexico is much lower than in the United States, even when one compares the views of Mexico's educated elite on economic issues at a time of presumed ideological ferment (1988) with the U.S. mass public's views over a wider array of issues at moments apparently free from ideological politics (the late 1950s).

PERSPECTIVES ON THE NATION AND THE SELF

Despite the lack of consensus over most issues and the lack of consistency across issues, Mexicans did agree on something: Mexico was going to hell. The proportion of Mexicans who believed in 1986 that the country was headed on the right track was minuscule; it was still only 38 percent on the eve of the 1988 presidential election.

In both 1986 and 1988 there was little variation among the categories included in table 3-8. In 1986 those with higher levels of political interest, the young, and males were more optimistic. In 1988 the gender gap on optimism remained but had narrowed; age no longer made much difference, nor did the remaining categories, which had also not made much difference in 1986. In 1988 only the level of political interest made a difference in explaining variance in optimism: the greater the interest, the greater the optimism. But even among the most interested Mexicans, pessimism reigned in both 1986 and 1988.

A key point about table 3-8 is the trend over time. Optimism doubled between 1986 and 1988. This has two implications. First, the country's mood had already begun to change in the closing years of the de la Madrid presidency—a mood change that would continue to improve under Salinas, as we shall note in a later chapter. Second, and more important, the Mexican electorate was not dumb. Between 1986 and 1988 Mexico's gross domestic product (GDP) grew by a cumulative 3 percent, in contrast to a −3.8 percent change in 1986. There was some reason for optimism. Mexico's popu-

Table 3-8. Is the Country Headed on the Right Track?
(percentage saying yes)

	1986	1988
Whole sample	18	38
Education		
Secondary or less	17	36
Preparatory	20	39
University	19	36
Political interest		
Great	19	41
Some	21	43
None	14	32
Age		
18–29	20	39
30–49	16	37
50+	14	37
Gender		
Female	14	35
Male	21	40
Class		
Upper	17	38
Lower/middle	18	38
Church attendance		
Weekly	16	39
Less than weekly	19	37

Source: *New York Times* Mexico survey, 1986; IMOP
S.A. (Gallup) poll, May 1988.
Note: N = 1,899 (weighted, 1986) and 2,960 (1988).

lation grew faster than GDP between 1986 and 1988, however, so GDP per capita changed by a cumulative −1.5 percent in those years. There was also reason for most Mexicans to remain pessimistic. The level of consumer price inflation in 1988 was half that of 1986 (further reason for optimism), but the level of average wages in manufacturing had remained unchanged between those two years and was still 28 percent below the 1980 level (continued reason for pessimism). In short, the Mexican electorate's judgment about the country's direction was about right.[15]

When asked more specifically about how the Mexican economy was doing (table 3-9 reports the percentage that answered "well" or "very well"), the respondents gave answers similar to those reported in table 3-8. In both 1986 and 1988, Mexicans were overwhelmingly pessimistic. Even in 1988

Table 3-9. Perceptions of Economic Well-Being, 1986 and 1988 (percent)

	National Economy Is Doing "Well" or "Very Well"		Personal Finances Are "Good" or "Very Good"	
	1986	1988	1986	1988
Whole sample	11	23	41	57
Education				
Secondary or less	10	21	35	50
Preparatory	16	26	50	66
University	10	25	53	67
Age				
18–29	14	26	49	63
30–49	9	19	35	53
50+	9	24	29	48
Gender				
Female	10	20	40	58
Male	13	26	41	56
Class				
Upper	11	26	25	71
Lower/middle	11	22	42	53
Church attendance				
Weekly	10	24	42	57
Less than weekly	12	22	40	57

Source: New York Times Mexico survey, 1986; IMOP S.A. (Gallup) poll, May 1988.
Note: These items were phrased as follows: "Would you say that the national economy is doing very well, well, badly, or very badly? Now speaking of you personally, how is your own economic situation? Would you say that it's very good, good, bad, or very bad?" N = 1,899 (weighted, 1986) and 2,960 (1988).

only 23 percent thought that the economy was doing well. In 1986, once again, there was more optimism among those with greater political interest and the young (and slightly more among males). By 1988 the gender gap had widened and a bit of a social-class gap had opened, but in both years most differences were minor. There was a doubling of optimism levels from 1986 to 1988, even if the 1988 level of optimism remained low.

What is noteworthy about table 3-9 is the juxtaposition between levels of optimism about the nation and the self. In 1986, 41 percent of Mexicans thought that their personal finances were good—four times the number of those who thought so about the state of the nation. By 1988, 57 percent of Mexicans thought that their personal finances were good—a level more than twice the number of those who thought so about the state of the nation. For each year and each analytic category listed in table 3-9, the level of optimism about personal finances was typically at least twice the level of optimism about the nation's economy.

In 1986, though gender and religiosity explained little about the variance in attitudes about personal economic well-being, everything else pointed to highly diverse perceptions about personal circumstances. Most curiously, the lower the social class, the higher the level of optimism. We doubt that this reflects objective reality. (This is a good opportunity to remind the reader that polls are mainly about what people think, not necessarily about how things really are!) The young, the university-educated, and those with greater political interest were considerably more optimistic.

Between 1986 and 1988, optimism about personal finances rose for each of the categories listed in table 3-9; the lowest increase was 11 percentage points. In 1988 the mood was euphoric among those with higher educational levels. So too it was with upper-class Mexicans, who this time were probably reflecting objective reality. The young and those with greater political interest remained very optimistic, while gender and religiosity continued not to matter.

To close this analysis, let us focus on attitudes in 1988 toward four issues (table 3-10): Would the economy be improving, inflation decreasing, unemployment decreasing, and personal income rising? Only one-sixth of Mexicans thought that inflation and unemployment were decreasing, and only 22 percent thought that the economy was improving, while 44 percent thought that their personal income was rising. Except among the university-educated, the proportion of Mexicans who thought that their personal income was rising did not reach 50 percent in any of the demographic categories. Again excepting the university-educated and also the upper-class respondents, the proportion of Mexicans who thought that the economy was improving did not reach 25 percent in any of the demographic categories. With regard to all four issues, pessimism was more marked among women, the least well educated, and those of lower social class.

With regard to unemployment, respondents were probably right in their pessimism. Data on unemployment in Mexico's largest cities, including the Federal District—whose citizens were the most pessimistic about it—varied little during the 1980s and would not improve soon. With regard to the economy as a whole, though GDP was increasing a bit, GDP per capita—a better measure of well-being—had been negative in 1986, again in 1987, and it would be so in 1988. With regard to inflation, respondents would soon be proved wrong, but their mistake was understandable. Mexican consumer price inflation had accelerated each year between 1984 and

Table 3-10. Little Optimism in 1988 about Future Economic Conditions (percent)

	Economy Improving	Inflation Decreasing	Unemployment Decreasing	Personal Income Rising
Whole sample	22	17	17	44
Region				
North	24	18	19	45
Central	18	18	17	42
South	23	18	17	42
Federal District	21	11	15	47
Education				
Secondary or less	14	11	12	35
Preparatory	23	20	18	47
University	31	24	23	50
Age				
18–29	21	15	17	51
30–49	22	18	18	41
50+	21	17	17	31
Gender				
Female	20	14	14	41
Male	24	19	20	47
Class				
Upper	26	20	23	45
Lower/middle	21	16	16	44
Church attendance				
Weekly	22	17	17	43
Less than weekly	21	16	17	45

Source: IMOP S.A. (Gallup) poll, May 1988.
Note: N = 2,960.

1987; then in 1988 it dropped sharply, to half the 1986 level and less than one-third the 1987 level.[16] At the time the poll was taken (May 1988), the full effects of the decline of the inflation rate had not been felt, nor was it clear that the decline already in evidence would be consolidated.

More important for our purposes is whether the degree of optimism or pessimism was a function of a kind of "rational expectation" based on economic ideology. Did the believers in neoliberalism have greater faith that the course that the Miguel de la Madrid government had charted, and that Carlos Salinas promised to continue, would improve Mexico's economic circumstances? If so, belief in consistent neoliberalism and economic ebullience would be associated.

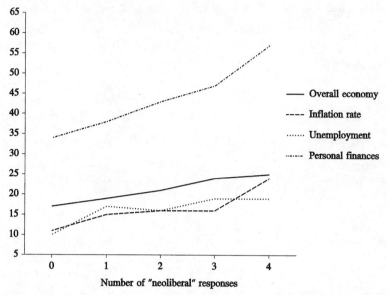

Figure 3-3. Optimism about Mexico's Economy, by Preference for "Neoliberal" Economics (percentage who were optimistic)

Source: IMOP S.A. (Gallup) poll, May 1988.

Note: "Neoliberal" attitudes are correlated at .06 with attitudes toward the Mexican economy; .06 with expectations regarding unemployment; .05 with predictions about inflation; and .13 with the respondent's own future economic situation. All correlations are significant ($p < .01$). $N = 2{,}382$.

The evidence summarized in figure 3-3 shows that there were statistically significant relationships between economic optimism and consistent neoliberal attitudes: the greater the extent of consistent neoliberalism, the greater the optimism about Mexican economic performance. This relationship is not very strong, however. The highest correlation reported in figure 3-3—the one between perceptions about one's own future personal finances and consistent neoliberalism—is only .13. To put it bluntly, even respondents who seemed to believe wholeheartedly in the new course that the government had charted in economic policy were not very upbeat about the nation's future.

In conclusion, Mexicans were profoundly worried about the direction of their country in general, and of the nation's economy in particular. They were pessimistic about trends in key indicators such as inflation and unemployment. But they were less gloomy in 1988 than in 1986. In both years

Mexican citizens showed a good grasp of reality, and a part of that reality was that Mexico was beginning to recover. Most important, as we turn to consider elections in subsequent chapters, the state of personal finances was far better than the state of the nation, and it is the state of pocketbook, more than that of the Treasury, that often shapes elections.

CONCLUSION

In the 1980s the perennial issues that faced Mexicans acquired a new or renewed meaning. The decade-long economic hardship focused their attention, not unlike the prospect of a hanging. The government's changes in economic policy marked a turning point in the nation's history. Not surprisingly, Mexicans were divided in their assessment of these policies. Our data show that there was significant issue polarization among Mexicans on the eve of the 1988 presidential election. As it also happened in the United States in response to the events of the 1960s, Mexicans showed consistency in their approach to several economic issues, denoting the existence of underlying economic ideologies, and they even displayed some consistency between some social issues (e.g., capital punishment) and economic issues.

And yet while the level of issue polarization was high, the level of issue consistency was not. Some issues such as the privatization of state enterprises were at best distantly related to other issues that are often thought to be part of a package of economic liberalization. Even among the economic issues that were related to each other, the strength of association was modest. Nor was there analytical consistency as various social categories approached different issues: education, social class, and political interest, for example, were not consistent explanations from one economic issue to the next. Despite the strong ideological "feel" of the 1988 presidential election campaign, the level of economic-issue consistency among Mexicans remained well below the level of economic-issue consistency in the United States during the 1950s. Even well-educated Mexicans were remarkably issue-inconsistent over the economy. And consistent neoliberal beliefs had only a modest effect in raising confidence in Mexico's economic future.

In his classic work *An Economic Theory of Democracy*, Anthony Downs argued that in conditions of uncertainty, political parties may rely upon ideologies in order to maximize votes. Rational voters, moreover, may decide how to vote by focusing on ideological appeals instead of comparing policies; voting on ideological grounds saves time because voters need not become experts on the specific issues that may separate the political parties.[17] In 1988, Mexican politics was surely marked by uncertainty, but partisan ideological appeals were likely to founder because Mexicans were not ideologues. Their views on specific issues did not overlap sufficiently to permit ideological appeals to succeed in maximizing votes. The views of Mexicans seem to vary more by issue than by worldview.

Mexicans held complex views about their nation's economy. Despite evidence of some ideological traits, the orientations toward issues were sufficiently different as to suggest distinct intellectual dimensions. If so, their connection to partisan choices should be expected to be equally complex. The next chapter undertakes to analyze that possible connection.

4 ❖ THE PARTISAN CONSEQUENCES OF CITIZEN ATTITUDES: VOTING INTENTIONS IN THE 1988 ELECTION

How do citizens who have long been governed by the same party in an authoritarian regime plan to vote when there seems to be a chance that they could turn the incumbents out of office? In such elections, do citizens focus mainly on the future of the ruling party and its incumbents? Are these elections ideologically competitive, with party choice shaped by attitudes on policy issues and social cleavages? How do such citizens respond to the entry of a new party to challenge the rulers, and how strong is such a new party likely to remain from one election to the next? We address these questions by focusing on Mexico's historic 1988 national elections.

In the July 1988 presidential elections, Mexico's electorate split into three large voting blocs.[1] The long-ruling Institutional Revolutionary Party (PRI) claimed just over half the votes for its presidential candidate, Carlos Salinas de Gortari. In 1982 the PRI and small allied parties had claimed 71 percent of the votes cast for presidential candidate Miguel de la Madrid; in the 1960s and 1970s the PRI and its allied parties always claimed more than 80 percent of the votes cast in presidential elections. In 1988 the long-established opposition party, the National Action Party (PAN), led by Manuel Clouthier, came in third, well behind a new political force, a coalition of several parties on the political left led by Cuauhtémoc Cárdenas. Cárdenas himself, and many of his close associates in the new coalition, had once belonged to the PRI.[2]

In this chapter we hope to show that the voting intentions of Mexican citizens as reported to our pollsters are best explained in terms of voter judgments about the prospects for the political regime's ruling party and the voter's past party preferences. The election directly poses the question of the prospects for democratization. Voters asked themselves, above all, whether they continued to support the ruling party or, as Mexican scholars sometimes call it, the "party of the state." These explanations are strongly significant statistically. We also argue that the organizational weaknesses among the parties of the left help to explain important aspects of the election outcome. The Cardenista coalition failed to mobilize voters who had chosen to abstain in the 1982 election. We also find that voter attitudes are not well explained by (1) attachments to social cleavages; (2) attitudes on policy issues; or (3) general assessments about the present circumstances of and the prospects for the nation's economy or personal finances.

We also argue that Mexico's 1988 election did *not* feature a "sectoral partisan realignment" as scholars typically define this expression. "A realignment may be defined as a significant shift in the group [or sectoral] bases of party coalitions, and usually in the distribution of popular support among the parties as a result. . . . . [Many] people who earlier would have been unaffiliated, or loyalists of one party, now affiliate with another."[3] (A "critical" sectoral realignment is caused by sharp and massive partisan changes; a secular sectoral realignment may occur more slowly.) The novelty in the 1988 election was a new menu of political parties, not a change in the group or sectoral bases of party coalitions, nor a rush of unaffiliated voters to the opposition, and certainly not a wholesale breakdown in partisan loyalties.

In the chapter's last section we probe these conclusions further. We propose and explain a two-step "model" of Mexican voting behavior. Mexicans decide first on their judgment about the ruling party. Lurking beneath that judgment there are also differences by issue, prospective economic assessments, and social cleavages that shape voter choices between opposition parties, and that therefore shape the electoral arena. Thus a potential realignment could be discerned, but it was held back by the overriding significance of judgments about the ruling party and its presidential candidates.

In this fashion Mexicans exhibit traits of strategic voting not unlike those found in multicandidate decision-making environments.[4] Voters ask first whether the ruling party will remain viable and capable of making national policy in the future. Only when the answer to that question is no do citizens turn to the opposition, and then they do so according to policy preferences, performance judgments, and social attachments.

ASSESSING ARGUMENTS

The Institutional Revolutionary Party has long been a bureaucratized organization proud of the oxymoron in its very name. The party claims legitimacy from both Mexico's historic revolution and its near opposite—the reality of institutional rule.[5] In this section we spell out the reasoning behind the choice of variables for subsequent analysis as well as the puzzles we hope to address. The following subsections elaborate on this chapter's opening questions.

The Ruling Party

When citizens long-governed by the same party in an authoritarian regime face a fairly open election, the fate of the regime's ruling party becomes the central question for many voters; even those who oppose the ruling party do not necessarily oppose all of its policies, nor does their vote embody the social cleavages often evident in competitive politics.[6]

We assess the importance of ruling-party factors through questions that ask respondents about their past voting behavior and about the nation's prospects if a different party were to govern. If Mexico's voters were not focused mainly on the fate of the ruling party, then attitudes toward specific issues, general expectations about present and future economic circumstances, and ties to social groups would have a more salient role, while views about the ruling party's future would matter much less. To distinguish between these hypotheses, we take into account the Mexican context.

First, in Mexico, questions pertaining to, say, freer trade or foreign investment do not a priori tap support for or opposition to the ruling party, because the leaders of one major opposition party, the PAN, have officially favored such general policies. Responses to these questions thus measure attitudes on specific issues, not necessarily attitudes toward the ruling party. If attitudes toward issues were to explain Mexican voting behavior, we would conclude that the hypothesis about the preeminence of ruling-party factors in explaining voter choice does not hold.

Second, judgments about retrospective and prospective economic circumstances help to explain voter choice in many European countries where the same party has not governed alone for generations.[7] In this study we distinguish between responses to questions about the prospective economic situation posed in general terms from questions about the country's prospective situation that are specifically related to what would happen if a party other than the PRI were to gain power. If general questions about economic expectations were to explain Mexican voting behavior, we would conclude that the hypothesis about the preeminence of ruling-party factors in explaining voter choice does not hold.

Third, as the "party of the state,"[8] the PRI claimed election victories virtually without fail until 1988, by means fair and foul—at times including coercion and fraud. The PRI has never accepted defeat in a presidential election. Until 1988 it had never accepted defeat for a Senate seat or, until 1989, for a governorship. The PRI has been integral to the authoritarian political regime. If asked about a future without the PRI in power, Mexicans understand that they are not being asked about the fate of a "mere party."

We asked voters whether the country's economic conditions or its social peace would be hurt or helped if a party other than the PRI were to gain power; we also asked about general expectations concerning PRI strength. If these questions were to prove insignificant, or less important than questions about demographic factors, issues, or general economic expectations in explaining voter choice, we would conclude that the hypothesis about the preeminence of ruling-party factors in explaining voter choice does not hold.

The Organization of the Ruling Party

Prior to the 1988 elections the PRI typically depended on indirect collective affiliation. Various organizations belonged to the three sectors—one each for workers and peasants, and a third more heterogeneous one for middle-class organizations—that have constituted the party since its major reorganization in 1938.[9] A worker, for example, would belong to a labor union that was itself a member of a national labor confederation; this confederation would in turn belong to the PRI's labor sector. The individual worker did not belong directly to the PRI, but by belonging to labor union organizations that were part of the PRI, the individual worker had an indirect affiliation with the ruling party independent of such a worker's personal partisan preferences. This internal party organization enabled top PRI leaders to channel support and to manage conflicts among its constituent organizations. Paradoxically, this also meant a party without direct members, a party that sought the support of organizations but not directly the support of the nation's citizens, a party always ready to govern but not necessarily to win honest elections.[10]

The impact of the PRI's internal structure on voting behavior was open to competing hypotheses. Did the PRI have a strong hold on individuals affiliated with the party in this indirect manner, or did the indirect affiliation weaken individual loyalties to the party, rendering once-PRI voters vulnerable to the appeals of a new opposition party many of whose leaders had once belonged to the PRI? The PRI had long drawn strength from its peasant and labor unions; thus it might be expected that lower-class Mexicans would vote PRI. Alternatively, the indirect nature of PRI "membership," the weakness of an internal party life, and the reputation of some labor and peasant leaders for bossing their members might mean that lower-class voters had no special attachment to the PRI. In the 1960s and 1970s there were local revolts at some work-centers seeking union democratization against traditional PRI-affiliated labor unions.[11] This disconnection between the PRI and its presumed affiliates might cancel the effects of demographic factors. Under this alternative, voting would be unrelated to union membership, social class, religion, region, and other demographic factors.

The Presidency

Mexico's political system has been highly centralized (see chapter 1); the presidency has been "at its epicenter."[12] Since the party's foundation, the president has always come from the PRI. We would be shocked if presidential performance failed to explain much about voting behavior in Mexico.

The Issues during the 1988 Election Campaign

As we saw in chapter 1, in the 1980s Mexico's economy was in deep trouble. In 1988, voters were intensely conscious of economic difficulties and had reason to worry about the country's and their own finances. In terms of economic policy orientations, the speeches of politicians suggested some convergence between the PRI and the PAN in support for freer markets, although the PAN candidate, Manuel Clouthier, argued that only the PAN truly favored freer markets. These speeches also indicated that voters who disagreed with market-oriented economic policies could vote for Cárdenas. At the same time, there was also some convergence between Cárdenas and Clouthier in their claim that only by defeating the PRI could Mexico democratize at long last, while Salinas argued that the PRI too stood for democracy. In this fashion each candidate made a distinct set of claims for the support of the electorate, but there was enough overlap among these claims that certain differences might become blurred in the eyes of the ordinary voter.

Cárdenas argued, "I think that this administration has been letting foreigners take over our fundamental decisions. It has acted not in the interest of the country but of foreigners who are against Mexico." He also said, "Possibly, the present administration and the program of Carlos Salinas are rational in some way, but it is a rationality which goes against the majority. It is a rationality that has made many Mexicans poor, that leaves important economic decisions to foreigners, that closes the channels of democratic expression. A rationality conducive to repression and dictatorship."[13]

Cárdenas's own economic policy proposals were complex. For example, he noted that "foreign investment can be of help. It can contribute to this country's development." He looked to foreign investment especially to promote exports. He also argued, however, that foreign investment had to be regulated carefully "in such a way that would not allow for loss of capital within the country," which might raise fear in the minds of some foreign investors about controls over profit remittances. Cárdenas at times also suggested that he believed that in some circumstances foreign investment could be "having a negative effect on the economy" in ways that might be "hurting our national sovereignty."[14] Such talk would appeal to economic nationalists worried about the de la Madrid administration's market openings, which Carlos Salinas promised to continue.

With regard to the foreign debt, Cárdenas argued that Mexico would "have to declare a moratorium on the debt," but that this should be done "in order to reach an agreement" with Mexico's creditors that would be more favorable for the country. In this fashion he sought to appeal to those who supported a debt moratorium while seeking at the same time not to break entirely with the international financial community, which nonetheless would be concerned by expressions such as "We have to pay what we legitimately have to pay. And we do not have to pay what is not legitimate to pay."[15]

During the 1988 election campaign, Salinas took strong exception to Cárdenas's characterization of his own views and of the de la Madrid administration's policies. "In fact," Salinas argued, "the fundamental decisions of Mexico's economic policy have been taken by Mexicans . . . for the interests of our fellow Mexicans." The positive results of the de la Madrid administration's policies were already evident in 1988, in Salinas's view: "Inflation was controlled, international reserves were built up, the country has the possibility of beginning to grow again, and you no longer have the social anger which existed in 1982."[16] Salinas differed specifically with Cárdenas concerning how to address the foreign debt problem. Salinas believed that "it's better to negotiate than to enter into confrontation" with the banks and other creditors.[17] In contrast, he argued, Cárdenas's economic policy proposals "have not been consistent," nor have they been "based on an integrated program."[18]

Salinas defended the de la Madrid administration's policies to free Mexican trade "because . . . to close our economy as had happened in decades past would imply [that Mexico would be left with] obsolete technologies, the creation of less employment per peso invested, and the defeat of the possibilities for all Mexicans to have a dynamic economy capable of generating employment." Instead, Salinas said, he would "follow a strategy of export promotion, [and] an industrialization tied into exports in order to strengthen the internal market."[19]

On the other hand, during the 1988 election campaign, Salinas also opposed the calls of some for Mexico to join a North American free trade agreement with the United States and Canada in order to ensure that U.S. markets would remain open to Mexican exports (Canada and the United

States had already signed a bilateral free trade agreement): "Listen—on the record—Canada and the United States have almost similar economies. The U.S. and Mexico have very dissimilar economies, it's so uneven the relationship that that's the reason why I have rejected the idea of entering a North American common market." But, he added, "I would like to talk and see the plan for a bilateral kind of agreement" that included the freer movement of both goods and labor.[20] (As president, Salinas reversed himself and took the lead to create the North American Free Trade Agreement— NAFTA—with both Canada and the United States; the NAFTA did not include the freer movement of labor.)

Salinas's opposition to a North American free trade agreement during the 1988 campaign may have sought to limit the number of defections of import protectionists to Cárdenas. Salinas also appealed to the political left by pledging that he would give high priority to "the challenge of social justice," because "we continue to have a very unequal distribution of income"; Mexico under his leadership, he said, would move toward a more "equitable distribution."[21]

On behalf of the PAN, Manuel Clouthier argued forcefully that the PAN was "the only real option" for those who wished to change Mexico because "we believe profoundly in democracy and democracy not only in politics but [also] democracy in the market and democracy in the . . . labor unions, democracy in the fields, democracy in the culture." In his view, both Cárdenas and Salinas were "statists," eager to retain government controls over the economy. In contrast, Clouthier argued, if elected his administration would deregulate the economy to free up the creative capacities of individuals. Clouthier would remove government barriers to private investments in a wide variety of economic sectors (including secondary petrochemicals—a proposal with which Cárdenas disagreed quite specifically because he would reserve such activities to state-owned companies);[22] he would privatize the state-owned banking system; and he would "let off all the controls of the . . . government." In the more competitive private economy and more democratic politics that would result, Mexicans would be "at peace." "I don't mean the peace of cemeteries," Clouthier said, the peace of a coercive government such as the one he believed Mexicans had, but a peace that would come from the rededication of Mexicans to work.[23]

During the 1988 election campaign, Salinas dismissed the PAN's economic policy arguments. He said that the PAN did not have a serious economic project for Mexico. Instead, Salinas campaigned against the PAN mainly by raising the fear that the PAN would generate political and social instability. Salinas claimed to be worried "above all" by "the persistent call to disobey the law" that he attributed to PAN leaders. Playing on Clouthier's call for a different kind of "peace"—not "the peace of the cemeteries," as we quote him above—the Salinas campaign sought to plant the notion that the PAN would provoke disorders contrary to the "social peace which the overwhelming majority of Mexicans demand."[24]

Salinas, finally, defended his own commitment to the promotion of democracy: "My vision of Mexico's future is tied into the challenges we face today . . . [the] democratic challenge. Mexican attitudes have changed. We have a more participatory community, more critical, better informed. That is going to be reflected in political participation. And that is [a] challenge to my party to modernize its processes, actions, [and] political work to continue deserving the confidence of the majority of Mexicans."[25]

Issue-oriented voting was certainly rational and conceivable in 1988. The three principal candidates disagreed sharply on various issues, though they modulated some of their positions. Cárdenas appealed to economic nationalists and asserted a role for the state in directing the economy. His call for a debt moratorium and his insistence on regulating foreign investment were consistent with his overall approach, but he also sought to appeal to those who would welcome foreign investment under certain conditions and who would promote exports. Cárdenas and Clouthier emphasized strongly their commitment to a more democratic Mexico whose fate should no longer be entrusted to a single party. Clouthier sketched perhaps the strongest claim to being a proponent of market-based economic policies. Salinas in fact shared as well a strong market orientation in his views of economic policy, as he would demonstrate during his presidency; in this way he fought off Clouthier's challenge. During the campaign Salinas explicitly rejected the idea of leading Mexico into a North American free trade agreement, in part to prevent import protectionists from defecting. He campaigned against the opposition in part by raising fears that their victory would threaten Mexico's "social peace"; he also sought to limit support for the opposition by asserting his own commitment to democracy and to the promotion of a more equitable distribution of income.

Compared with elections in the United States, for the most part these three candidates provided a choice, not an echo. The overlaps in some policy positions, however, permitted each candidate to include among his supporters voters whose views of economic policy and even of the nation's democratic prospects diverged.

The Opposition, Cleavages, and Parties

Did the shaping of Mexico's electoral arena in 1988 conform to broader patterns of the construction of partisan cleavages? As Seymour Martin Lipset and Stein Rokkan argued in their classic work, in the genesis of party systems there are often territorial and religious bases for opposition because of a clash between the central nation-building political coalition and territorially or religiously defined oppositions.[26] Scholars of Mexico have found ecological correlations between demographic variables and party voting.[27] In Mexico the PRI markedly centralized power in the capital city and at moments in its history sponsored anticlerical policies.

The PAN might embody these territorial and religious cleavages. The PAN has had a long if generally unsuccessful electoral trajectory opposing the PRI. The PAN is a real political party, with its own members, activists, programs, and goals. Especially in some northern states such as Chihuahua—though, as we shall see, not everywhere—there is a genuine vibrancy to its internal life.[28] It may have won the 1986 gubernatorial elections in Chihuahua (though the official results gave the governorship to the PRI). In the PAN's history, fidelity to Roman Catholicism has played a significant role.[29] The PAN has also seemed stronger among middle-class voters. Thus we expected that high individual voter loyalty to the party, plus region, church attendance, and social class, would help to explain voting preferences for the PAN.[30]

During the 1988 election campaign, PRI candidate Carlos Salinas thought that the PAN was vulnerable to the charge that it cared mainly for the middle class and the rich. With Clouthier's candidacy, Salinas averred, the PAN "presented a program which, I am worried, may affect rights guaranteed by our constitution" to workers, and also to peasants in *ejidos* (collective farms, tilled individually).[31] In that way Salinas sought to solidify support for his candidacy from the PRI's peasant and labor sectors.[32]

The Cardenista coalition was new in 1988. Formed around the person of Cuauhtémoc Cárdenas, a former PRI governor of the state of Michoacán and son of former president Lázaro Cárdenas, Cardenistas lashed out at the PRI's lack of internal democracy—such practices as having the incumbent president de facto "appoint" his own successor, or having most PRI candidates for governor and Congress be chosen by a few leaders or by the president himself. We expected Cardenistas to oppose the PRI, the official candidate, import liberalization, the sale of state enterprises, and continued servicing of the foreign debt. Consistent with the Lipset-Rokkan argument, the Cardenista coalition had some features of a socialist party in part because it included various parties that bore the name "socialist" and because it included the old Mexican Communist Party. This coalition's newness led us to ask how they got their votes. Did they mobilize the previously unmobilized? Did they take voters as well as leaders from the PRI? Had PAN voters in the past been "closet leftists" who had voted for the PAN mainly because there was no viable left-wing alternative but who in 1988 at last had one?

THE CRISIS OF THE RULING PARTY

In anticipation of the 1988 presidential elections, in August 1986 a group of leading PRI politicians formed the Democratic Current (*Corriente Democrá-tica*) to advance a broad program of political, economic, and social change.[33] One important goal was to challenge the unwritten but consistent political "rule" that the outgoing president of Mexico in effect chooses his own successor. In May 1987 former PRI party president Porfirio Muñoz Ledo formally proposed the former PRI governor of the state of Michoacán, Cuauhtémoc Cárdenas, as a candidate for the PRI presidential nomination. One goal of Democratic Current politicians was to oblige the PRI to follow its own formal party statutes. These statutes required that the party's candidate be chosen by the party's national convention after an internal campaign within the party; during that within-party campaign would-be candidates would have to announce their candidacy publicly and register formally as PRI precandidates. The national convention would have a real choice among various candidates prior to choosing its official nominee.

President Miguel de la Madrid and the PRI leadership chose to open the PRI nomination process to a limited degree.[34] The PRI leadership announced that six men were especially worthy of consideration for the nomination; Cárdenas was not among them. In July 1987 the six "acceptable" precandidates spoke before the party's National Executive Committee; the sessions were broadcast over national television. These sessions represented a significant political opening, but subsequent events showed that the actual choice of the PRI's candidate was not much different from that in elections past.

At 9 P.M. on the eve of the PRI's National Executive Committee meeting of October 3, the party's official registry for precandidates was open. The party president proposed Carlos Salinas de Gortari as the sole acceptable precandidate; leaders of the PRI's three constituent "sectors" immediately supported the motion. Twelve hours later the Executive Committee decided "unanimously" that Carlos Salinas de Gortari would be the sole precandidate to be presented to the PRI's national convention in November. In effect the process vitiated the party statutes and led directly to the departure from the PRI of many Democratic Current politicians.[35] Cárdenas, Muñoz Ledo, and others within the PRI joined with other existing small parties in the opposition to form the largest challenge ever to the longstanding PRI rule.

Table 4-1.　Attitudes toward the PRI's Position in Mexican
Elections, 1986 and 1988 (percent)

	1986	1988
Preference for a more competitive party system	62	63
Satisfaction with one-party dominance	37	28

Source: New York Times Mexico survey, 1986; IMOP
S.A. (Gallup) poll, May 1988.
Note: This item was worded as follows: "Which of these
two phrases best describes your own opinion? (a) The Mexican political system should be changed so that candidates
of other parties will be able to win more often. (b) The
existing system works well and should be left as it is." N =
1,899 (weighted, 1986) and 2,960 (1988).

This path-breaking elite struggle seemed politically feasible in part because Mexicans already favored a more competitive political system. As
evident in table 4-1, by 1986 and continuing into 1988 an overwhelming
majority of Mexicans already preferred a more competitive party system in
which candidates from parties other than the PRI would be able to win
more often. The percentage of those who said that they were satisfied with
the existing system dropped to below one-third between 1986 and 1988.
The PRI was vulnerable to opposition challenges as it headed into the 1988
election.

Consistent with this preference for more open politics, voter identification with the PRI dropped steadily between 1983 and 1988, as evident in
figure 4-1. In 1983 nearly one-quarter of Mexican respondents stated that
they did not have a partisan preference. Support for the PAN rose steadily
in the 1980s. Support for other parties fell during the mid-1980s but
boomed by the eve of the 1988 election. By 1988 virtually all respondents
had taken a partisan stand.[36] In 1988 the combined support for the opposition parties nearly equaled the expressed support for the PRI. Considering
that some who expressed a preference for the PRI might have felt intimidated by the polling process, it is possible that there was an opposition
majority in the wide electorate prior to the 1988 elections.

Among the most likely voters in 1988, however, there remained a PRI
majority over the combined opposition (table 4-2). Moreover, the consequences of a three-party race became apparent: the PRI was likely to win a
smashing victory in a political system whose electoral law allocated the

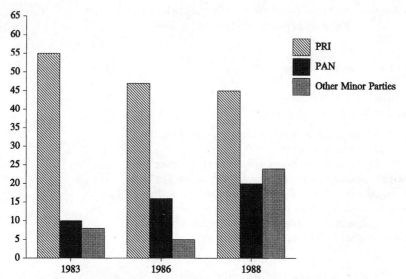

Figure 4-1. Mexican Party Preferences in the 1980s (percent)

Source: Miguel Basáñez poll, March 1983; New York Times Mexico survey, 1986; IMOP S.A. (Gallup) poll, May 1988.

Note: N = 7,051 (1983), 1,899 (weighted, 1986), and 2,960 (1988).

presidency, all Senate seats, and most seats in the Chamber of Deputies by means of the "first-past-the-post" rule.

The precariousness of the PRI's position becomes evident in table 4-3, which compares the 1988 presidential elections that were held in both Mexico and the United States. In both countries, in 1988 the incumbent party won with a candidate other than the victor in the prior presidential election. Commentators on U.S. elections often refer to the relative weakness of party loyalties in the United States. The longstanding clout of the PRI, in contrast, might suggest a much higher degree of party loyalty in Mexico. In fact, in 1988, Reagan voters in the United States were more loyal to Bush than were de la Madrid voters in Mexico to Salinas. The continuity coefficient for the PRI was appreciably lower than that for the Republicans. This finding lends preliminary support to the view that the PRI was a "party without members"; at least it requires us to examine carefully the significance of individual allegiance to the PRI.

In sum, in 1988 the PRI was at risk of losing the national election if the opposition were to unite. Even with a divided opposition, the PRI could suffer important election setbacks. The question then arises: On what basis

Table 4-2.   Candidate Preferences Leading up to the 1988
              Presidential Election and Official Results
              (percent)

	Gallup Poll	Official Results
Salinas (PRI)	55	50
Clouthier (PAN)	20	17
Cárdenas (PFCRN, PARM, PPS, PMS)	22	32
Other	2	1

Source: IMOP S.A. (Gallup) poll, May 1988; Embassy of Mexico to the United States.

Note: Respondents who were not registered to vote or did not have a clear candidate preference have been dropped from this table. N = 1,914 (65 percent of the total sample).

Table 4-3.   The Stability of the PRI Bloc, in Comparative Perspective
              (percent)

	Mexico: Voted for de la Madrid in 1982?	
	No	Yes
Intend to vote for Salinas in 1988?		
No	87	24
Yes	13	76
Total (N)	100 (351)	100 (962)

	United States: Voted for Reagan in 1984?	
	No	Yes
Intend to vote for Bush in 1988?		
No	92	18
Yes	8	82
Total (N)	100 (410)	100 (632)

Source: IMOP S.A. (Gallup) poll, May 1988; American national election study, 1988.

Note: This table includes only those respondents who were registered to vote in 1988 and reported voting in the previous presidential election. In the Mexican sample the correlation between vote choices is .57 (Kendall's tau); in the United States the correlation is .72.

could opposition politicians construct coalitions to defeat or at least to embarrass the PRI?

THE BASES FOR PARTISAN REALIGNMENT?

Ideology, Issues, Democratic Values, and Turnout

Could the underlying ideological bases of Mexican politics have shifted? We examined this question in the previous chapter in terms of attitudes toward specific issues. We found fairly high issue polarization but much lower levels of issue consistency. Here we turn to a somewhat different matter: Is there a potential for partisan realignment evident in the linkage, or lack thereof, between parties and self-declared ideological orientation?

Cárdenas apparently thought so. On November 29, 1987, he officially launched his campaign for the presidency. He broke with the PRI and took much of the Democratic Current with him. He accepted the presidential nomination from four small opposition parties and continued discussions with other opposition parties that would later also endorse his candidacy. He appealed to a broad array of people from different walks of life (though not to business executives); he raised issues that would resonate especially on the political left. He closed his speech saying, "Let us fulfill our commitment as revolutionaries."[37]

Was Cárdenas right in his political gamble? As shown in table 4-4, in 1986 most Mexicans had no difficulty in placing themselves on a left-right ideological scale. Whereas most voters on the right readily identified with the PRI or the PAN, 42 percent of centrists and 35 percent of leftists expressed no partisan preference. Moreover, nearly one-fifth of left-wing voters preferred parties other than the PRI and the PAN. These data indeed suggest the possibility of an ideological realignment. Heading into the 1988 election, these unaffiliated centrist and leftist "floating" voters could be mobilized by politicians who appealed to the left but who had careers that also showed certain establishment credentials to appeal to the center: Cárdenas and the PRI's Democratic Current.

On the other hand, Clouthier and Salinas did not think that there were many votes to be found on the extremes of the political spectrum. During the 1988 election campaign, Clouthier argued that "we are not a right-wing party and we are not a left-wing party."[38] Carlos Salinas too positioned himself between the "option of the right-wing which is to ignore fundamental [social and economic] rights of Mexicans which are even in our Constitution" and the option of the political left, "which is a confusion between socialism, trotskyism, stalinism, communism, [and] a little bit of anarchism, too." "And before those two extremes," concluded Salinas, "we are, I have reiterated, the progressive center because," this inveterate reader of public-

Table 4-4.   Partisan Preferences and Ideological Orientation in 1986
(percent)

	Left	Center	Right
PRI	26	42	63
PAN	20	13	19
Other	19	3	3
Not sure/no preference	35	42	15
Total (weighted N)	100 (178)	100 (1,014)	100 (669)

Source: New York Times Mexico survey, 1986.
Note: Ideological orientation was measured by asking respondents,
"Do you lean toward the right, the center, or the left in most matters?"
Virtually all (98 percent) could place themselves on this scale.

opinion polls argued correctly, "it is there where the majority of Mexican opinion is."[39] The evidence presented in table 4-4 confirms that many more Mexicans thought of themselves as being on the right than on the left but that well over half of all Mexicans thought of themselves as being in the center. Clouthier and Salinas had a better feel for public opinion than did Cárdenas.

Moreover, the evidence of an anti-PRI "silent majority" waiting to be mobilized is modest at best. As the evidence in table 4-5 shows, Salinas received support from 51 percent of those eligible to vote in 1982 who had not voted in that election, whereas Cárdenas got only 28 percent of those voters; Salinas also drew well among voters too young to have voted in 1982. Cárdenas drew twice as many votes from former PRI voters as he did from those 1982 nonvoters who were nonetheless eligible to vote; he drew twice as many votes from all former voters (PRI plus PAN) as he did from all 1982 nonvoters (those who had been too young to vote in 1982 plus those who were old enough to vote but did not). Cárdenas's relative electoral success came not from an enlargement of the political arena but from a reshuffle of voters. The electorate did not expand much in 1988, and to the extent that it did, the electoral benefit did not just redound to the opposition. In the absence of a more substantial expansion of the electorate, the case for an ideological base for partisan realignment is weak.

Could the underlying policy bases of Mexican politics have shifted instead? Did the voters respond to more specific issue schisms? In chapter 3 we presented evidence of substantial issue polarization. Did this polarization translate into partisan preferences? The answer is no. The differences reported in table 4-6 are remarkably modest. Support for the PAN was unrelated to economic issues. PAN supporters were found in comparable proportions among those who supported and those who opposed capital pun-

Table 4-5. Voting Behavior in 1982 and Candidate Choice in 1988: Did the Electorate "Expand"? (percent)

| | 1982 Voting Behavior | | | |
| | Voters | | Nonvoters | |
1988 Candidate Choice	de la Madrid (PRI)	Madero (PAN)	Inactive	Too Young
Salinas (PRI)	76	12	51	46
Clouthier (PAN)	9	60	20	22
Cárdenas (PFCRN, PARM, PPS, PMS)	13	28	28	28
Other	1	1	1	4
Total (N)	99 (962)	101 (270)	100 (240)	100 (294)

Source: IMOP S.A. (Gallup) poll, May 1988.

Note: Respondents who were not registered to vote or did not have a clear candidate preference in 1988 have been dropped from this table. The first and second columns do not total 100 percent because of rounding error.

ishment, foreign investment, import liberalization, and continued payment of the foreign debt. PAN supporters did favor privatizing state enterprises.

Cardenistas were quite sharply divided in their issue preferences. By modest margins, support for the Cardenista coalition was higher among those who favored capital punishment and those who held negative views on foreign investment, freer imports, servicing the foreign debt, and privatizing state enterprises.

Supporters of Salinas were also sharply divided in their issue preferences. By equally modest margins, support for Salinas tended to be higher among those who opposed capital punishment and those who favored foreign investment, freer imports, and the continued payment of the foreign debt but also the retention of state industries.

Although the candidates had at times etched out quite different positions on these issues, as we noted earlier they had also carefully clouded some of their views to appeal across the divide of issue polarization. Our evidence suggests that the "clouding effect" prevailed. The lack of correspondence between issue polarization and candidate polarization further weakens the possibility that ideological differences might have accounted for the vote shift in the 1988 presidential election. Mexicans were deeply divided in their views on issues and in their views on parties and candidates, but these two sources of division did not overlap.

Ronald Inglehart's writings on advanced industrial democracies remind us, however, that the left-right ideological spectrum and the economic issues we have considered so far need not be the only sources of electoral

Table 4-6.　Issue Preferences and Candidate Choice in 1988 (percent)

	Salinas	Clouthier	Cárdenas	N
Favor capital punishment?				
Yes	54	21	25	824
No	58	21	21	957
Foreign investment is:				
Positive	57	21	21	1,065
Negative	50	20	27	563
Both	50	19	26	114
Importation of foreign goods should be:				
Made easier	56	22	21	950
Limited	53	19	25	847
Continue paying foreign debt?				
Yes	58	20	20	1,335
No	47	21	29	477
Retain state industries?				
Yes	56	16	25	854
No	52	25	21	859

Source: IMOP S.A. (Gallup) poll, May 1988.

division. New "postmaterialist" issues may arise to divide the electorate.[40] In 1988 in Mexico one such issue was common crime. The evidence on attitudes toward capital punishment reported in table 4-6 (above) suggests, however, that attitudes toward crime have no greater discriminating power than do attitudes toward economic issues.

Another source of electoral division might have been attitudes toward democratic values. The challenge to the PRI from the PAN and from the Cardenistas emphasized their opposition to the authoritarian nature of the political regime. Supporters of the opposition might have had a higher level of interest in politics and been opposed to boss rule by a few strong leaders, as had long happened in Mexico's strongly presidentialist political system. In chapter 2 we found a long-term increase in interest in politics; Mexicans scored high even when compared with the advanced industrial democracies about which Inglehart has written. We also found that Mexicans had become less supportive of rule by just a few strong leaders.

Could it be that these shifts in political culture toward the values of democracy were more prevalent among opposition voters? Once again, the answer is no (table 4-7). Candidate choice is unrelated to attachments to democratic norms. Respondents who had a high level of interest in politics

Table 4-7. Attachments to Democratic Norms and Candidate Choice in 1988
(percent)

	Salinas	Clouthier	Cárdenas	N
Political interest				
Great	55	19	24	338
Some	57	21	21	471
Little	54	21	22	611
None	56	19	23	481
"A few strong leaders would do more than all the laws and talk"				
Agree	54	20	23	1,137
Disagree	55	21	22	646

Source: IMOP S.A. (Gallup) poll, May 1988.

or distrusted rule by a few strong leaders were no more likely to support the opposition. Salinas's own repeated commitments to advancing democracy in Mexico may well have worked.

In sum, through no fault of their own, some Mexican opposition leaders may have committed a strategic mistake. They observed that Mexicans were ideologically divided and polarized over issues. They also observed an emerging trend supportive of democratic values. They further noted that Mexican voter turnout had been low in earlier elections. They concluded, quite reasonably, that there was an ample basis on which to construct an opposition. They were wrong only in part, but in the part that mattered most to their candidacies.

As we have seen, all of these premises were correct except for the assumption that these attitudinal factors were linked to candidate choice and to party preference. Mexicans were indeed more democratic, but Mexican democrats were not more supportive of the opposition; some Mexican democrats backed Salinas too. Mexicans were deeply divided over issues, but those divisions fractured the candidate and party coalitions as well, in part because candidates at times appealed across the issue divide. Salinas raided free-marketeers from Clouthier and held on as well to statists who did not defect to Cárdenas. Mexican nonvoters turned out to be not oppositionist enough. What, then, explains voting intentions in 1988?

Economic Expectations

As is often the case in Western Europe and North America, Mexicans may vote motivated by general economic perceptions and expectations, though not necessarily connected to more narrowly defined policy issues (table

Table 4-8.   Economic Perceptions and Candidate Choice in 1988 (percent)

	Salinas	Clouthier	Cárdenas	N
Current Mexican economic performance				
Good	66	16	16	462
Bad	52	22	24	1,404
Future Mexican economic performance				
Improve	68	12	19	465
Worsen	45	27	26	674
Current personal financial situation				
Good	59	18	22	877
Bad	50	21	26	757
Future personal financial situation				
Improve	58	18	22	877
Worsen	52	24	23	461

Source: IMOP S.A. (Gallup) poll, May 1988.

4-8). Those who believed that the nation's and their own economic circumstances were bad or would worsen were more likely to vote for opposition
candidates. In particular, a majority of Mexicans who thought that the nation's economic performance would worsen in the future indicated a preference for opposition candidates. Those who had more hopeful expectations were strongly supportive of the Salinas candidacy. Nonetheless,
Salinas had support even from about half of those who had negative views
of the economy's and their own present or future economic circumstances.
Equally important, the two opposition candidates seemed about equally
capable of capitalizing on prospective economic discontent. These general
economic views, especially of the economy's prospective performance, tap
support for the opposition overall but do not distinguish well between Cárdenas and Clouthier supporters.

Organizational Strength and Socioeconomic Representation

A different explanation of the upsurge of support for the opposition focuses
attention on a concept explored earlier in this chapter, namely, that the PRI
may be a party without members. To the extent that it represents specific
interests, the PRI has been the party of the state; it represents the elites
above all. It is an instrument of governance. It has the resources and the
clout to mobilize support in the mass public, but that support does not run

very deep, especially among non-elites. The PRI's internal party life, as we noted at the opening of this chapter, might be so weak that the party itself might thus be organizationally disadvantaged in a more competitive election.

In contrast, the PAN's internal party life might be expected to be much stronger. Identifying with an opposition party did not bring benefits to individuals other than the satisfaction of supporting a cause they valued; PAN members might be expected to be more dedicated to the party as an organization. This factor could also distinguish between Clouthier and Cárdenas supporters. Cárdenas was in the process of putting together a somewhat heterogeneous coalition; Clouthier was backed by a party with a long life. If we were to find that the PAN had a very active organizational life, that might separate it from both the PRI and the Cardenistas.

On the contrary, we found that in 1983 the PAN's internal party life was quite weak (table 4-9). Only one-tenth of its supporters always attended party meetings, while more than half never did. The PAN was more a "mind-set" than a party. Alas, self-identified PAN members were less likely to "fly to the assemblies," as Jean-Jacques Rousseau might have wished, than self-identified PRI members.

In 1983 the PAN was in the midst of an organizational transformation. The "old" PAN had been ideologically coherent; it had been zealous of its autonomy and, to maintain it, had relied for financing mainly on membership contributions. PAN leaders had been local community leaders; the party honored its local cadres. The "new" PAN—as Mexican scholars call it, *neo-panismo*—was much more pragmatic, and therefore more interested in winning elections; it relied for financial support on business contributions. Its political campaigns came to rely more on the mass media; its new political leaders, such as Manuel Clouthier, were important businessmen. One result of this transformation may have been the weakening of internal party life.[41]

In 1983 the PRI too had a weak organizational life, though not as weak as the PAN's. Only one-fifth of PRI self-identifiers always attended party meetings. The proportion of PRI members who reported never attending party meetings outweighed those who said that they always did.

For both the PAN and the PRI, males, those with a university education, those with high income, and government employees were much more likely to participate in the internal life of their parties. In the PRI, older people were also much more likely to participate. (Of course, the importance of education and income in the making of Mexican political activists renders them quite similar to activists in other countries.)[42] In general, mere institutional affiliation did not automatically produce this mode of political

Table 4-9.   The Strength of Internal Party Organization during the Early 1980s
(percent)

| | How Often Did Supporters Attend Partisan Events? | | | |
| | PRI | | PAN | |
	Always	Never	Always	Never
Whole sample	20	27	9	53
Education				
Secondary or less	18	13	8	53
Preparatory	16	30	10	48
University	23	19	12	56
Age				
18–25	15	34	6	59
26–35	18	26	12	45
36–50	24	18	10	52
51+	33	17	10	67
Gender				
Female	13	38	7	61
Male	22	22	10	49
Monthly income (pesos)				
Less than 10,000	18	35	7	59
10,000–40,000	19	25	9	52
40,000–80,000	22	20	14	49
More than 80,000	25	17	13	54
Employment				
Government worker	27	20	14	49
Nongovernment worker	16	28	9	54
Unemployed	9	46	5	59

Source: Miguel Basáñez poll, March 1983.
Note: This item was worded as follows: "Do you attend events organized by your party—such as conferences or meetings—always, nearly always, at times, or never?" N = 3,902 (PRI) and 737 (PAN). In total, 7,051 respondents were included in the survey.

participation, although—contrary to expectations—it seemed to produce it more in the PRI than in the PAN. The PRI was an elite-based party, but so was the PAN.

This particular configuration of relationships suggests that Mexico ranks among those countries—among them the United States and India—in which socioeconomic factors are important determinants of political participation in part because parties have not sufficiently mobilized their own lower-class members. Because socioeconomic factors are so strong, Mexico's "haves" are overrepresented in the activist population within the par-

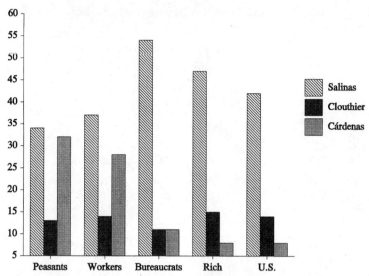

Figure 4-2. Perceptions of Which Candidate Best Represents the
Interests of Various Constituencies (percent)

Source: IMOP S.A. (Gallup) poll, May 1988.
Note: N = 2,960.

ties. There is inequality in access to participation among party activists.[43]
On this point, Mexico had not changed much since the 1950s, when the
association between social structure and political participation was also
found to be strong and when the effect of the interaction between social class
and organizational involvement on participation inequalities was similar.[44]

This strong elitist foundation for partisan life, though present in both the
PRI and the PAN, most clearly shaped public perceptions of the PRI, because it was after all the governing party. The data presented in figure 4-2
show that in 1988 Salinas was perceived as best representing the interests
of bureaucrats, the rich, and the United States. Clouthier was not identified
with any group in particular; he was seen as just as likely to represent the
rich as the poor. Salinas received strong competition from Cárdenas in the
perception of representativeness of the interests of workers and peasants.
Equally noteworthy, Salinas was perceived to be concerned about groups
across the social-class spectrum, whereas Cárdenas was perceived to be
concerned mainly about a lower-class constituency.

Given the elitist bases of the PRI and the PAN and the class-shaped public perceptions of the candidates, did socioeconomic cleavages shape candidate choice? The evidence in table 4-10 suggests that the answer might

Table 4-10. Demographic and Social Determinants of Candidate Choice in 1988
(percent)

	Salinas	Clouthier	Cárdenas	N
Education				
Primary	63	17	18	677
Secondary	56	18	25	415
Preparatory	47	24	27	400
University	51	23	23	415
Age				
18–29	50	22	26	741
30–49	57	20	22	848
50+	64	17	17	325
Gender				
Male	53	20	25	973
Female	58	21	20	941
Class				
Professional	58	21	18	324
Middle	46	21	29	298
Working	59	15	24	325
Union member?				
Yes	64	14	22	442
No	53	22	23	1,472
Region				
North	59	24	15	479
Central	56	17	24	474
South	67	12	20	446
Federal District	42	25	29	515
Population of city/town				
Less than 20,000	62	17	20	836
20,000–100,000	57	14	28	212
100,000–1 million	54	22	22	407
More than 1 million	44	28	25	459
Church attendance				
Weekly	59	21	18	953
Less than weekly	54	19	25	793
Never	45	22	33	163

Source: IMOP S.A. (Gallup) poll, May 1988.

be yes. Salinas drew more support from women, towns with fewer than twenty thousand people, southern Mexico (itself quite rural), older voters, union members, the less well educated, and churchgoers. Salinas was especially weak in the Federal District, even though the party of the state might have been expected to be stronger among elites and government employees. That is, the party of the elites drew the most support from non-elites. It comes through as a "traditionalist" party.

Cárdenas's best source of support was religiosity, or more precisely the lack thereof. He did best among voters who never went to church; they were twice as likely to vote for him as those who went to church every week. Cárdenas drew more support from voters with levels of education above the primary, from men, and from young voters. He had substantial support among middle-class Mexicans, even more than among working-class Mexicans. He was weakest in northern Mexico and strongest in Mexico City. Union membership did not matter in explaining support for him.

Clouthier drew support from the youngest voters, the better educated, the middle and professional classes, and those who did not belong to unions. He was quite weak in southern Mexico. Contrary to the PAN's reputation as a Roman Catholic party, gender and religion did not explain support for the PAN. This was the profile of a secular, center-right party—another illustration of what Mexican scholars often call *neo-panismo* to identify the impact of secular business elites who exercised great influence on the PAN in the 1980s.

In sum, socioeconomic factors mattered for both candidate choice and the nature of political participation, but they did so in complex ways. The internal organizational life of the PRI and the PAN is quite weak. The PRI was a party with few committed self-identified "members," but the PAN had even fewer. The PRI drew its activists from the elites but the bulk of its electoral support from the non-elites. The PAN's inner organizational life, much weaker than the PRI's, was just as biased in social-class terms. The Cardenistas might speak in the name of workers and the poorly educated, and Cárdenas was broadly perceived as representative of the interests of poor Mexicans, but Cardenismo was weaker electorally among those kinds of voters whom it wanted and was perceived to represent.

The 1988 party contenders, it should be noted, were national parties; they did not draw their support from just one segment of the electorate. To be sure, they drew disproportionately from certain regions and certain social categories, but each party drew some support from nearly everywhere. The nationalization of Mexican party politics may have been an unexpected outcome of the 1988 presidential election.

Table 4-11. Perceptions of the PRI's Viability and Candidate Choice in 1988 (percent)

	Salinas	Clouthier	Cárdenas	N
In ten years, will the PRI be stronger or weaker?				
Stronger	73	12	14	619
Same	64	17	18	470
Weaker	34	30	34	669
National economic performance if another party wins				
Better	31	30	36	749
Same	64	18	16	525
Worse	82	9	9	396
Will there be an increase in social unrest if another party wins?				
Yes	61	18	20	1,068
No	45	25	28	683
Presidential approval rating, on a 10-point scale				
Very high (9 or 10)	79	10	11	364
Favorable (7 or 8)	62	17	19	721
Mediocre (4 to 6)	38	30	30	473
Poor (1 to 3)	26	33	37	206

Source: IMOP S.A. (Gallup) poll, May 1988.

Institutional and Candidate Expectations

Given the institutional role of the PRI in the Mexican political system as well as the centrality of the presidency, how did Mexicans assess the likely future of the regime's institutions and the candidates who sought to lead them? We find that there was a strong association between presidential approval rating and party support (table 4-11). Those who approved of the president's performance supported the PRI quite strongly; support for the opposition increased as presidential approval ratings dropped. This factor identified support for the opposition but did not distinguish between Cárdenas and Clouthier.

PRI supporters were found especially among those who believed that the PRI would get stronger over time, and that the economy would worsen and social unrest would increase if some other party were to gain power. Supporters of the opposition were much more likely to be found among those who held the opposite views. On this score there is again little difference between the opposition parties. These are among the strongest relationships we found.

In 1988 Mexicans faced the first really competitive presidential election of their lives and of their nation's history. We asked them about their perceptions of the personality traits of the presidential candidates; these are reported in table 4-12. These four items tap into the dimensions that political psychologists most often use when they assess candidates in the United States, namely, strength, competence, integrity, and empathy.[45]

There was little differentiation among these traits; Salinas did well on all four. He was seen as the strongest, most intelligent, most honest, and most caring; his margin over his opponents was strong across these items. He was weakest on honesty and caring, where Cárdenas came within range of posing a challenge. The four factors were quite closely correlated (on average, the items in table 4-13 are intercorrelated on the order of .76). We infer that beliefs about the personality of each candidate were tightly bound with the general assessment of him; as a result, the traits of each candidate did not vary much. Thus it comes as no surprise that a summary trait index based on these four items was highly correlated with candidate choice (table 4-14). This index identified remarkably well the link between the voter and the chosen candidate.

What, then, might explain voter intentions in 1988? We conclude, preliminarily, that attitudes toward the ruling party's future strongly shaped voter choice, as did attitudes toward individual candidates and the incumbent president. Together these factors delineate the roles of the ruling party and the presidency as well as those of incumbents and would-be incumbents.

General judgments about present and prospective economic performance were also important in explaining voter intentions, though they were not nearly as effective discriminators as the question that connected the economy's future with the prospects that a party other than the PRI would gain power. There was, however, little connection between attitudes toward issues and party choice, and between attachment to democratic values and party choice. Certain socioeconomic factors contributed also to some degree to explaining voter choice. Internal party life was generally weak, especially so in the PAN. Mexico ranks among those countries where political participation is affected by socioeconomic status and where partisan organizations do not mitigate such class differences.

With regard to the opposition parties, we reached two important preliminary conclusions. First, the PAN is not a confessional party. Second, Cardenismo failed to mobilize previously unmobilized voters—for example, those who could have voted in the 1982 presidential elections but

Table 4-12. Perceptions of Personality Traits (percent)

	Salinas	Clouthier	Cárdenas
Has the best leadership qualities	42	14	22
Is intelligent	36	10	18
Is honest	27	11	19
Cares about people like you	33	12	23

Source: IMOP S.A. (Gallup) poll, May 1988.
Note: N = 2,960.

Table 4-13. Correlations among Personality Trait Perceptions: Ratings of Salinas

	Has the Best Leadership Qualities	Is Intelligent	Is Honest
Is intelligent	.71		
Is honest	.75	.76	
Cares about people like you	.77	.78	.81

Source: IMOP S.A. (Gallup) poll, May 1988.
Note: The coefficients above are polychoric correlation estimates derived via maximum likelihood. All are strongly significant ($p < .001$). Ratings of Clouthier and Cárdenas are similarly structured. N = 2,960.

Table 4-14. Correlations among Personality Trait Ratings and Candidate Choice in 1988

Summary Trait Index	Candidate Choice		
	Salinas	Clouthier	Cárdenas
Salinas	.69	−.52	−.52
Clouthier	−.54	.71	−.24
Cárdenas	−.44	−.23	.75

Source: IMOP S.A. (Gallup) poll, May 1988.
Note: The coefficients above are polychoric correlation estimates derived via maximum likelihood. All are strongly significant ($p < .001$). N = 1,914.

chose not to do so—sufficiently to overcome the PRI's lead. Instead, Cárdenas appears to have based his campaign on a reasonable but seriously flawed strategy: the premise that the growth in generalized attachments to democratic values and the polarization over issues would create a large pool of voters who would vote for him. This did not happen.

Table 4-15. Predicting Support for Opposition Candidates in 1988

	Clouthier	*Cárdenas*
Previous PRI voter	−.70 (.29) **	−1.13 (.24) **
Previous PAN voter	2.48 (.38) **	1.03 (.37) **
Not previously mobilized	.11 (.35)	−.08 (.30)
Favor capital punishment	.07 (.10)	.15 (.09)
Increase foreign investment	.21 (.12)	.14 (.11)
Limit imports	−.05 (.11)	−.04 (.09)
Pay foreign debt	.11 (.12)	−.22 (.11) *
Retain state industries	.03 (.11)	.16 (.10)
Political interest	−.03 (.11)	.01 (.09)
Preference for "strong leaders"	.07 (.13)	−.05 (.12)
Current national economy	.07 (.14)	.02 (.13)
Future national economy	−.31 (.15) *	−.06 (.10)
Current personal finances	.04 (.17)	−.14 (.15)
Future personal finances	−.21 (.10) *	−.06 (.09)
Educational level	−.04 (.06)	.08 (.05)
Age	.01 (.01)	.01 (.01)
Female	−.10 (.24)	−.16 (.21)
Professional class	−.27 (.34)	−.73 (.31) *
Working class	−.39 (.35)	.06 (.28)
Union member	−.81 (.28) **	−.12 (.28)
Population of city/town	.10 (.08)	.02 (.07)
North	−.10 (.31)	−.70 (.29) **
South	−.80 (.34) **	.12 (.28)
Federal District	−.25 (.31)	−.18 (.23)
Church attendance	.08 (.07)	−.12 (.06) *
PRI getting stronger	−.42 (.13) **	−.34 (.12) **
Economy—other party	.91 (.16) **	.93 (.14) **
Social unrest—other party	.43 (.21) *	.28 (.18)
Presidential approval	−.09 (.05) *	−.14 (.04) **
Personality trait index: Clouthier	1.07 (.10) **	.14 (.12)
Personality trait index: Cárdenas	.17 (.10)	.75 (.07) **
Constant term	−2.67 (1.23) *	−1.23 (1.07)

Source: IMOP S.A. (Gallup) poll, May 1988.

Note: The coefficients above are multinomial logit estimates. Standard errors appear in parentheses. *LLF* = −1,493.0 (initial) and −763.6 (at convergence). The model correctly predicted 78 percent of the cases. $N = 1,359$.

$* = p < .05.$ $** = p < .01.$

ANALYZING AND EXPLAINING PARTISAN CLEAVAGES

Why did Mexicans plan to vote for the opposition parties? Because we are interested in modeling discrete choices among a set of partisan alternatives, a multinomial logit specification for regression analysis is appropriate. Table 4-15 presents the results of this analysis, where the relative importance of demographic, economic-expectation, issue-attitude, and political and institutional factors can be judged.[46]

We seek to explain the intention to vote for the PAN's presidential candidate, Manuel Clouthier, and for Cuauhtémoc Cárdenas, who headed a coalition that included four political parties on the ballot: the Mexican Socialist Party (PMS) included the old Communist Party; the People's Socialist Party (PPS), the Authentic Party of the Mexican Revolution (PARM), and the Frente Cardenista National Renovation Party (PFCRN)—the last previously known as the Socialist Workers' Party (PST)—had long been in coalition with the PRI, but this time they bolted to the opposition.[47]

The Parties, the Presidency, and the Presidential Candidates

The only variables that identify statistically significant relationships to explain the intention to vote for both opposition candidates are those that refer to the parties, the presidency, and the presidential candidates:

1. The more likely a voter was to have voted PRI in a prior presidential election, the less likely this voter was to support any opposition candidate in 1988.
2. The more likely a voter was to have voted for an opposition party in a previous election, the more likely this voter was to support an opposition candidate in 1988.
3. The greater the belief that the PRI would get stronger, the lower the likelihood of voting for an opposition candidate.
4. The greater the belief that the economy would improve if a party other than the PRI were to gain power, the greater the likelihood of voting for an opposition candidate.
5. The greater the approval for incumbent president Miguel de la Madrid, the less the support for the opposition.
6. The greater the esteem for the personality traits of a particular candidate, the greater the likelihood of voting for that candidate.

A core political division existed between the PRI and the opposition parties. The fate of the political regime's ruling party was the central decision facing each voter. First and foremost the voter asked, Am I for or against the PRI and the president?

This important finding casts doubt on the hypothesis that Mexico witnessed a critical sectoral realignment in the 1988 election, because the evidence of a shift in the group or sectoral bases of politics is weak. Those who had not been previously mobilized politically did not support one candidate more than another, contrary to what might be expected during a realignment. Moreover, party loyalty was strong and persistent across elections, not at all what would be expected at a time of realignment.

The Role of Issues, Democratic Values, and Retrospective and Prospective Economic Assessments

Consistent with the argument above, and with the discussion earlier in this chapter, for the most part the 1988 election was not about policy issues. There is no statistically significant relationship between attitudes toward policies and the likelihood of voting for Clouthier or Cárdenas (except that there is a modest association between the likelihood of voting for Cárdenas and a preference for not continuing payments on the foreign debt). Also consistent with the argument that issues matter little, the variables measuring attachment to democratic values—level of political interest and preference for strong leaders—are not statistically significant.

Voters' views about the current condition of the nation's economy or their own finances had no direct impact on their choices. On balance, these findings are inconsistent with a mode of analysis that emphasizes that citizens vote "retrospectively," that is, that they vote to reward or punish incumbent performance.[48]

Voters' views about the future of the nation's economy or about the future of their own finances had no direct impact on voting for Cárdenas. There was a negative association between expectations about the future of both the nation's economy and one's own finances, on the one hand, and the likelihood of voting for the PAN, on the other. That is, those who thought that the economy and their finances would get better were less likely to vote PAN. These results suggest that Mexico's 1988 presidential election had some similarities to many European elections in which voter behavior can be forecast from expectations about the economic future. Nonetheless, expectations about the economic future did not explain the Cardenista vote and were not a major explanation of voting for or against the PAN.

Compare the results on two variables: general expectations about the nation's economic future and expectations about the nation's economic future if a party other than the PRI were to gain power. The latter was a powerful and systematic predictor for all parties. The former was not statistically significant in the case of the intention to vote for Cárdenas. It was only moderately significant in the case of the intention to vote for Clouthier; in this instance the coefficient for the variable concerning the economy's future if a party other than the PRI were to gain power was more than three times that for the variable measuring general expectations about the economy's future.

We conclude, therefore, that Mexicans did not plan to vote in terms of general retrospective or general prospective assessments of the economy or their finances, or in terms of specific economic policy issues.[49] Instead, they focused on a particular kind of prospective judgment: the connection between the future of the "party of the state" and the impact of its fate on the future of the economy.[50]

Political Cleavages

This argument about the preeminence of ruling-party factors in Mexican elections must be tempered, however. There were differences between the opposition parties, which hinted at the development of distinct political cleavages. Consider the PAN. Union members were much less likely to support the PAN. The PAN was also much weaker in southern Mexico. As just noted, voters were less likely to vote for its presidential candidate if they thought that the economic future was likely to improve. Nonetheless, the PAN in 1988 had emerged as a national party, a substantial political accomplishment. It drew strength from throughout Mexico's northern and central regions, including the Federal District of Mexico City; from cities and towns big and small; and from all educational, generational, class, and gender categories. Nor was it more or less likely to draw support on the basis of church attendance.

Cardenismo too had emerged suddenly as a national party, although it was more narrowly based than the PAN. Cardenistas were less likely to attend church; they were also much weaker in the north; and they were less likely to draw support from professionals. Unlike the PAN voters, they were unmotivated by prospective economic assessments, but they were more likely to stop payments on the foreign debt. This was perhaps a socialist party in the making.

As noted in an earlier section, the assessment of the personality traits of each presidential candidate is strongly associated with voter choice. The lack of differentiation among those traits suggests, however, that the specific traits of the candidate were less important than the voter's perception of the candidacy as a whole: a would-be president from the opposition. In any event, the index of personality traits also helps to separate the Clouthier from the Cárdenas and the Salinas voters.

Was There an Ecological Realignment?

An ecological realignment occurs when there are "changes in the relative size of one or more social groups or economic strata. In this case, the bases of party support do not necessarily undergo marked changes. Rather, the relative size of various demographic or attitudinal groups changes, bringing with it a shift in the fortunes of two or more parties." In Japan and in Italy the long-term decline of the rural sector reduced the relative size of that conservative constituency, and as a result, support for the conservative parties fell in both countries.[51]

Wayne Cornelius and Ann Craig have argued that the same has happened in Mexico. "One of the key factors accounting for the long-term decline in the official party's effectiveness as a vote-getting machine," they write, "is the massive shift of population from rural to urban areas that has occurred in Mexico since 1950." They document the decline in the size of the rural areas and the decline in the PRI's national vote share. They (and others) have shown that the more rural the district, the higher the PRI's share of the vote.[52] We show that connection too for the 1988 election (see our table 4-10). In this sense an ecological realignment certainly occurred. Our evidence suggests, however, that the partisan impact of this ecological realignment should not be overstated.

As shown in table 4-15, in 1988 there was no statistically significant relationship between urbanism and ruralism, on the one hand, and voter choice, on the other. Even the evidence that Cornelius and Craig present shows that the PRI's share of the vote declined proportionately in rural and in urban areas, suggesting that something other than place of residence was tugging at the political loyalties of Mexicans. The continuing decline in the size of the rural sector has negligible partisan effects once the rural sector's support for the ruling party declines at the same speed as the urban sector's support for the ruling party.

Cornelius's own other work provides a clue to this puzzle. He demonstrated that it was untrue that rural migrants to the cities were automatic political radicals and argued instead that the patterns of political mobilization in the specific context of urban neighborhoods were the more important explanation for political behavior.[53] So too is the case more generally, we think, with urban and rural voters in Mexico in the 1988 election. There was nothing automatic about the views of rural folk or urban folk in the

1988 election. Powerful political forces divided urban Mexicans among themselves and rural Mexicans among themselves. The partisan meaning of the urban-rural distinction was not dominant because the patterns of politics in specific communities shaped voter choice. Urban and rural voters too focused above all on the fate of the ruling party and its meaning for themselves.

We conclude that there was a long-term ecological realignment that helps to explain the reduction in the PRI's vote totals over time, but we also show that the rural-urban distinction had a statistically insignificant partisan effect in the 1988 election. Other variables that cut across the urban-rural divide were far more important, especially the expectations about the future of the ruling party.

Organizational Factors

There was an important organizational story in the 1988 election. The PRI is indeed a party with voters loyal to it in election after election, even if, as we saw earlier, they are neither very active within the party nor as loyal partisans as U.S. Republicans. The statistical results on the importance of continued voting for the same party are strongly significant for the PRI and the PAN: each is very likely to draw from its same pool of voters in successive elections. But the PAN voter believed in occasional defections; in 1988 the Cardenista coalition drew quite significant support from voters who had previously supported the PAN. Many past PAN voters were sophisticated strategic voters. Prior to 1988 many PAN voters were motivated by their opposition to the ruling party but not by the PAN's views on particular issues. They voted for the PAN because that was the only way to oppose the PRI. Once a viable Cardenista option appeared in 1988, many 1982 PAN voters flocked to Cárdenas. In a more ideologically competitive election focused no longer on the fate of one party but on the ideas of various parties, policy issues, economic expectations, social ties, and candidates, this massive PANista vote-switching would be less likely to happen.

The Cardenista coalition's organizational skills were insufficiently developed, however. Although many Cardenista leaders had come from the PRI, voters who had supported the PRI in previous presidential elections were significantly likely *not* to vote Cardenista. Cardenistas could not effectively raid PRI supporters, who were more loyal to the PRI than comparable past PAN voters were to the PAN. Moreover, the Cardenistas did a poor job of mobilizing voters who had been eligible to participate in the 1982 presidential election but had chosen not to do so: the coefficient linking these previously inactive citizens to the new partisan insurgency is insignificant.

A TWO-STEP "MODEL" FOR MEXICAN VOTING BEHAVIOR 1

The results from table 4-15 suggest that the Mexican voter approached the 1988 elections by focusing, above all, on the fate of the PRI and the presidency, which are intimately interconnected. We believe, however, that a more ideologically competitive election lurked just behind this behavior; such voters behaved strategically, reasoning through two different decisions during the election. First, they made their judgment on the ruling party. Second, once some Mexicans got past their judgment on the ruling party, they made other kinds of voting decisions, which were shaped indeed by demographic and issue factors. These factors divided the PRI from the opposition and the opposition parties among themselves. To clarify these relationships, we seek to explore the interplay between ideological predispositions and beliefs about the PRI's long-term institutional viability. Thus we report in table 4-16 on the hypothetical probabilities of voting for the opposition parties. These probabilities are derived from the regression analysis presented in table 4-15.

At the top of table 4-16, the expected voter choices have been computed for two types of populations. The first row reports on those who believed that the PRI was becoming weaker and that opposition parties could do a good job of getting the economy to grow and maintaining social peace. The second row reports on those who believed that the PRI was becoming stronger and that opposition parties could not do a good job of getting the economy to grow and maintaining social peace. Among those who thought that the PRI was becoming stronger and that the economy and social peace would suffer if a party other than the PRI were to gain power, the probability of voting for Clouthier was 5 percent, the probability of voting for Cárdenas was 7 percent, and the probability of voting PRI was 88 percent. Among those who thought that the PRI was becoming weaker and that the economy and social peace would not suffer if an opposition party were to gain power, the probability of voting for Clouthier rose to 34 percent, the probability of voting for Cárdenas jumped to 36 percent, and the probability of voting PRI dropped to 30 percent; among these voters, Cárdenas would have been elected president.

We modeled, then, two kinds of voters. One we call a left-wing voter. Such a person would come from the working class and would belong to a union, would never attend church, and would oppose foreign investment, freer trade, continued payment of the foreign debt, and privatization of state enterprises. The other we call a right-wing voter. Such a person would come from the professional class and not belong to a union, but would at-

Table 4-16. Ideological Predispositions and Beliefs about the PRI's
Long-Term Viability in 1988: Some Expected Probabilities
of Voting for the Opposition

	Prefer Clouthier	Prefer Cárdenas
PRI becoming weaker	.34	.36
PRI becoming stronger	.05	.07
Voters with right-wing dispositions		
PRI becoming weaker	.53	.16
PRI becoming stronger	.08	.03
Voters with left-wing dispositions		
PRI becoming weaker	.06	.67
PRI becoming stronger	.01	.13

Source: IMOP S.A. (Gallup) poll, May 1988.
Note: These probabilities were derived from the estimated logit coefficients presented in table 4-15 ($N = 1,359$). A voter's perception of the
PRI's future viability is defined by three items: the expected strength of
the PRI in the next ten years; whether the national economy would prosper
under an opposition party; and whether there would be increased social
unrest if another party took control of the Mexican government. Left-wing
or right-wing predispositions are indicated by four factors: socioeconomic
status (professional versus working class); religiosity (weekly versus no
church attendance); union membership; and economic policy preferences.
All other independent variables in table 4-15 have been set to their mean
values.

tend church once a week and favor the four policies opposed by the left-
wing voter. Turn, then, to the bottom four rows of table 4-16.

Right-wing and left-wing voters who believed that the PRI was getting
stronger and that the economy and social peace would be hurt if a party
other than the PRI were to gain power were quite unlikely to vote for any
opposition party. They remained faithful to the PRI. What happens, however, if voters are ready to be governed by a party other than the PRI?

Among right-wing voters who believed that the PRI was getting weaker
and that the economy and social peace would not suffer if an opposition
party were to gain power, the probability of voting for Clouthier rose to
53 percent, while the probability of voting for Cárdenas was 16 percent.
Among left-wing voters who believed that the PRI was getting weaker and
that the economy and social peace would not suffer if an opposition party
were to gain power, the probability of voting for Clouthier was 6 percent,
while the probability of voting for Cárdenas rose to a whopping 67 percent.

Among voters ready to live without the PRI, therefore, the PAN benefited substantially among right-wing voters and lost considerably among left-wing voters. Cárdenas benefited enormously among left-wing voters but lost more than half his vote among right-wing voters. Nonetheless, Cárdenas's support among right-wing voters was more than double the PAN's support among left-wing voters; this suggests strategic voting by right-wing voters ready to support Cárdenas because he seemed more likely than Clouthier to beat Salinas. In 1988, among voters ready to replace the party in power, issues and demographic cleavages mattered. Provided voters thought that the PRI was becoming weaker and that the economy and social peace were not in danger if an opposition party were to win, then such voters were much more likely to support the opposition. These voters were also more likely to split between the opposition presidential candidates in ways that conform to the evolution of a political party and cleavage system in the midst of sectoral realignment. The prospects for such a realignment, we now see clearly, were dimmed by the strength of the institutional variables, especially the assessment of the future of the PRI and its impact on the country.

Moreover, the strategic voting behavior of many Mexican voters was impressive. Such voters reasoned through two separate electoral decisions: a negative judgment on "the party of the state," and then a choice of an opposition vehicle. And a minority of these voters continued to exhibit strategic behavior even though it meant voting for a candidate with whom they differed in terms of policy preferences and social attachments. Some right-wing and, to a lesser degree, some left-wing voters made electoral judgments that maximized the likelihood of the PRI's defeat—thereby reinserting traits that focused on the fate of the ruling party even after we sought to dampen their impact.

CONCLUSION

After decades of single-party rule and well-founded suspicions about the conduct of their rulers and the fairness of their elections, in 1988 Mexican citizens approached the national election by focusing on the fate of the party that had long governed them. First and foremost they asked themselves, Am I for or against the "party of the state" and its leader? The most statistically significant and consistent explanations for voting intentions were related to these concerns: What would happen to the economy if a party other than the PRI were to win, is the PRI getting stronger or weaker, how does one judge the president's performance, and what are past patterns of partisan choice? PRI supporters strongly believed in the continued viability of their party's rule, and this belief shaped their voting behavior.

In this fashion Mexican voters rendered a judgment on the political regime at election time.

General expectations about the economy's future were significant only in shaping the vote with regard to the PAN; they did not shape the vote for the left. Prospective economic expectations become a powerful explanation only when the question explicitly connected the economy's future to the fate of the PRI. (Retrospective assessments on the state of the economy had no direct impact on voting.)

Consistent with an explanation of voter behavior focused on the ruling party's fate, attitudes on policy issues hardly mattered. These conclusions differ markedly from the way most Mexican politicians and journalists, and many scholars, interpreted the 1988 election, namely, as an ideological struggle or a judgment on the economic policies of the de la Madrid presidency. In the previous chapter we showed that the level of issue consistency in the Mexican public was relatively low. Mexicans were not ideologues. In this chapter we find as well that attitudes toward policy issues do not help to explain voting patterns in 1988. Candidate coalitions and issue coalitions were not the same. Candidate coalitions included people who held diverse views on the central issues of the day; similarly, issue coalitions drew supporters from all major political parties.

For the most part this makes Mexicans typical, not unusual. That issues have little impact on the voting choice is not surprising from a broad comparative perspective (ideological identifications, however, have at times been more important for some West European electorates and for Chileans).[54] Nor are our findings surprising when Mexico is compared with other large Latin American countries, such as Brazil or Argentina, where the public votes on the basis of considerations other than policy issues or broad ideologies.[55]

A related implication of our findings is that no newly politicized bloc of voters entered Mexico's "political space." In 1988 the principal effect of the entry of Cardenismo was to reshuffle the voters among existing parties, not to mobilize the previously unmobilized or to shift the partisan allegiance of demographic or economic groups or sectors. Nor have highly charged issue-oriented conflicts or voting behavior based on general economic expectations—as opposed to economic expectations tied to the ruling party's fate—replaced the key basis for division: whether to retain or reject the PRI.

Some scholars have noted that the entry (or reentry) of a large and politically mobilized "popular sector" has problematic consequences for the prospects for stabilizing democracy and effectively implementing economic adjustment policies;[56] in Mexico's ongoing search for democracy, little of the sort had yet occurred. The "popular sector" independent of the

PRI, though vibrant in terms of social movement activities,[57] had not had much impact on voting intention, nor had it been able to derail the economic policies of the de la Madrid government. Mexican civil society was "resurrecting";[58] in the immediate aftermath of the 1988 election, many citizens protested vigorously against the electoral fraud they perceived, but so far such citizen behavior has had at best only a modest impact on voting intentions (this point is explored more fully in chapter 6).

We have also shed light on two points important to Mexicanists: (1) The PRI has indeed retained the loyalty of its voters despite its peculiar internal structure and weak internal party life; it is a much stronger political party than some commentaries suggest. (2) The PAN is not a confessional party, nor is its internal party life unusually vibrant; consequently, the prospects for turning the PAN into a Christian Democratic party, similar to those in Europe or in other Latin American countries, remained weak.

There may be, nonetheless, an ideologically more competitive election and a sectoral partisan realignment lurking just beneath this focus on the fate of the ruling party. To find it, however, requires a heuristic exercise to identify these voters and model their hypothetical behavior. We developed a two-step "model" to understand the strategic components of the behavior of some Mexican voters who reasoned through two quite different steps. These voters decided, first, on their view of the ruling party. Many voters simply stopped there. The voting behavior of those open to the possibility of being governed by another party, however, resembled what might be expected in an ideologically competitive election. Policy issues mattered. Social cleavages mattered. Views of the presidential candidates mattered. There were important differences between the PRI, the PAN, and the Cardenistas. A sectoral partisan realignment was under way among these voters. There is also evidence of continuing and substantial strategic voting behavior among a minority of both right-wing and left-wing voters (but especially the former).

We have argued that Cárdenas's political movement might have been a socialist party in the making. Cardenismo, however, found it difficult to transform this potential into reality. Some left-wing Mexicans were prepared to consider voting for Cárdenas if and only if they were to make a prior negative judgment on the existing political regime—and not enough did. In addition, Cardenistas could not make sufficient inroads into the working class (whether measured in those terms or simply as union membership). In his sympathetic study of the development of social democratic parties, Przeworski argued that "the organization of politics in terms of class is not inevitable." Moreover, "the relative salience of class as a determinant of voting behavior is a cumulative consequence of strategies pursued by political parties of the Left."[59] Cardenistas found this out the hard way. Mexican voting behavior had not been automatically framed for them in terms of social class, and they did not succeed in developing effective enough strategies to mobilize support based on social-class categories.

Our analysis helps us answer the question of whether the 1988 election featured a critical sectoral partisan realignment in the sense that this expression is used in the scholarly literature, namely, to denote a shift in the group or sectoral bases of party coalitions in one election: we think no such shift occurred.[60] The significance of institutional and candidate factors, especially the importance of judgments about the fate of the ruling party, undermined the prospects for a sectoral partisan realignment in the 1988 elections and weakened the impact of the long-term ecological realignment, that is, the impact of the decline in the rural sector's share of the population.

In 1988 the *group* or sectoral bases of politics did not change much; there is no Mexican equivalent of the changes begun in the late 1960s in the United States and in West Germany, where U.S. southern whites became more likely to vote Republican and German middle-class folk became more likely to vote Social Democrat.[61] Nor did the opposition disproportionately mobilize previously unaffiliated voters. In turn, as we shall see in the next chapter, this absence of a shift in the group composition of party coalitions and the opposition's organizational weakness would make it easier for the PRI to reassert its predominance in 1991. The principal shift in the 1988 election was a change in the menu of parties offered to the electorate.

For Mexico, the 1988 election suggested that the reshaping of its political arena was under way, however, and that a fundamental realignment could occur in the future. Mexicans differed on issues; the various parties expressed various social cleavages. But the full flowering of these issue and social cleavages in the political arena awaited further democratization. The overwhelming focus on the PRI's fate in the 1988 election still prevented the full emergence of the representative and contestatory roles that parties perform in ordinary elections in other countries. Such a change seemed far more likely after the 1988 election. The possible birth of a new era was announced by Carlos Salinas himself in the election's immediate aftermath: "The age of what is practically a one-party system is over. We are at the beginning of a new political era."[62]

5 ❖ THE PARTISAN CONSEQUENCES OF CITIZEN ATTITUDES: VOTING INTENTIONS IN THE 1991 ELECTION

Contrary to the expectations of many, including president-elect Carlos Salinas de Gortari, the era of virtual one-party government did not end in Mexico in 1988. By the time of the August 1991 nationwide elections for Congress and several governorships, the ruling Institutional Revolutionary Party (PRI) had made an impressive comeback (table 5-1). The National Action Party (PAN) endured as Mexico's second largest political party, but it failed to expand its electoral base; the PAN's congressional candidates got 17.7 percent of the recorded votes in 1991 (they had received 17.5 percent of the recorded votes for congressional candidates in 1982).[1]

Still led by Cuauhtémoc Cárdenas, the political left had witnessed the decline and fragmentation of its electoral strength. By 1991 the parties that had supported Cárdenas in 1988 had lost nearly half of their share of the recorded votes; nonetheless, the left's share of the 1991 recorded votes was the second highest in Mexico's recent history. The party that Cárdenas founded after the 1988 elections and with which he remained formally affiliated—the Party of the Democratic Revolution (PRD)—remained the largest party of the left, twice the size of the next-largest left-wing party. In addition to the PRD, however, seven small parties, the largest of which had been Cárdenas allies in 1988, also occupied the electoral space available to the political left. (As noted in chapter 1, several of these minor parties had been aligned with the PRI before the 1988 elections.) When the votes were recorded after the 1991 election, the smallest of these parties garnered 0.6 percent of the national vote while the largest got 4.4 percent, for a total recorded vote of 12.7 percent cast for the minor parties.[2]

How and why the Mexican public changed so as to make these outcomes possible is the story of this chapter. Those who were waiting for a political regime transition, or at least for a major electoral realignment, had to wait much longer. In 1991 there was also even less reason than in 1988 to expect a partisan realignment. Even more than in 1988, in 1991 the voting intentions of Mexican citizens are best explained in terms of voter judgments

Table 5-1.   Partisan Preferences Leading up to the 1991
             Midterm Elections and Official Results
             (percent)

	Gallup Poll	Official Results
PRI	68	61
PAN	15	18
PRD	7	8
Other	9	13

Source: IMOP S.A. (Gallup) poll, July 1991; Embassy of
Mexico to the United States.
Note: Respondents who did not have a clear partisan
preference have been dropped from this table. N = 2,029 (66
percent of the total sample).

about the prospects for the political regime and the voter's past party preferences; this finding is quite consistent with the analysis in the previous
chapter. Mexican voters asked themselves, above all, whether they continued to support the "party of the state."

As in 1988, so too in 1991: Mexican voter attitudes were not explained by
attachments to social cleavages, attitudes on policy issues, or assessments
of the present and future circumstances of the nation's economy and one's
own finances; in fact, in 1991 these variables mattered even less. (The
reader might review the alternative explanatory hypotheses presented in
chapter 4.)

The 1991 election differed in two important respects from that of 1988.
One is the splintering of the Cardenista coalition even though the pool of
potential Cardenista voters remained large. That is, from 1988 to 1991,
opinion alignments remained more stable than party alignments. The other
difference is the denationalization of opposition parties in 1991: instead of
national parties, the opposition parties had shrunk into regional parties.

Were Mexicans reverting to authoritarianism in 1991? At the outset we
wish to recall the findings of chapter 2 in order to dismiss such an explanation. Even though the 1991 election was not a presidential election, and
thus the level of interest in politics might have been expected to decline, in
fact interest declined very little; the gains made in attentiveness to politics
from the late 1950s to the late 1980s were consolidated in 1991. The willingness of Mexicans to discuss politics freely had increased substantially since
the late 1950s as well. Support for rule by "a few strong leaders" instead of
reliance on law had declined between the late 1950s and the late 1980s and
continued to decline in 1991. We believe, therefore, that in 1991 Mexicans

did not return to the political culture of authoritarianism even if they chose to support the PRI much more strongly than in 1988. Their decision in 1991 was partisan, not cultural.

THE RESHAPING OF THE POLITICAL ARENA

Immediately after his inauguration, Carlos Salinas wanted to leave no doubt that he was president of Mexico, no matter how controversial his election. In January 1989 he ordered the arrest of Joaquín Hernández Galicia (known as "La Quina"), the longtime boss of the national petroleum workers' union; subsequently jailed, La Quina was accused of presiding over a corrupt and violent empire. In February Salinas ordered the arrest of Eduardo Legorreta, a financier accused of fraudulent manipulation of the Mexican stock market especially during the fall 1987 financial panic. In April the president's agents orchestrated the removal of Carlos Jonguitud, the longtime boss of the national teachers' union. In June the arrest of the former head of the Federal Security police—the alleged "intellectual author" of the murder of journalist Manuel Buendía—lengthened the list of efforts to cleanse Mexican politics. The president's popularity soared in public-opinion polls.[3]

Salinas's strategy regarding the opposition parties was astute as well as differentiated: the carrot for the PAN, the stick for the PRD. Salinas sought to coopt the PAN and to marginalize Cardenismo, and in the process to fragment each of these political coalitions. After prolonged and complex negotiations, in October 1989 most of the PAN's members of Congress joined the PRI (and several minor parties) to approve constitutional amendments required to reform the electoral law; the changes were enacted in 1990.

Several of these changes were important. New high-tech photograph identification credentials would be issued to the entire electorate in order to reduce the incidence of old-style vote fraud at local polling places on election day. The new Federal Elections Institute (IFE) was founded as a permanent body, staffed with a professional corps of officials, and with some provisions for greater independence from the PRI; nonetheless, through the representatives it controlled, the PRI in fact continued to enjoy a majority on the IFE's General Council. The IFE was given broad authority to centralize certain electoral tasks whose performance had been dispersed and which were therefore more likely to have been subject to fraud. In addition, a new Federal Electoral Court was created; parties could lodge complaints at this court and appeal the official election count.[4] These electoral law reforms were Salinas's principal response to the allegation that his own election had been the result of fraud; it was also the price the PAN exacted for accepting Salinas's right to rule and to cooperate with his administration in the approval of economic legislation. Although the PAN's top leadership was firmly committed to this reform of the electoral system, a profound split emerged within the PAN over the wisdom and appropriateness of this partial collaboration with the PRI.[5] In October 1992 some longstanding PAN leaders would persuade their faction to leave the party over these and other issues related especially to PAN-PRI collaboration.

The same 1989 agreement over the electoral clauses in the Constitution, and agreements over other issues, fostered a change in the political alignment of several of the minor parties: they eased away from their cooperation with Cárdenas and edged back to their longstanding collaboration with the PRI, which had been only briefly interrupted in time for the 1988 election.

The clearest difference in the Salinas government's treatment of the major opposition parties became evident in its response to sharply contested elections in 1989 in the states of Baja California Norte, Michoacán, and Guerrero. In June 1989, for the first time in Mexican history, the government recognized that the PAN had won a state governorship; the PAN's Ernesto Ruffo became governor of Baja California Norte.

On the same day, however, serious, credible charges of fraud were levied against the government and the PRI in the state assembly elections in Michoacán, where the PRI's main adversary was Cárdenas's PRD.[6] The PRD made similar charges of fraud in the December 1989 elections for state assembly and mayors in the state of Guerrero.[7] Between 1988 and 1991, PRD leaders and activists were victims of sporadic official repression in various states and municipalities, and also within officially sponsored labor and peasant organizations.[8] In these ways the national government and the PRI conveyed the message that a vote for the PRD was likely to be wasted. The government sought also to weaken the PRD by coopting some of its individual leaders (in contrast to the effort at coopting the PAN as a whole); for example, just days before the August 18, 1991, nationwide congressional elections, the PRD leader in the Chamber of Deputies, Ignacio Castillo Mena, was lured to defect from the PRD by being appointed Mexican ambassador to Ecuador.

Salinas also attempted to reinvent the PRI, but that task proved too daunting, and the resulting changes had only minor effects by the 1991 election. At its Fourteenth National Assembly in September 1990, the PRI decided that its candidates would be chosen at the local level, not at the state, sectoral (e.g., labor or peasant federation), or national level. Candidates for Congress would be chosen by party conventions whose members would have been elected democratically; candidates for state and local offices would be chosen directly in party primaries. Only in exceptional cases would the PRI leadership choose the local candidates. In fact, the "exception" proved to be the rule: only 4.3 percent of the PRI's 1991 candidates for the Chamber of Deputies and none of its candidates for the Senate were chosen through party primaries or nominating conventions. Candidates were typically hand-picked in time-honored fashion by the leadership at party conventions not preceded by primary elections. Similarly, attempts to choose PRI candidates for governor by more democratic means led to violence in the state of Morelos and to severe dissension in the state of Colima; after 1991 the choice of the PRI gubernatorial candidates reverted to appointment by President Salinas. In November 1994 the PRI in Jalisco chose its candidate for governor through a party convention of local leaders, reopening thereby the prospects for the PRI's internal democratization. From 1990 to 1994, however, the main observable change was the weakening of the clout of the sectoral organizations, and the shift in power to President Salinas in the choice of candidates for governors and senators and to the state governors in the selection of candidates for lower offices. This was no doubt an important political change but hardly a democratizing one.[9]

Nonetheless, as PRI party president Luis Donaldo Colosio argued forcefully, in preparation for the 1991 elections the PRI improved its capacity to contest elections by adopting the paraphernalia of parties in electorally more competitive political systems: sustained public-opinion polling, closer contact with local constituencies, and better organizational support from Mexico City for candidates in close elections. The PRI also began to move away from its past practices of nominating old-line bosses to sinecures as members of Congress and from seeking to impose outsiders as the alleged congressional representatives of districts in which the candidates had not even lived before their election. Instead, Colosio explained, "in 1991, emphasis was placed on finding people with well-established roots in the communities they sought to represent. We tried to run candidates who were well known and well liked at home."[10]

Another dimension of Salinas's reshaping of the political arena stemmed from the major steps in economic policy that were summarized in chapter 1. The Salinas government greatly accelerated the privatization of state enterprises. In 1989–90 the government privatized the telephone system, the airlines, the nation's largest copper mine (Cananea), several major sugar mills, and its automobile- and truck-manufacturing company (DINA); it continued the privatization of petrochemical firms. In 1990–92 the government reprivatized the banking system and proceeded to privatize steel mills, insurance companies, and other firms. In 1989 the Salinas government reached a comprehensive settlement of Mexico's international public debt obligations and began to adopt measures to liberalize greatly the rules governing foreign direct investment. In June 1990 the U.S. government accepted the Salinas government's proposal to negotiate a free trade agreement between the two countries; as extended to include Canada, the North American Free Trade Agreement (NAFTA) would become the crowning jewel of the Salinas administration's economic reforms.[11] Some claimed that Salinas had "stolen" the PAN's economic program. No matter. After 1988, Mexico's economic growth rate accelerated; optimism soared, as we shall see, as did domestic and international praise for Mexico's president.

The PAN's View of Mexican Politics

One view of the role of the PAN in Mexican politics after the 1988 elections was best expressed by longtime PAN leader, the president of its National Executive Committee, Luis H. Alvarez, who had been the PAN's candidate for president as a thirty-eight-year-old in 1958 (Manuel Clouthier, the PAN's 1988 presidential candidate, died in 1989 in an automobile accident). After the 1988 elections the PAN, led by Alvarez, sought to participate in and contest elections, winning not only the governorship of Baja California Norte but also the municipal elections in important Mexican cities in different regions, such as in the cities of León, San Luis Potosí, Mazatlán, Saltillo, and Mérida.

To win those elections the PAN had to develop a capacity to monitor them and to defend the honest counting of the vote. The PAN sought to nominate candidates who would actually win elections, not just stand as witnesses or martyrs at the altar of PRI electoral fraud. The PAN attempted to strengthen itself as a partisan organization. In the same vein, it pragmatically discussed issues, and engaged in tactical collaboration, at the national and local levels at times with the PRI and at other times with the PRD and other parties. As Alvarez would put it in the immediate aftermath of the 1991 congressional and local elections, the PAN had to be ready "to be at the same time government and opposition" because PAN members had come to govern states or municipalities in which some ten million Mexicans lived. The number of votes recorded in favor of the PAN had increased between 1985 and 1988, and again between 1988 and 1991.

On the other hand, Alvarez was no less committed to opposing the PRI and to defeating it in elections. He was motivated by a felt need to change the political system fundamentally and to stop the reliance on electoral fraud on the part of the PRI and the government. But Alvarez explicitly rejected the proposition that the PAN should eschew a dialogue with the government, because "those who chose that path got very little electoral support." Results, more than abstract principle, were the PAN president's key political motivation.[12]

Alvarez sought to lay claim to a politically complex position. He believed that the Salinas concepts of "modernization and related ideas" were "acceptable and even necessary" and seemed "on the surface to have been taken from the PAN's political platform." For example, Alvarez wrote, "We applaud the decision to sell state-owned enterprises." He argued, however, that the similarity was superficial. The Salinas reforms, he claimed, sought "only to insure [the PRI's] permanence in power," whereas the PAN sought the fuller democratization of Mexican society, economy, and politics.[13]

An alternative view of the PAN's role was expressed by the Foro Doctrinario y Democrático, a PAN faction whose leaders would leave the party in October 1992. The Foro's members included former PAN party president and 1982 presidential candidate Pablo Emilio Madero as well as other PAN officials and members of Congress. For them, the PAN had sold out on the excuse of pragmatism. The PAN had soiled itself by making deals with the PRI and the government; it had abandoned its ideological doctrine and its commitment to the nation's fundamental democratization. As the PAN had become more a party ready to win elections, it also had become, they claimed, more bureaucratized and less democratic internally.

Foro leaders also objected to the growth of business influence in the PAN's affairs, a continuation of the *neo-panismo* discussed in the previous chapter. Business executives had routinely become the PAN candidates for major offices, sidelining longtime PAN members. Foro leaders criticized the selective approach to PAN programs suggested by the presence of these new business members of the party. Foro leaders complained as well about the chorus of praise from PAN national leaders for President Salinas's economic policies. Thus in the Foro's view the PAN had stopped being a genuine opposition party. In the eyes of critics within the PAN, support for Salinas, for his government's economic policies, and generally for pragmatic behavior constituted the PAN leadership's trinity of sins.[14] A decisive question, therefore, is whether the PAN electorate would abandon the PAN because it had deviated from its ideas, had become too closely identified with the PRI, or was simply too sharply divided internally.

Cárdenas and the Political Left

After the 1988 presidential election Cárdenas's key plank was to question the legitimacy of Salinas's election: "We have no assurance that the election of 6 July 1988 was clean. We have every assurance that it was an election dominated by electoral wrongdoing and that it was fraud that put the majority of candidates who currently form the bulk of both houses of Congress into power. It was also fraud that decided who would occupy the seat of executive power."[15] For that very reason the Salinas administration found it much more difficult to deal with the PRD than with the PAN. Cárdenas himself analyzed the results of the June 1989 elections in Michoacán (denial of PRD victories by the government) and Baja California Norte (acceptance of PAN victories by the government) as reflecting the broad perception that not the PAN but "the PRD represents a true alternative to the PRI and the people who are now in power."[16]

In economic matters the PRD and Cárdenas criticized the Mexican government's policies; theirs was a position on the left, but one far less radical than was often supposed and certainly less so than in 1988. For example, Cárdenas and the PRD no longer favored a moratorium on the payment of Mexico's international debt—as shown in the previous chapter, Cárdenas did in 1988—but they criticized the terms reached in the Mexican government's public debt settlement with its creditors; the size of the debt was reduced too little. Nor did Cárdenas oppose all privatizations of state enterprises, though he did "not consider it valid that . . . the government should indiscriminately transfer its business interests to the private sector and, in particular, to transnational corporations." Cárdenas opposed the privatization of profit-making state enterprises, such as the largest airline, Mexicana de Aviación, the largest copper mine (Cananea), and many petrochemical firms.[17] He did not regard this as "modernization," he said; "we see it simply as a form of favoring certain economic interest groups." Above all, he favored the state's continued direct involvement in what he called "strategic activities," no doubt including the petroleum sector that his father, President Lázaro Cárdenas, had nationalized in 1938.[18]

After the U.S. and Mexican governments announced their wish to negotiate a free trade agreement, Cárdenas opposed it on the grounds that such a relationship would leave Mexico as a "low wage, high unemployment economy, with large impoverished sectors, high concentration of income in the hands of a few, and an overwhelming subordination to the U.S. economy."[19] He criticized the marked increase in imports whose effects were to dismantle Mexico's industrial capacity. On the other hand, Cárdenas and the PRD did not reject a free trade agreement outright. The PRD "proposed a social charter as a fundamental part of the NAFTA." This social charter would emphasize dispute settlement procedures, labor mobility, environmental protection, compensatory investments, and other features derived in part from the agreements reached between the European Community and its less economically developed members—Portugal, Spain, Greece, and Ireland. (In fact, at U.S. insistence the NAFTA draft text had to be renegotiated in 1993 to strengthen its provisions to protect labor and the environment.) The PRD preferred a continental free trade agreement, especially one "that would begin with the recognition of the existing differences in degrees of development and productivity of the economies and social conditions." One goal of the agreement would be "the decrease and eventual eradication of these differences."[20]

Cárdenas continued to argue that Mexico had not emerged from the economic crisis since Salinas had become president; the real income of Mexican workers continued to decline, and unemployment was still increasing, as were pressures to migrate to the United States, while Mexicans enjoyed few political freedoms.[21]

Other voices on the Mexican left presented an array of views. As a thoughtful Mexican commentator, Carlos Monsiváis, pointed out, after the 1988 elections the PRD faced the problems of becoming an opposition party, opening itself "to factionalism, to power struggles, [and] to repetition of formulas of revolutionary behavior that had become increasingly hollow." Though the PRD was committed to democracy, its leaders had found it difficult "to rid themselves of the traces of authoritarianism."[22]

This critique would eventually take form within the PRD's "Democratic Reform Current" faction. Its members worried about the lack of internal democracy in the PRD as well as about the party's apparent strategy of opposition for opposition's sake; therefore, they criticized the posture of complaining about the proposed free trade agreement with the United States and Canada without simultaneously proposing a truly better alternative.[23]

Aspects of the PRD's political platform were quite polemical. For example, the Salinas administration proposed a substantial change in the relations between the Roman Catholic church and the state, which required a constitutional amendment. The PRD announced its opposition to most of those changes not merely as issues in public policy but in terms of the very nature of the Roman Catholic church. The PRD's official position with regard to the amendment of the Constitution's church-state clauses opened with the following words: "We are not unaware of the Church's vertical structures; we are not unaware that the hierarchy is the same as sacred power; we know of the anti-democratic structures within the Roman Catholic church."[24] These views help to explain why those who never went to church were much more likely to vote for Cárdenas in 1988 (chapter 4) and would remain his backers in 1991. On such a plank the PRD alienated many faithful churchgoers.

In sum, the reshaping of Mexico's political arena leaves us with several hypotheses as we ponder the distribution of public opinion before the August 1991 nationwide congressional and local elections. Carlos Salinas had become a stunningly powerful figure in Mexican politics, much more so than his predecessor Miguel de la Madrid. Salinas had implemented many significant changes in government and politics. On the other hand, his assault on some of the powerful political bosses on which the PRI's power had once depended raised the question of whether the supporters of these bosses might have withdrawn their support for the PRI. Could it be that PRI voter loyalty would play a lesser role in 1991 at the same time that presidentialism seemed even more important?

Cárdenas and other leaders of the left continued to emphasize the illegitimacy of the 1988 elections as well as their opposition to the government's economic policy. The left's leaders still focused on the national economic crisis born in the 1980s, and they were still suspicious of foreigners, whether in trade or in other ways. In Congress the left had a well-defined adversarial position toward the Roman Catholic bishops. For the leaders of the left, issues mattered.

The PAN, albeit divided, sought to win elections. All of its factions emphasized the party's commitment to democratizing Mexico. The PAN strongly believed in the importance of free and fair elections. Its factional split focused especially but not exclusively on such topics as collaboration with the PRI and the role of business influence in the PAN. The fact of internal division suggested the possibility that the PAN might have become an appreciably weaker organization despite the wishes and efforts of its top leaders.

The prospects that voter loyalty might prove weaker in 1991 than in 1988 as an explanation of voter choice were suggested by problems in the three main party coalitions. The PAN was divided. So was the left, within which there were divisions both within the PRD and between it and the smaller parties. And perhaps the old-line PRI loyalists too might be ready to bolt.

With regard to policy issue cleavages, circumstances in 1991 resembled those of 1988. There were marked differences in the policy positions of the three main parties, but there were also important overlaps. Cárdenas, for example, stood out for his opposition to the Salinas administration's NAFTA proposal, but he insisted that he was not in principle opposed to a "better" trade agreement. The PAN vigorously contested the PRI in many elections, but the PAN's support for many of the Salinas administration's economic policies dulled the edge of its political sword in combat with the ruling party.

Both the PRD and the PAN sharply condemned the antidemocratic practices of the ruling party, but Salinas could point out that between 1988 and 1991 the electoral law had been reformed and the government had recognized hundreds of opposition electoral victories in congressional and municipal elections, and finally even in a gubernatorial election; even the Salinas administration seemed to stand for more democracy. Did such issue overlap prevent in 1991 as it had in 1988 the convergence between issue polarization and partisanship? Or did the Salinas administration's economic policy single-mindedness and Cárdenas's sustained challenge to it polarize partisanship more sharply in 1991 according to the issues?

ECONOMIC OPTIMISM: THE TURNAROUND

By the time of the August 1991 national elections Mexicans had become much more tolerant, indeed more supportive, of one-party rule and much less eager to bolster opposition parties. As the evidence in table 5-2 shows, in 1991 most Mexicans still preferred a more competitive party system, but the level of support for such an essential feature of democratic politics fell to its lowest point since the mid-1980s. In contrast, satisfaction with one-party dominance rebounded from its 1988 low to return to the 1986 level. Given our earlier analysis of rising long-term democratic trends (chapter 2), we believe that this is a political judgment on the choice of parties in 1991, not a regression to the political culture of authoritarianism. But if the prevalence of authoritarian values does not explain the rise in support for the PRI in 1991, then what does?

Table 5-2. Attitudes toward the PRI's Position in Mexican Elections, 1986 to 1991 (percent)

	1986	1988	1991
Preference for a more competitive party system	62	63	54
Satisfaction with one-party dominance	37	28	36

Source: New York Times Mexico survey, 1986; IMOP S.A. (Gallup) polls, May 1988 and July 1991.

Note: This item was worded as follows: "Which of these two phrases best describes your own opinion? (a) The Mexican political system should be changed so that candidates of other parties will be able to win more often. (b) The existing system works well and should be left as it is." N = 1,899 (weighted, 1986), 2,960 (1988), and 3,053 (1991).

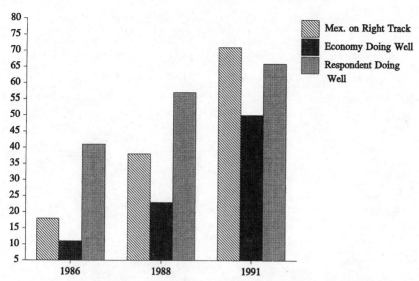

Figure 5-1. Perceptions of National and Personal Well-Being (percent)

Source: *New York Times* Mexico survey, 1986; IMOP S.A. (Gallup) polls, May 1988 and July 1991.

Note: N = 1,899 (weighted, 1986), 2,960 (1988), and 3,053 (1991).

One important explanation for the greater support for the PRI is that Mexicans had become much more satisfied with economic performance (figure 5-1). By 1991 nearly three-quarters of Mexicans thought that the country was on the right track, about four times more than had thought so only five years earlier. In 1991 a majority of Mexicans thought that the nation's economy was doing well; this percentage was more than five times greater than in 1986. In 1991 two-thirds of Mexicans thought that their personal finances were good, also an appreciable increase from 1986. Although economic optimism increased steadily from 1986 to 1988 to 1991, on balance the sharpest rise occurred after Salinas's election as president.

Because the rise in optimism was so pronounced, and because Cárdenas made the case that workers and other lower-income Mexicans were still suffering, we decided to examine the efficacy of this electoral strategy: Did Mexicans of different social classes and regions of the country perceive the changed economic circumstances differently? For the most part the answer is no. As the results reported in table 5-3 show, Mexicans of all levels of education and political interest, of both genders, and of all age groups, social classes, religious practices, and regions were much more likely in 1991 than in 1988 to think that the national economy was doing well. The increase in optimism is smaller in the answers to questions about personal

Table 5-3.　Perceptions of Economic Well-Being, 1988 and 1991 (percent)

	National Economy Is Doing "Well" or "Very Well"		Personal Finances Are "Good" or "Very Good"	
	1988	*1991*	*1988*	*1991*
Whole sample	23	50	57	66
Region				
North	21	54	61	73
Central	25	45	54	59
South	24	48	60	59
Federal District	24	51	58	71
Education				
Secondary or less	21	48	50	59
Preparatory	26	53	66	74
University	25	52	67	77
Political interest				
Great	22	51	60	69
Some	23	55	62	70
None	20	41	52	58
Age				
18–29	26	55	63	74
30–49	19	47	53	62
50+	24	46	48	57
Gender				
Female	20	46	58	65
Male	26	54	56	66
Class				
Upper	26	59	71	85
Lower/middle	22	49	53	64
Church attendance				
Weekly	24	49	57	68
Less than weekly	22	51	57	64

Source: IMOP S.A. (Gallup) polls, May 1988 and July 1991.

Note: These items were phrased as follows: "Would you say that the national economy is doing very well, well, badly, or very badly? Now speaking of you personally, how is your own economic situation? Would you say that it's very good, good, bad, or very bad?" N = 2,960 (1988) and 3,053 (1991).

finances, but that was because the level of optimism about personal finances was already high in 1988. Economic optimism increased for every category listed in table 5-3, no matter what the question, except that in Mexico's southern region the percentage claiming that personal finances were good remained essentially unchanged, though still high, from 1988 to 1991.

There were, however, some differences in exuberance. As the Mexican left might have suspected, in 1991 optimism about the nation's economy and about personal finances was highest among the better educated, among upper-class respondents, and among those from northern Mexico, who benefited more from the deepened economic relationship with the United States. From the government's perspective, the high level of optimism among the youngest adults was especially valuable: a new generation of Mexicans had come to believe in the nation's and in their own economic future.

As noted in chapter 1, Mexico's gross domestic product per capita had improved between 1988 and 1991, but not by much; and although real average wages in manufacturing had increased substantially, the real minimum wage had not. On these three economic indicators Mexicans were still worse off in 1991 than they had been ten years earlier. Moreover, Mexico's deficit on the balance-of-payments current account had been worsening in the early 1990s, reaching $13.9 billion in 1991.[25] Cárdenas knew this and may have fashioned his electoral strategy accordingly. Most Mexicans thought, however, that they and the nation were doing far, far better. The "Mexican miracle" in 1991 was to be found, therefore, not in the vibrancy of the real economy's performance but in the Salinas government's spectacularly effective public relations job: an acceptable though modest economic recovery had been transformed into a political triumph.

Mexicans were also upbeat about the future of the nation's economy and their own personal finances. Once again there was a marked increase in levels of optimism about the economic future—at times a remarkably large shift—for both questions and all variables presented in table 5-4. With regard to the future, the increased optimism about personal finances was much more substantial than when Mexicans were asked merely about the present. There was therefore no perceptual basis for the political approach followed by Cardenistas in 1991. Even if Cárdenas was correct that many Mexicans were not in good economic shape, most Mexicans disagreed with his assessment; even the less well educated, those from the middle and lower classes, and certainly the young believed that their own personal finances would improve markedly.

Table 5-4. Increasing Optimism in 1991 about Economic Conditions (percent)

	National Economy Will Be Stronger		Personal Finances Will Improve	
	1988	*1991*	*1988*	*1991*
Whole sample	22	43	44	70
Region				
North	24	54	45	72
Central	18	45	42	66
South	23	38	42	69
Federal District	21	36	47	73
Education				
Secondary or less	20	38	39	65
Preparatory	23	51	51	78
University	25	52	50	78
Political interest				
Great	31	56	50	74
Some	23	47	47	74
None	14	33	35	64
Age				
18–29	21	46	51	80
30–49	22	42	41	67
50+	21	41	31	56
Gender				
Female	20	37	41	68
Male	24	49	47	72
Class				
Upper	26	59	45	71
Lower/middle	21	41	44	70
Church attendance				
Weekly	22	44	43	67
Less than weekly	21	43	45	73

Source: IMOP S.A. (Gallup) polls, May 1988 and July 1991.

Note: These items were phrased as follows: "Within [three or six] years will Mexico's economic situation be better, worse, or about the same? How do you expect your own economic situation to be in [three or six] years—much better, a little better, slightly worse, or much worse?" N = 2,960 (1988) and 3,053 (1991).

ATTITUDES TOWARD ECONOMIC ISSUES

This wild optimism swayed some Mexicans in their attitudes toward some specific economic policy issues. In comparison with 1988, by 1991 more Mexicans supported such key Salinas administration economic policies as facilitating the importation of foreign goods and favoring foreign investment.[26] In the previous chapter we found that the connection between issue preferences and partisan preferences was too faint. This shift in public opinion since 1988 suggests that issues could have played a different political role in 1991.

Majorities of Mexicans from all analytical categories listed in table 5-5 favored foreign investment; support for foreign investment had also increased in each of those categories between 1988 and 1991. The support for freer imports was also evident across the analytical categories presented in table 5-5, but between 1988 and 1991 the level of support remained basically unchanged in central Mexico, in the Federal District, and among those with little interest in politics. (Mexicans felt more positive about foreign investment than about freer imports.) Between 1988 and 1991 the level of support for both of these Salinas policies increased the most among upper-class respondents and among northerners; in 1991 the upper class and the northerners had also the highest absolute level of support for both policies. The size of the shift suggests that the nature of the pro-Salinas coalition may have changed and that issues might have played a different role in the 1991 elections.

THE REBIRTH OF THE PRI

How did this increased optimism about the current and future economic prospects for the nation and the self, and this greater support for Salinas's economic policies, affect perceptions of the PRI? The evidence in table 5-6 shows that the PRI benefited greatly. Compared with 1988, in 1991 a great many more Mexicans believed that the PRI would become stronger in ten years; many fewer believed that it would become weaker. The proportion of Mexicans who thought that the nation's economic performance would improve if a party other than the PRI were to win the elections dropped considerably, whereas the proportion who thought that national economic performance would suffer under those electoral circumstances increased. In the 1988 elections these two variables were among the most significant shapers of vote choice; thus the changes reported in table 5-6 go a long way toward explaining the improvement in the PRI's fortunes. In both 1988 and 1991, moreover, majorities of Mexicans believed that social unrest would increase if a party other than the PRI were to win.

Table 5-5. Changes in Economic Policy Preferences, 1988 to 1991 (percent)

	Favor Foreign Investment		Favor Foreign Imports	
	1988	1991	1988	1991
Whole sample	53	62	50	56
Region				
North	62	74	50	67
Central	54	59	54	53
South	47	59	49	56
Federal District	49	56	47	49
Education				
Secondary or less	49	57	50	54
Preparatory	58	65	52	57
University	61	70	48	60
Political interest				
Great	60	69	55	64
Some	59	66	49	59
None	48	53	51	49
Age				
18–29	56	63	50	57
30–49	53	62	50	56
50+	48	57	50	53
Gender				
Female	50	59	49	54
Male	57	64	51	58
Class				
Upper	56	78	51	68
Lower/middle	53	60	50	55
Church attendance				
Weekly	52	64	50	55
Less than weekly	55	61	49	57

Source: IMOP S.A. (Gallup) polls, May 1988 and July 1991.

Note: These items were phrased as follows: "Should the government facilitate the importation of foreign goods into Mexico or limit importation? [1988 sample]. Regarding foreign imports, in your opinion are they good or bad for our country? [1991 sample]. In your opinion, is investment on the part of foreign companies good or bad for our country? [both samples]." $N = 2,960$ (1988) and 3,053 (1991).

Table 5-6.   Changing Perceptions of the PRI's Viability, 1988 to 1991
              (percent)

	1988	1991
In ten years, will the PRI be stronger or weaker?		
Stronger	30	43
Same	26	25
Weaker	35	22
National economic performance if another party wins		
Better	39	28
Worse	19	24
Will there be an increase in social unrest if another party wins?		
Yes	55	54
No	35	35
Presidential approval rating, on a 10-point scale		
Very high (9 or 10)	30	43
Favorable (7 or 8)	29	40
Mediocre (4 to 6)	20	11
Poor (1 to 3)	14	3

Source: IMOP S.A. (Gallup) polls, May 1988 and July 1991.
Note: N = 2,960 (1988) and 3,053 (1991).

A key to many of these changes was, of course, the shift in the public perception of Salinas himself. In 1988 a majority of Mexicans had a favorable view of candidate Salinas, but in 1991 the proportion who held a favorable view of President Salinas had risen to 83 percent. By 1991 very few Mexicans thought poorly of him. The president's coat-tails were powerful; he had helped to improve the image of his party, the support for his issues, and even the general assessment of economic circumstances and prospects more than the facts warranted. His political achievement was no less stunning than his achievement in reorienting economic policies.

Mexican citizens were asked to indicate what the Salinas administration's "main" achievement had been; the results appear in table 5-7.[27] Overall, the most important items are the administration's general economic policies— fighting inflation, stabilizing prices, working on the foreign debt, and generating more jobs—and especially its espousal of a free trade treaty with the United States and Canada. The "Plan de Solidaridad" is also credited with being as important an achievement as the free trade treaty.

Table 5-7.   What Has Been the Greatest Achievement of the Salinas Administration? (percent)

	PRONASOL	Providing Public Services	Free Trade Treaty	Other Economic Policies
Whole sample	11	9	11	15
Region				
North	9	5	16	16
Central	9	10	9	13
South	16	11	9	13
Federal District	9	8	10	15
Population of city/town				
Less than 20,000	13	10	9	11
20,000–100,000	12	9	11	15
100,000–1 million	9	6	14	18
More than 1 million	8	8	11	16
Education				
Secondary or less	11	10	9	11
Preparatory	11	6	16	17
University	10	6	13	24
Class				
Upper	5	5	16	24
Lower/middle	11	9	11	14

Source: IMOP S.A. (Gallup) poll, July 1991.
Note: PRONASOL = National Solidarity Program. N = 3,053.

President Salinas created the high-profile National Solidarity Program (PRONASOL) to bring together various government distributive programs and to bypass the political opposition (which after the 1988 election controlled about 48 percent of the seats in Congress), the traditional apparatus of government- and PRI-affiliated labor and peasant confederations, the state agencies that had been in charge of most such programs, and many local governments that were either corrupt or had been won by the opposition in the 1988 elections. PRONASOL saved government funds because it cut through these various organizational layers. Its very design simultaneously decentralized government spending away from the bureaucracy and middle-level politicians and instead created a special political tie between President Salinas and Mexico's poorest.[28]

PRONASOL grants financed small social and community infrastructure projects. The plan was politically effective because its programs worked and had visibly high impact: sewerage and potable water, street paving, food distribution, electrification, support for peasant producers, health clinics, school buildings, and so on. To appeal specifically to the rural areas, no more than 25 percent of each grant could be spent on projects in a municipality's main town; the remainder had to be spent in outlying areas. Mexican government funds were supplemented by grants from the World Bank, which averaged over $100 million per year, for spending in Mexico's four poorest states: Oaxaca, Chiapas, Guerrero, and Hidalgo.[29]

Thanks to a massive public relations campaign preceding the August 1991 elections,[30] PRONASOL was perceived to be the Salinas administration's single most successful program by a significant fraction of the public, as table 5-7 indicates. PRONASOL also allocated disproportionate amounts of money to win back for the PRI areas where the center-left opposition (especially the PRD) was strong, such as the state of Michoacán, where bypassing local municipal governments was a way to skip PRD mayors and deny them political credit. (This strategy had the paradoxical effect, however, of rewarding areas that had voted for the opposition.)[31]

The evidence in table 5-7 indicates that PRONASOL's design was indeed closely related to its political effects. Lower- and middle-class Mexicans, people living in towns with fewer than twenty thousand people, and residents of the south (a largely rural region) were much more likely to believe that PRONASOL was the Salinas administration's main achievement. They were also more likely to have mentioned, in more general terms, that the provision of public services—street paving, the construction of bridges and schools, and the providing of public transportation—was the main accomplishment; these public services were often delivered through PRONASOL too, even if the program was not mentioned specifically.

In contrast, the free trade treaty and the other economic policies of the Salinas administration were more likely to be mentioned as the main achievement in northern Mexico and in the Federal District, in the larger cities and towns, by the better educated, and by upper-class respondents.

Respondents voiced perceptions that were closest to their own situation. That is, poor people most affected by public works projects in rural areas valued those programs more than they did the macroeconomic policies, whereas the better-off respondents valued the latter much more. The combination of macroeconomic policy changes and micro-targeted social assistance programs were a politically potent combination that enhanced Salinas's clout and revivified the PRI's fortunes. He and his party had become all things to all people.[32]

Table 5-8.   Correlations among Voter Expectations in 1991:
            If the PRI Gets Stronger, Do the Opposition
            Parties Weaken?

	PRI Will Become Stronger	PAN Will Become Stronger
PAN will become stronger	−.36	
PRD will become stronger	−.34	.26

Source: IMOP S.A. (Gallup) poll, July 1991.
Note: The coefficients above are polychoric correlation estimates derived via maximum likelihood. All are highly significant ($p < .001$). $N = 2,382$.

THE PARTY OF THE STATE VERSUS THE PARTIES OF THE OPPOSITION

In some countries voters perceive the major parties as getting weaker simultaneously. For example, in the United States, the United Kingdom, and the Netherlands there was a sustained and far-reaching partisan dealignment from the late 1960s through the 1970s; support for all major parties declined.[33] All parties lost support as voters became more independent, more willing to make up their minds at the last minute, and less willing to base their vote on a standing decision in favor of a specific party. In such circumstances a party often gains votes by appealing to the pool of independents, not necessarily by taking votes directly from another party.

Mexico is different.[34] In Mexico in 1991 the gains for the ruling party reflected the losses of the opposition parties—what is called a "zero-sum" relationship. In table 5-8 we show the correlations between the perception that the PRI will get stronger and the ratings of opposition party strength. These correlations are highly significant statistically. They show that perceptions of the PRI's strength in 1991 came directly at the expense of a weakened PAN and PRD.

Just as important, the zero-sum relationship occurred only between the party of the state and the opposition as a whole, not between the PAN and the PRD. There is a positive correlation between the PRD getting stronger and the PAN getting stronger. These parties did not take supporters from each other; they took them from, or they lost them to, the PRI. Similarly, the PRI's growing support did not hurt just one party in the opposition; it hurt both. (The results in table 5-8 are also supported by those in table 5-2, which also suggested a bipolar relationship between ruling party and opposition.) This finding is consistent with our argument in the preceding chapter that

Mexican voters decide first between the PRI versus the opposition—a judgment on the political regime's ruling party—and only later and secondarily do they choose between the opposition parties.

ANALYZING AND EXPLAINING PARTISAN CLEAVAGES

How, then, did Mexicans plan to vote for the opposition parties in 1991? We proceed in the same fashion as in the comparable section of the preceding chapter. Table 5-9 presents the multinomial logit estimates and standard errors.[35] We seek to explain the intentions to vote for the PAN, the PRD, and seven other small opposition parties. The PRD included the cadres of the old Mexican Socialist Party (PMS)[36] in addition to many other supporters of Cuauhtémoc Cárdenas. The seven minor opposition parties, in the order of their officially reported electoral strength in 1991, are as follows. There were the three former Cárdenas allies, namely, the Frente Cardenista National Renovation Party (PFCRN), the Authentic Party of the Mexican Revolution (PARM), and the People's Socialist Party (PPS); together these three parties got 8.3 percent of the recorded vote in 1991, and each of them was able to elect its own national deputies. The other four parties together got 4.3 percent of the recorded votes in 1991 but were not able to elect any national deputies; they are the Mexican Ecologist Party (PEM), the Workers' Party (PT), the Mexican Democratic Party (PDM), and the Revolutionary Workers' Party (PRT).[37]

The Parties and the 1988 Presidential Candidates

The only variables that identify statistically significant relationships to explain the intention to vote for all three opposition clusters (PAN, PRD, and other) are those that refer to the parties, the presidency, and the 1988 presidential candidates:

1. The more likely a voter was to have voted for Salinas in the 1988 presidential election, the less likely this voter was to support any opposition party in 1991.
2. The more likely a voter was to have voted for an opposition presidential candidate (Cárdenas or Clouthier) in 1988, the more likely this voter was to support an opposition party in 1991.
3. The greater the belief that the PRI would get stronger, the lower the likelihood of voting for an opposition party.
4. The greater the belief that the economy would improve if a party other than the PRI were to gain power, the greater the likelihood of voting for an opposition candidate.
5. The greater the approval for incumbent president Carlos Salinas, the lower the likelihood of support for the opposition.

Table 5-9.   Predicting Support for Opposition Parties in 1991

	PAN	PRD	Other
Previous Salinas voter	−2.14 (.31) **	−2.19 (.37) **	−2.30 (.33) **
Clouthier voter	2.56 (.34) **	.21 (.52)	.35 (.45)
Cárdenas voter	−.41 (.51)	1.75 (.39) **	1.28 (.36) **
Abstained in 1988	−.21 (.27)	−.52 (.33)	−.84 (.30) *
Increase foreign investment	.07 (.13)	−.23 (.14)	−.03 (.13)
Limit imports	−.08 (.11)	−.15 (.14)	.05 (.12)
Protect environment	.14 (.14)	.31 (.17)	.07 (.15)
Political interest	.01 (.10)	.14 (.12)	−.16 (.11)
Discuss politics openly	−.14 (.09)	−.19 (.11)	−.18 (.10)
Preference for "strong leaders"	−.20 (.11)	−.07 (.14)	−.19 (.12)
Current national economy	−.15 (.16)	−.17 (.19)	−.10 (.17)
Future national economy	−.10 (.13)	−.25 (.16)	.11 (.15)
Current personal finances	−.47 (.19) *	−.44 (.22) *	−.36 (.21)
Future personal finances	−.04 (.11)	.20 (.13)	−.07 (.11)
Educational level	.04 (.06)	−.02 (.07)	−.05 (.06)
Age	−.02 (.01)	.01 (.01)	−.01 (.01)
Female	−.23 (.22)	−.60 (.27) *	−.45 (.42)
Professional class	−.32 (.35)	−.33 (.44)	−.44 (.42)
Working class	.46 (.27)	.17 (.31)	−.21 (.30)
Union member	−.21 (.25)	−.05 (.29)	−.25 (.28)
Population of city/town	.42 (.10) **	.08 (.11)	.12 (.11)
North	1.19 (.28) **	.41 (.37)	−.25 (.41)
South	.28 (.34)	−.19 (.39)	.83 (.32) **
Federal District	.40 (.30)	.74 (.38) *	.92 (.34) **
Church attendance	.01 (.07)	−.16 (.08) *	−.10 (.07)
PRI getting stronger	−.65 (.12) **	−.61 (.15) **	−.68 (.14) **
Economy—other party	.87 (.14) **	.74 (.17) **	.48 (.15) **
Social unrest—other party	.11 (.10)	.20 (.12)	.18 (.11)
Presidential approval	−.12 (.06) *	−.17 (.06) *	−.12 (.06) *
Constant term	.12 (1.25)	.95 (1.50)	2.62 (1.35) *

Source: IMOP S.A. (Gallup) poll, July 1991.
Note: The coefficients above are multinomial logit estimates. Standard errors appear in parentheses. $LLF = -1,556.0$ (initial) and $-1,005.9$ (at convergence). The model correctly predicted 78 percent of the cases. $N = 1,607$.
* = $p < .05$.   ** = $p < .01$.

These five factors are basically identical to those identified in chapter 4 as the most important explanations for voting intentions in the 1988 elections. This finding suggests a considerable stability in Mexican electoral behavior from the late 1980s into the early 1990s. In 1991 a core political division continued to exist between the PRI and the opposition parties. The question of the ruling party's future remained the central decision facing each voter: Is the PRI likely to remain capable of governing effectively?

There is a very strong statistical association between having voted for Salinas in 1988 and intending to vote for the PRI and against all opposition parties in 1991. There is a comparably strong association between having voted for Clouthier in 1988 and intending to vote for the PAN—and for no other party—in 1991. There is a similarly strong link between having voted for Cárdenas in 1988 and intending to vote for the PRD in 1991. These findings should put to rest the view that old-line PRI bosses might have punished Salinas's PRI at the polls; perhaps they tried it, but the voters did not respond. Similarly, despite the factional schisms within the PAN, PAN voter loyalty remained quite strong.

In 1991 the 1988 Cardenista vote divided. There is also a powerful link between having voted for Cárdenas in 1988 and intending to vote for the other small parties in 1991. This suggests a rather stable opinion alignment on the left thanks to voter loyalty to that alignment: the 1988 Cardenista voter sought to remain loyal in 1991 to one of the parties of the 1988 Cardenista coalition. The divisions evident in 1991 on the political left are best explained not in terms of a shift in voter blocs away from or toward the parties of the left, but in terms of the schisms among these parties. Despite factional infighting, many 1988 Cardenista voters attempted to remain 1991 Cardenista voters, but the hitherto Cardenista parties had splintered for their own internal reasons.

The Role of Issues, Democratic Values, and Retrospective and Prospective Economic Assessments

There are other important similarities in voting intentions between the 1988 and the 1991 elections. In neither election can the voting intentions of Mexicans be explained with reference to their attitudes on policy issues. In 1991 there was no statistically significant relationship between attitudes on the issues and the likelihood of voting for any of the opposition parties.[38] This consistent finding was not altered by the addition in 1991 of a question asking respondents to rate the importance of environmental protection. Among the respondents wishing the Salinas administration to accord its highest priority to cleaning up environmental pollution (61 percent of the sample), 68 percent were PRI voters; among those less committed to an environmental cleanup, 69 percent also supported the PRI—an insignificant difference. (The Mexican Ecologist Party received only 1.4 percent of the recorded votes.)

In 1991 as in 1988, Mexicans were divided over various policy issues, but there was no systematic overlap between the split over the issues and the partisan split. In both years there was sufficient convergence between the issue positions of the various parties to prevent a close match between issue polarization and party polarization. Voters found it difficult to connect their policy preferences to their candidate preferences.

Citizens of varying policy persuasions belonged to all partisan coalitions, and citizens of varying partisan preferences held diverse views on national policies. Each of the party coalitions was divided on the issues; each of the issue coalitions was divided among the parties. Cárdenas and the PRD had continued to believe that issues mattered for the electorate; these findings suggest that they misjudged the voters.

Nor did the level of commitment to democratic values shape the vote choice in 1991. In 1991 there was no statistically significant relationship between the level of political interest, the willingness to discuss politics openly, or the preference for strong leaders over relying on the rule of law, on the one hand, and partisan choice, on the other. Mexican democrats and Mexican authoritarians peopled all the political parties.

In 1991, voters' views about Mexico's and their own economic future, or their views about the current state of the national economy, had no statistically significant direct association with vote intention; in 1988, expectations about the economic future had had some direct impact on the intention to vote for the PAN. In 1991 there was a modest statistically significant relationship between perceptions of one's current financial situation and the intention to vote for either the PAN or the PRD. That is, those who thought that the current state of their personal finances was good were less likely to vote PAN or PRD, while those who thought that their personal finances were bad were more likely to vote PAN or PRD—a case of retrospective voting, of the shaping of the voter decision in terms of views about the present and the recent past, not about future expectations.

Compared with 1988, voter intentions on these matters changed in two ways. First, in 1988 there was no direct relationship between any of these general economic views and the likelihood of voting for Cárdenas, whereas there was a modest relationship in 1991. Second, in 1988 the finding with regard to the PAN focused on future expectations, not on retrospective judgments, whereas in 1991 the likely PAN vote was associated with a retrospective judgment.

As in chapter 4, consider the results on two variables that look to the economy's future: general expectations about the economy and expectations about the economy if a party other than the PRI were to win the elections. The latter remains a strong and powerful predictor for all parties in both elections. The general expectations about the economy have no direct statistically significant effects at all in 1991, although in 1988 they mattered a bit with regard just to the PAN.

Which general economic variable might matter somewhat has also changed. Perhaps because Mexicans in 1991 were so bullish on Mexico, they made some retrospective judgments based on their current personal finances to inform their likely 1991 vote. In essence some Mexicans asked themselves, Why are my own finances lagging when Mexico is apparently doing so well and its future seems so promising? Why should I tolerate inequality?[39]

Nonetheless, our principal finding remains unchanged. For the most part, in both elections Mexicans did not plan to vote in terms of retrospective or prospective general assessments about the economy or their own finances, or on specific issues related to the economy or the environment, or on the basis of their attachments to democratic values. Instead, they focused on their views about the future of the "party of the state"—including its continued governance of the economy—and on their partisan attachments.

Political Cleavages

In 1991 the opposition parties shrank to become mainly regional parties. The PAN drew its support mainly from the north and from the larger cities and towns, whereas in 1988 it had drawn votes from all parts of Mexico, both urban and rural (although it had been much weaker in the south). In 1991 the PRD drew its support mainly from the Federal District, whereas in 1988 Cárdenas had drawn votes from all parts of Mexico except the north. The other small parties drew well from both the Federal District and southern Mexico.

In the previous chapter we noted that there has been a long-term ecological realignment in Mexican elections; over time, the size of the rural sector has shrunk. Because the PRI has always received many more votes in the rural areas—true also in both 1988 and 1991—the decline in the size of the rural sector has, on average, lowered the total national vote for the PRI. We also noted in chapter 4, however, that the urban-rural distinction was statistically insignificant in the 1988 election. That is, it did not help to explain voter intentions; urban Mexicans as well as rural Mexicans were divided among themselves more than urban folks were separated from rural folks. Instead, both kinds of Mexicans focused most of all on the fate of the ruling party.

Why, then, is the urban-rural distinction so strongly significant in explaining the vote for the PAN in 1991? The answer has little to do with long-term changes in the relative sizes of the urban and rural sectors. The simple explanation is that the PAN lost its rural base.

Between 1988 and 1991 the voting trends for the PRI and the PRD operated more or less uniformly across communities of varying sizes. That is, the increase in support for the PRI in small towns was about as large as it was in big cities; between 1988 and 1991 the PRI picked up 16 percentage points in small towns and 13 percentage points in cities with population over one million. Moreover, the loss in support for the PRD in 1991 compared with the vote for Cárdenas in 1988 was also about as large in small towns as in big cities; in 1991 the PRD got exactly 15 fewer percentage points both in small towns and in cities with population over one million.

Now consider the PAN. Between 1988 and 1991 the PAN lost 12 percentage points in small towns (down to 9 percent), but it lost only 6 percentage points in cities with population over one million (down to 22 percent). In cities of between one hundred thousand and one million people, the PAN held steady (22 percent in 1988 and 20 percent in 1991). In short, the explanation for the strong association between the size of the community and the vote for the PAN in 1991 is unrelated to decades-long shifts in the size of the rural sector; instead, it reflects the collapse in support for the PAN in the smaller towns and rural areas in 1991.

Opposition Voter Profiles

In 1991 the PAN vote had a modest dimension of retrospective voting, but the main factors in explaining it were three: regional concentration; long-standing habits of voting PAN and strong expectations that the economy would improve if a party other than the PRI were to govern; and opposition to the PRI and the incumbent president. Above all, the PAN voter was a regional partisan.

The modal PRD voter was a Mexico City male who did not attend church—consistent with the PRD's expressed programmatic hostility to the Roman Catholic bishops—and felt that his personal finances were not in good shape. These statistically significant factors had only a modest explanatory impact, however. For the PRD as for the PAN, the main way to explain the vote was also in terms of partisanship: in 1991 the likely PRD voters were those who had supported Cárdenas in 1988, disapproved of Salinas's performance as president, and believed that the PRI would weaken and that the economy would improve if a party other than the PRI were to govern.

The profile of voters for the other small parties was close to the profile of PRD voters. Supporters of these small parties and the PRD had voted for Cárdenas in 1988, disapproved of the way Salinas had performed as president, and believed that the PRI would get weaker and that the economy would perform better if a party other than the PRI were to win. Voters for these parties came disproportionately from the Federal District. In all of these ways the PRD voter profile matched that of the voter for the small parties.

There are five differences, however, in the voter profiles of these two kinds of "Cardenista" opposition to the PRI. The small parties got a disproportionate number of votes in southern Mexico; for them, church attendance, gender, and judgments about their current personal finances were statistically independent of the voter choice. The small parties were the least likely of all parties to have mobilized new voters in 1991. In short, the voter for the small parties was principally a 1988 Cardenista who did not wish to vote PRD in 1991. The voter for the small parties was even less motivated by potential issues (such as the role of the church or economic assessments).

For reasons explained earlier in this chapter, the prospects for the opposition parties weakened between the 1988 and the 1991 elections. The opposition parties retreated to regional bastions. The left divided, and its various factions drew votes from each other. The opposition parties became vehicles of protest against the ruling party; whether one chose one vehicle over another is best expressed in terms of prior political affiliation in 1988 and, within the left, favor or distaste for the PRD.

Organizational Factors

Organizational factors remained important in 1991. The PRI drew from faithful voters in 1991 just as it had in 1988; in this sense the PRI had the loyalty of voters who wanted to be its "members" even if the PRI's internal structure, in practice, did not favor such individual affiliation. The PAN too drew from faithful voters in both years. The PRD and the other small parties benefited from those who had voted for Cárdenas in 1988.

This last point is the most important organizational story in 1991 because it helps to explain the political left's crushing defeat. As we saw, the divisions within the left are not well explained by different voter profiles for different left-wing parties; their voter profiles match enough and make them jointly different from the PAN and the PRI. Moreover, neither the PRD nor the other small parties were able to raid the PAN or the PRI very

Table 5-10. Partisan Preference and the Timing of Vote Decisions in 1991 (percent)

	PRI	PAN	PRD	Other
Pre-election poll: How sure are you that you will vote for your preferred party?				
Very	71	67	62	55
Somewhat	22	26	24	30
Not very	7	8	14	15
Exit poll: When did you decide to vote for your preferred party?				
Yesterday or today	17	17	21	23
Within the last month	13	15	17	19
After candidate announcements	15	24	25	21
Relied on a standing commitment	56	44	37	38

Source: IMOP S.A. (Gallup) poll, July 1991; IMOP S.A. (Gallup) exit poll, August 18, 1991.

Note: N = 1,995 (July) and 25,348 (August).

much. As was the case for the Cardenistas in 1988, the PRD in 1991 was not able to bring in a new pool of supporters. And as noted earlier, the small parties were significantly unable to mobilize support among those who had been able to vote in 1988 but had chosen not to do so; they performed much worse than the Cardenistas in 1988 or the PRD in 1991. These small parties did not expand the electorate; instead, they contributed to a fratricidal conflict within the left. This is a recipe for losing elections.

To underline the PRD's problems in 1991 but also to call attention to the fragile nature of the vote for the other small parties, we turn to table 5-10. The pre-election poll asked voters about the certainty of their vote for their preferred party. The results show that PRI voters were the most strongly committed, followed by PAN voters and then by PRD voters. The voters for the other parties were the least committed before the election; barely half of their presumed voters were committed to voting for such parties.

In 1991 Gallup was able to conduct an exit poll (see details in appendix 2). The poll asked about the timing of the voting decision. The results in table 5-10 show the PRI's impressive strength, deriving a majority of its votes from citizens who had made a standing decision to support the party even before the names of candidates were announced. Over one-third of the voters for all parties had made a standing decision to support the PRI even before candidates were announced. To overcome the PRI, the opposition needed the loyalty of its members and the organizational capacity to mobilize new voters. The PAN received much loyalty from its voters, though it was more conditioned on the quality of its candidates. On the other hand, nearly four out of ten PRD voters decided quite late in the campaign. This tardiness is even more evident in the case of the minor parties. Over one-fifth of those who voted for the PRD or the minor parties made up their minds within the twenty-four hours prior to voting. The parties of the left lacked strong loyalties; they also failed to mobilize the previously unmobilized. This is a weak basis on which to build party strength, and it helps to explain the left's election defeats.

A TWO-STEP "MODEL" FOR MEXICAN VOTER BEHAVIOR 2

In the previous chapter we suggested that a more ideologically competitive election lurked just beneath the key decision whether to support or oppose the ruling party. That is, once a Mexican voter made that first decision, demographic and issue factors played an important role in shaping other voting decisions. We report in table 5-11 the hypothetical probabilities of voting for the opposition parties. These probabilities are derived from the regression analysis reported in table 5-9. We follow the same procedure as in the comparable section of chapter 4.

At the top of table 5-11 the expected voter choices have been computed for two types of populations. The first row reports those who believed that the PRI would become weaker and that the opposition parties could do a good job of getting the economy to grow and maintaining social peace. The second row reports on those who believed that the PRI would become stronger and that the opposition parties could not do a good job of getting the economy to grow and maintaining social peace. In 1991, among those who thought that the PRI would become stronger and that the economy and social peace would suffer if a party other than the PRI were to gain power, the probability of voting for any opposition party was between only 1 and 2 percent.

Among those who thought that the PRI would become weaker and that the economy and social peace would not suffer if a party other than the PRI were to gain power, the probability of voting PAN rose to 26 percent, of voting PRD to 14 percent, and of voting for the other small parties to 16 percent; among these voters the PRI got only 44 percent of the votes. Note, however, that the PRI would have won the 1991 election even among these voters because the opposition was fragmented into so many parties. (In 1988, among these kinds of voters Cárdenas would have been elected president, as chapter 4 indicates.) Even if the parties of the left had been united in 1991, they would still have lost the election to the PRI among these voters. Therefore, the opposition parties had lost considerable support among the voters most favorable to opposition appeals. They had lost

Table 5-11. Ideological Predispositions and Beliefs about the PRI's
Long-Term Viability in 1991: Some Expected Probabilities
of Voting for the Opposition

	PAN	PRD	Other
PRI becoming weaker	.26	.14	.16
PRI becoming stronger	.02	.01	.02
Voters with right-wing dispositions			
PRI becoming weaker	.21	.05	.12
PRI becoming stronger	.02	.01	.01
Voters with left-wing dispositions			
PRI becoming weaker	.25	.25	.14
PRI becoming stronger	.03	.02	.02

Source: IMOP S.A. (Gallup) poll, July 1991.

Note: These probabilities were derived from the estimated logit coefficients presented in table 5-9 ($N = 1,607$). A voter's perception of the
PRI's future viability is defined by three items: the expected strength of
the PRI in the next ten years; whether the national economy would prosper
under an opposition party; and whether there would be increased social
unrest if another party took control of the Mexican government. Left-wing
or right-wing predispositions are indicated by four factors: socioeconomic
status (professional versus working class); religiosity (weekly versus no
church attendance); union membership; and policy preferences regarding
foreign investment, foreign imports, and environmental protection. All
other independent variables in table 5-9 have been set to their mean values.

so much support that only if the entire opposition—not just the left—had
been united could the PRI have been defeated among these voters.

We modeled, then, two kinds of voters. One we call a right-wing voter.
Such a person would come from the professional class, would not belong
to a union, and would attend church every week; this person would favor
foreign investment and freer imports but would not accord high priority to
improving the quality of the air and water. The other we call a left-wing
voter. Such a person would come from the working class and belong to a
union but would not attend church; this person would not favor foreign
investment or freer imports but would accord high priority to improving
the quality of the air and water. Turn, then, to the bottom four rows of
table 5-11.

Right-wing and left-wing voters who believed that the PRI would get
stronger and that the economy and social peace would be hurt if a party

other than the PRI were to gain power were quite unlikely to vote for any opposition party. Just exactly as in 1988, they remained faithful to the PRI.

Past the decision concerning the ruling party, in 1991 the PAN actually lost some likely support among right-wing voters but held its own among left-wing voters. The other small parties lost only a bit of likely support among either right-wing or left-wing voters. The PRD nearly doubled its share of the votes among likely left-wing voters but lost nearly two-thirds of its votes among likely right-wing voters; these swings are a pale version of the 1988 Cardenista performance, however.

In 1991 the PRI would have won the election among likely right-wing voters, capturing 62 percent of the votes. The PRI would also have won the election among likely left-wing voters, garnering 36 percent of the votes— enough to prevail given opposition party fragmentation. In contrast, in 1988 Cárdenas would have won by a landslide among likely left-wing voters, and the PAN's Clouthier would have won a majority among likely right-wing voters.

To put the point sharply, in 1991 only the PRD voters responded, albeit modestly, to issue and social cleavage motivations as had been more generally the case in 1988. The voters for the minor parties in 1991 were late deciders, and not much motivated by these ideological issues.

In 1991 the likely left-wing voters were the more frequent strategic voters, that is, voters who supported the opposition party they considered most likely to beat the PRI, even though they disagreed with that opposition party's stance on the issues. Past the decision about the ruling party's fate, the probability that left-wingers would vote for the PAN was 25 percent, while the probability that right-wingers would vote for the combination PRD/other parties was only 17 percent. (In 1988 the likely right-wing voters were the more frequent strategic voters; these right-wingers intended to vote for Cárdenas, even though they disagreed with his policy views, because he was perceived as the candidate most likely to beat Salinas.) This net balance of the distribution of strategic voters explains why the PAN performed better in 1991 among all voters than among right-wing voters; strategic left-wing voters voted for the PAN, even though they disagreed with its policy views, because in 1991 the PAN was perceived as the party most likely to beat the PRI.

In 1991, Mexican oppositionists often engaged in strategic voting. Among left-wing voters the likelihood of voting PAN was the same as the likelihood of voting PRD, presumably because many left-wingers were less interested in promoting an ideological vision than in trying to defeat the PRI. Among right-wing voters 17 percent were likely to vote for an opposition party other than the PAN, while only 21 percent were likely to vote for the PAN; among right-wingers too the motivation to defeat the PRI was nearly as strong as the commitment to advancing their ideological cause.

Past the judgment about the ruling party, in 1991 as in 1988, issues and demographic cleavages mattered. If voters thought that the PRI would become weaker and that the economy and social peace would not be in danger if a party other than the PRI were to win, then they were more likely to support the opposition. But the fragmentation of the opposition parties in 1991 meant that the PRI would win the election even among these voters, and even among left-wing voters unless all the opposition parties were to unite. The PRI would win by a landslide among likely right-wing voters who otherwise might have supported the opposition.

Yet another key finding is that issues and demographic cleavages mattered less in 1991 than in 1988. The frequency of strategic voting behavior was more pronounced in 1991 than in 1988 because so many left-wing and right-wing voters were ready to engage in such behavior. In 1991, therefore, Mexico moved away from the more normal electoral contestation typical of democratic politics and focused more narrowly on an up-or-down decision on the fate of the political regime.

CONCLUSION

In 1991 as in 1988, Mexicans asked themselves, first and foremost, whether they favored continued rule by the "party of the state"—the party that had long embodied the political regime. In 1991 that was the only question most Mexican voters asked themselves: their answer was yes. The PRI was especially strong among those voters who had been repeatedly loyal to it from one election to the next. The party of the state had self-identified "members." The political regime had been rejuvenated.

For the minority of Mexican voters who preferred to change the political regime, issues, general economic assessments, and sociodemographic cleavages had less to do in 1991 than in 1988 with shaping their choices among opposition parties; this choice was shaped best by prior partisan affiliation. The ideological and issue content of the election had declined. Among voters who also had to choose between the PRD and the small parties, the decision was typically a late one, more spontaneous than focused; the voters for the small parties were generally less ideological than the PRD voters, and in particular less secular than the PRD voters and less likely to be expressing personal financial distress blamed on the government.

An important organizational story in 1991 was the crumbling of the left-wing opposition. The left-wing parties got fewer votes overall and became more regionally restricted than in 1988. The parties of the Cardenista coalition fragmented, fought each other, and in the process lost an impressive amount of support. The divisions of the opposition, and especially the divisions on the left, virtually ensured PRI victories even among the kinds of voters who were most responsive to opposition appeals. Nonetheless, for the most part the differences between the parties of the left were not substantive. Opinion alignments as they affected voter choice were fairly stable from 1988 to 1991. A large pool of potential left-wing voters awaited the organizational reconstruction of Cardenismo.

The 1991 campaign strategy pursued by Cárdenas and his party, the PRD, was flawed. Their campaign was based on the premise that lower-class Mexicans did not share the economic optimism of wealthier Mexicans and that a large enough pool of Mexicans agreed with the left on the issues to oppose the Salinas government. Neither assumption was correct. In turn, Cárdenas and his party failed to strengthen the PRD's organizational capacities and participated in the division within the 1988 Cardenista coalition. It was not just that Salinas and the PRI beat them; they defeated themselves. Looking toward the future, Cárdenas and his allies had to focus on organizational matters much more if they wished to win elections.

For the PAN, the 1991 election demonstrated its staying power as well as the fact that its internal factional turmoil did not provoke voters into defection. Those who had voted for the PAN in 1988 were likely, for the most part, to remain faithful to it in 1991. The PAN demonstrated yet again in 1991 that it was not a confessional party. And yet a party that commanded consistently not much more than one-sixth of the electorate could not be expected to mount a credible national challenge to PRI dominance, even though the PAN had proved that it could win many local elections and congressional seats. For the PAN to grow, however, the best strategy did seem to be the one identified by its president, Luis H. Alvarez, after the 1988 elections, namely, to position itself as an alternative governing party. Once Mexican voters come to believe that a party other than the PRI could govern effectively—fostering economic growth and maintaining social peace—the PAN did well among right-wing voters and drew strategic left-wing voters.

From the perspective of democratization, the 1991 election was a disappointment because the political space was not enlarged. No new waves of voters washed onto the shores during this national election. The main effect of partisan competition was to reshuffle the voters, not to mobilize the previously unmobilized. Nor did the election engage citizens in a discussion of issues that might have been connected to their support for parties.

The 1991 national election reinstated virtual one-party government. After the 1988 election the PRI had 52 percent of the seats in the Chamber of

Deputies and sixty of sixty-four senators; after the 1991 election its share of the Chamber of Deputies rose to 64 percent, and it picked up an additional Senate seat. The parties that had supported Cárdenas in 1988 lost one-third of their deputies and two of their four senators, while the PAN dropped from 101 to 89 deputies and picked up its first senator ever. In concluding chapter 4 we noted that a critical realignment had not occurred in the 1988 election but that one might be possible in the future. When the future arrived in 1991, the prospects for a critical realignment and for sustained multiparty competition receded further.[40]

The 1991 election strengthened the Salinas government's capacity to govern. It would use that strength to continue the policies of economic adjustment and reform begun in the 1980s. In this sense the election indirectly performed the role that elections may perform in democracies:[41] to reject or to ratify the president's program, even if specific issues or ideologies had little direct impact on voter intentions. The Salinas government sought and received a deeper and broadened though general mandate to reshape Mexico.

The 1991 election in Mexico above all rendered a judgment on the presidency of Carlos Salinas de Gortari and his party. The electorate applauded the president's achievements; his adversaries fought among themselves. And yet the magnitude of the official party's victory cast doubt on the credibility of the official results. Did the PRI win so big because of electoral fraud? To this topic we devote the next chapter.

6 ✧ EVALUATION OF THE ELECTORAL PROCESS: PERCEPTIONS AND PRACTICE OF ELECTORAL FRAUD

At 7:30 P.M. on election day, July 6, 1988, the National Electoral Registry's screens lit up. Mexico's secretary of government (*Gobernación*), Manuel Bartlett, who also chaired the Federal Elections Commission, had ensured that the registry would have a state-of-the-art computer, telephone equipment, and expert staff—the registry's director had a Ph.D. in mathematics from the University of London—to handle the count for the presidential and other elections held on that day. The central computer would flash the information about the count in each district onto the registry's screens for all national and international observers to see.

The first results came from one polling place in Tula, about thirty miles outside of Mexico City. The numbers showed that Carlos Salinas de Gortari, the candidate of the long-ruling Institutional Revolutionary Party (PRI), had won. However, representatives from opposition parties present in the room checked the numbers they had received from their party observers at the Tula site; these observers reported that opposition leader Cuauhtémoc Cárdenas had won this site. And then, poof! The screens went off. The computer had failed, the public were told.[1] The computer's shutdown was both fact and symbol of election fraud.

Despite the lack of a public official count, hours later PRI party president Jorge de la Vega Domínguez proclaimed that Salinas had been elected president of Mexico. For one week after the election the Federal Elections Commission failed to issue official results. The PRI and the opposition parties released their conflicting counts, each claiming quite different numbers. Finally, on July 13 Secretary Bartlett formally announced Salinas's victory.

On July 16, 1988, Cárdenas addressed a gigantic crowd gathered in Mexico City's historic central square, the Zócalo, to protest election fraud. The opposition leaders, he stated, had "reached the agreement not to recognize public authorities who might emerge from the electoral fraud." He continued: "If the government were to ratify [the election result] technically . . . it would be staging a coup d'état to impose a usurper government, which would lack legitimacy.''[2] At one moment during the meeting Cárdenas called for a moment of silence to honor two of his campaign workers who had been murdered hours before the election; the huge crowd fell silent, holding their arms up with their fingers displaying the V for victory.[3]

Electoral fraud was not invented in Mexico on election day 1988, but that election illustrates why Mexico had not yet effected a transition to democracy based on free and fair elections.[4] In June 1994 the then-director of the Federal Elections Institute (IFE), Arturo Núñez, admitted that the computer system had been forced to fail in 1988—an order that could have been given by at most a handful of people at the very top of the Mexican government.[5] The complexity of the fraud through this and other means, the secrecy of the count, and the government's decision to bar opposition observers from access to the actual ballots and to prevent a verifiable public count were key elements in the government's and the PRI's use of power to impose their own count on the nation. The PRI was not ready to lose the presidency in 1988. It would win by all means, fair and foul. In so doing it would reduce the likelihood that Mexicans would trust in the validity and credibility of elections. Thus the PRI made it harder to rely upon elections to democratize, or even to govern, Mexico.

We cannot improve on the work that Mexican scholars have done in documenting electoral fraud in Mexico.[6] In particular, we cannot document the incidence of fraud, or lack thereof, better than they have. Our task is more modest. We seek to analyze what Mexicans think about electoral fraud and how such beliefs affect their political behavior.[7]

We have found that the perception of electoral fraud lowered the likelihood of voting on election day. Fraud-induced nonvoters, moreover, were disproportionately likely to support the opposition; thus fraud-induced nonvoting also helped to distort the election results. On every dimension, therefore, electoral fraud in Mexico has had antidemocratic consequences. It violates Mexico's Constitution and formal laws, and it deprives Mexican citizens of their fundamental rights. It depresses participation, and it prevents Mexicans from choosing as they truly prefer.

REALITIES AND IMAGES: VIGNETTES FROM THE 1988 PRESIDENTIAL CAMPAIGN

Fraud in this book refers principally to what may happen on election day and during the subsequent counting of the ballots. Nonetheless, electoral fraud can begin well in advance of an election; political leaders can set it in motion by preventing or by making it difficult for the opposition to contest the election and by presenting false images to the electorate during the campaign. In this section we present some vignettes from Mexico's 1988 presidential election campaign that do not involve fraud but that suggest the complexity posed by reality and image during that campaign.[8] (See also two vignettes in chapter 1.)

On the morning of Friday, May 27, Carlos Salinas attended a rally at Mexico City's huge National Auditorium. The rally had been organized by the PRI-affiliated labor union of government workers for the Federal District of Mexico City. As an old-line labor leader spoke before the crowd that packed this auditorium, Salinas sat up at the podium facing several rows of people who seemed very enthusiastic; they had been hired to look enthusiastic, however, and were trained to cheer, clap, and make friendly noises—they were equipped with noisemakers—at the right moment. Behind the hired cheerleaders there was a mass of sullen-looking workers who filled up more than two-thirds of the seats. Those seated near the rear would boo whenever Salinas and the PRI were mentioned; they were at this rally against their will, but their jobs were on the line. Salinas spoke for only about five minutes; the anger in the hall did not dissipate.

The rally was designed to convey an image of support despite the reality of opposition. It was not electoral fraud in the technical sense, but this rally was surely fraudulent. And yet in this case Salinas was also one victim of the fraudulent rally. There had been a struggle for power in the labor union. One faction maneuvered to place its candidate to speak just before Salinas did in order to give the impression that Salinas endorsed him. The crowd was angry at this appearance, and so was Salinas, helpless to remedy the situation.

That evening there was a different fraudulent spectacle. State-owned television channel 13 gave a full, lengthy, and accurate version of everything Salinas had done during the day—except that there was no mention of his having attended the rally at the National Auditorium. The evening news had been doctored. Channel 13 also made no mention of any other presidential candidate; its political bias was blatant.

Mexico's largest television network, the privately owned TELEVISA, was not appreciably fairer. Its flagship channel 2's evening news program did report on the Salinas, Cárdenas, and Clouthier campaigns. Salinas was shown campaigning, and his own words were heard. Cárdenas and Clouthier, however, were not heard to utter a word; their pictures were shown, but the anchorman spoke over them. The viewer of the program came away with a strongly favorable image of Salinas.

On Saturday, May 28, Salinas attended a discussion on mining issues in the rural state of Hidalgo, north of Mexico City. The meeting was held at a mine. When the presidential caravan arrived, Salinas could see the miners, wearing their yellow hard hats with their lights on; they formed two lines to make way for him and his entourage. They applauded Salinas as he passed by, headed for the amphitheater set up just in front of the mine. But as the miners walked toward the area where the meeting was going to be held, the doors were shut, leaving them outside. In anger, they nearly rioted. Someone had the good sense to reopen the doors to let the miners stand in the back of the meeting area.

At the front, Salinas sat at the podium with the business leaders of the private mining sector, the heads of government mining agencies, and the old-line leader of the miners' union. In front of this podium were seats for the invited national and foreign guests, the press, and the local elites. The miners stood at the rear. This was a striking visual image of social and political stratification.

In his speech Salinas called attention to this embarrassment. The most important people, he said shrewdly, were those left standing in the back. In calling attention to the gaffe he made it clear that he had been victimized again, this time by inept campaign planning, and hurt by an image that this time accurately reflected reality.

At midday on Friday, May 27, Salinas visited the Federal District's third district, roughly in the center of Mexico City. This was a poor area, hard-hit by a major earthquake in 1985; the government had helped to rebuild the community. Salinas sat at the podium; the crowd seemed genuinely honored and pleased that he was visiting them. Several people spoke frankly and openly about their problems and concerns. These were common folks—including an old heavy-set woman who, just before introducing Salinas, confessed that she was really nervous. Salinas responded, speaking about the need for better public safety in the neighborhood. He talked about gangs but also about corrupt police officers who broke the law to prey on ordinary citizens; he was remarkably candid. As his speech was ending, Salinas said that he had noticed that more people had wanted to speak but had not been able to do so. Therefore, he said, he would walk into the crowd and invited all who wanted to talk to him face to face to come forward; several did so.

This meeting was a bodyguard's nightmare. Anyone could have shot the candidate. The lack of security became apparent when Salinas was physically unable to leave the area because of the crush of people. There were not enough security personnel to rescue him. Well-wishers could have trampled him. Finally, as the crowd parted a bit, he made it out, receiving in his hand messages from people in the crowd who were requesting personal favors.

This time too the image matched the reality, but it put Salinas in a most favorable light. He addressed the concerns of the urban poor about whom he had learned both at the meeting and also through his steady public-opinion polling. He had risked injury by wading into the crowd, but he demonstrated his great skill at interpersonal relations. He conveyed personal honesty.

Ordinary Mexicans found it difficult to sort out political image and reality. Was the real Salinas the honest, take-charge straight talker of the third district neighborhood discussion? Or the helpless politician at the National Auditorium? Or the equally helpless would-be president of a highly stratified society who tried to make the best of a bad situation? Or the censor of the television evening news? In some sense he was all of these. Despite evidence that there was much to praise, the balance of the imagery was vulnerable to suspicion; no wonder Mexicans often distrusted the political system and perceived its elections to be marred by fraud and its government tainted by corruption. To these perceptions we turn.

THE PERCEPTIONS OF ELECTORAL FRAUD AND THEIR CONSEQUENCES

A core concept of democratic political theory is majority rule. In political systems under representative democracy, elections are the vehicle for citizens to choose their governors. In 1959 Mexicans were asked whether they believed that the way people vote is the main thing that decides how the country was run. In 1959–60 the same question was asked in Great Britain, West Germany, the United States, and Italy. The Gallup poll asked the same question of Mexicans in 1988 and in 1991. The results appear in table 6-1.

In the late 1950s Mexicans were the least likely to believe that elections determined the identity of the nation's rulers. The proportion who disagreed that elections decided how the country was run was highest in Mexico. The percentage disbelieving that elections decided how Mexico was run reached a high of 45 percent on the eve of the 1988 presidential election. In 1991 the proportion had returned to a level nearly identical to that of 1959. In short, Mexicans have been much more suspicious of their electoral system than citizens of several advanced industrial democracies, and those misgivings have endured. Not surprisingly, in 1990 Miguel Basáñez found that 83 percent of Mexicans wanted their government to be more open to the public, while only 30 percent believed that "political reform [was] happening too fast."[9]

In 1988 a substantial majority of Mexicans believed that electoral fraud was widespread; as the evidence in table 6-2 shows, fewer than one in ten Mexicans believed that there was no fraud in Mexican elections. Only 30 percent believed in Salinas's pledge of free and fair elections. That proportion was replicated in 1991, when only 30 percent of respondents agreed

Table 6-1. Perceptions of the Mexican Electoral System, in Comparative
Perspective (percent)

	Voting Decides How the Country Is Run		
	Agree	Disagree	N
Civic Culture countries, 1959–60			
Great Britain	83	15	963
West Germany	75	12	995
United States	71	25	970
Italy	62	13	995
Mexico	65	30	1,295
Mexico, 1988	52	45	2,960
Mexico, 1991	62	32	3,053

Source: The Civic Culture study; IMOP S.A. (Gallup) polls, May 1988
and July 1991.
Note: The sample size reported for Mexico in 1959 is a weighted N.

that the elections would be clean and that the results would be respected.
In 1991 approximately one out of every six Mexicans believed that the final
electoral results at the local, state, and national levels would be seriously
corrupted through electoral fraud; one-third of Mexicans believed that the
results of state and local elections would be seriously marred by fraud.
Heading toward the August 1994 presidential election, in late 1993 about
41 percent of Mexicans believed that the forthcoming national election
would be "dirty."[10] These Mexicans clearly did not believe that those who
would govern them had earned the right to do so through elections.

In 1991 the modal position was held by 45 percent of the respondents. It
was rather nuanced; these respondents believed that there would be some
fraud, whose magnitude and significance would vary, but they also believed that the national results of the election would be essentially accurate.

For decades there have been substantive and procedural problems with
Mexican elections.[11] Mexico has also had a long history of corruption in
public office. Though Mexicans have not liked these facts, they have been
accustomed to such problems. Perhaps for this reason, in recent years in
relative terms most Mexicans have not seen political corruption as one of
the country's major problems.

In both 1986 and 1991, political corruption ranked well behind Mexico's
other economic and social problems on the mass public's list of the nation's
most important problems, as the evidence in table 6-3 makes clear. (For
both years table 6-3 reports answers given to open questions that asked

Table 6-2.   Perceptions of Electoral Fraud (percent)

Asked in 1988: *How Prevalent Is Fraud in Mexican Elections?*	
Widespread	59
Some	26
None	8

Asked in 1988: *Do You Trust the Salinas Pledge for Fair and Honest Elections?*	
Yes	30
No	61

Asked in 1991: *Which of the Following Statements Best Represents Your View of How the Federal Elections Next Month Will Be Conducted?*	
The elections will be clean, and the results will be respected	30
There will be some fraud, but it will not affect the results at the local, state, or national levels	29
There will be more serious fraud affecting local and state elections, but not the national results	16
Fraud will be a very great problem, and the final electoral results at all levels will be corrupted	17

Source: Franz A. von Sauer, "Measuring Legitimacy in Mexico: An Analysis of Public Opinion during the 1988 Presidential Campaign," *Mexican Studies/Estudios mexicanos* 8 (Summer 1992): 269–70 (based on a nationwide poll conducted by Consultores 21, S.A., in June 1988); IMOP S.A. (Gallup) poll, July 1991.

Note: N = 1,397 (1988) and 3,053 (1991).

respondents to name the nation's main problems.) In both years inflation ranked first; this concern was less pronounced in 1991, accurately reflecting the inflation rate's decline. The foreign debt was the second most frequently mentioned problem in 1986, but—again reflecting the decline in its objective importance—it was much less worrisome in 1991. Concerns about unemployment, air pollution, and drug abuse had increased greatly between 1986 and 1991, as had concern with common crime; there were good objective grounds for increased worry in all of these cases.

Table 6-3.   Concern with Political Corruption (percent)

	Asked in 1986: What Is the Main Problem We Have in the Country Today?
Inflation/cost of living	52
Foreign debt	16
Inept government	10
Unemployment	8
Drug abuse	2
Overpopulation	2
Political corruption	2

	Asked in 1991: What Are the Three Principal Problems We Face Today in This Country?	
	First Problem Mentioned	Total Problems Mentioned
Inflation/cost of living	20	37
Unemployment	14	31
Air pollution	12	22
Drug abuse	7	17
Foreign debt	6	8
Political corruption	4	10
Illiteracy	3	10
Delinquency/robbery	2	9
Overpopulation	2	5

Source: New York Times Mexico survey, 1986; IMOP S.A. (Gallup) poll, July 1991.

Note: N = 1,899 (weighted, 1986) and 3,053 (1991).

The salience of political corruption increased slightly between 1986 and 1991, from 2 percent calling it the main problem in 1986 to 4 percent mentioning it first when asked to describe Mexico's principal problem in 1991. This jump is not statistically significant, nor is it substantively important. Political corruption remained a relatively low priority for Mexicans. Furthermore, when prompted in 1991 to mention additional problems facing the country, the proportion of respondents mentioning political corruption rose just to 10 percent of the 1991 sample. In both years political corruption tied for fifth place among the country's most serious problems.

Given the comparatively low level of concern with political corruption, it should not be surprising, therefore, that the variable "voting decides

Table 6-4.   Perceptions of Fraud and Voter Turnout (percent)

	Do the Following Reasons for Not Voting Pertain to Many People, to Some People, or to Only a Few?		
	Many	*Some*	*Few*
Voting doesn't matter, since the same party always wins	66	21	11
People don't believe that the elections would be honest or clean	59	24	13
It doesn't matter who wins the election, because all politicians are alike once they are elected	58	23	15
People aren't interested in politics	33	35	29
People are too lazy to vote or have other things to do on election day	29	32	35

Source: IMOP S.A. (Gallup) poll, July 1991.
Note: N = 3,053.

policy" does not help to explain voter choice in either the 1988 or the 1991 elections. We included this variable in the regression analyses (not shown here) that seek to predict party choice along the lines reported in tables 4-15 and 5-9; the coefficients were not statistically significant.

It would be mistaken to conclude, however, that perceptions of fraud have no electoral importance. In 1991 Mexicans were asked to explain why people do not vote in elections (table 6-4). The most common response was that voting does not matter because the same party always wins. This was accurate enough, though it also suggested an alienation from voting as a result. A related response that also suggested alienation was the belief that it does not matter who wins because all politicians are ultimately alike. (The respondents did not give much credence, however, to the view that Mexicans did not vote because they were uninterested in politics or because they were too lazy or had other things to do on election day.) Most important for our purposes is that 59 percent said that they believed that many people did not vote in elections because the elections were not perceived to be honest or clean. That is, these citizens explained electoral abstention as a direct consequence of the perception that electoral fraud was broadly prevalent. Perceptions about fraud were, in their view, an important explanation for the failure to vote.

Electoral turnout, or its insufficiency, has been a serious problem in Mexico. There were two broad categories of nonvoters, namely, those who had failed to register to vote and those who, though registered, failed to vote on election day. Between the 1958 and 1982 presidential elections, the percentage of the voting-age population who had failed to register to vote fell from about 28 percent to about 15 percent; between those same elections the percentage of registered voters who failed to vote oscillated somewhat, but it never fell below one-fifth of the voting-age population. Combining these two variables, the overall abstention rate fell from 48 percent of the voting-age population in 1958 to about 36 percent in 1982—an improvement, but still quite a high rate of electoral abstention.[12]

What explains the likelihood of voter turnout, therefore? Using both the 1988 and 1991 pre-election surveys, in table 6-5 we present regression weights to predict participation. An item that asked respondents to state when the PRI would lose an election (asked only in 1988) is used here to tap into the sentiment that "voting does not matter, since the same party always wins." In addition, we include in both models a measure of cynicism about the responsiveness of individual political candidates, levels of citizen interest in politics, a host of demographic factors that might be related to turnout, an indicator of consistency[13] among economic preferences, and the "voting decides how things are run in this country" item from table 6-1. As shown in table 6-5, only three variables are statistically significant in both elections to explain the likelihood of voting:

1. The higher the level of political interest, the greater the likelihood of voting.
2. The greater the belief that voting decides how Mexico is run, the greater the likelihood of voting.
3. Residents of the Federal District are more likely to vote.

Our first finding contradicts to some degree the perception of the majority of 1991 poll respondents. As we saw in table 6-4, respondents did not believe that level of political interest had much impact on the likelihood of voting. In fact, level of political interest is the single most important and consistent explanation for the likelihood of voting in 1988 and 1991.

Our second finding is consistent with the perception of the majority of 1991 poll respondents who believed—accurately—that perceptions of electoral fraud would dampen the likelihood of voter turnout. This is exactly what we show in table 6-5. This variable's explanatory importance increased between 1988 and 1991.

The important depressing effect that perceptions of electoral fraud have on electoral turnout is highlighted by our equally consistent finding for both years that perceptions about the behavior of politicians after the elec-

Table 6-5. Predicting Participation: A Model of Voter Turnout

	1988	1991
Does voting decide how Mexico is run?	.15 (.06) *	.22 (.05) **
Do candidates act differently after elections?	.05 (.07)	.01 (.06)
When will the PRI lose an election?	−.01 (.04)	N/A
Consistency in economic preferences	.05 (.12)	.05 (.09)
Political interest	.27 (.05) **	.18 (.04) **
Educational level	.06 (.02) **	−.03 (.02)
Age	.38 (.04) **	.03 (.04)
Female	−.04 (.10)	.30 (.10) **
Professional class	.10 (.16)	.07 (.14)
Working class	.01 (.14)	.25 (.12) *
Union member	.16 (.11)	.02 (.10)
North	−.17 (.13)	−.10 (.11)
South	−.16 (.13)	.16 (.12)
Federal District	.48 (.14) **	.30 (.12) *
Church attendance	−.01 (.03)	.11 (.03) **
Constant term	−2.00 (.40) **	−.92 (.35) **

Source: IMOP S.A. (Gallup) polls, May 1988 and July 1991.

Note: The coefficients above are maximum likelihood logit estimates. The dependent variable is coded 1 if the respondent was a likely voter and 0 otherwise. Standard errors appear in parentheses. Initially the LLF equaled −1,667.7 (1988) and −1,916.6 (1991); at convergence the LLF equaled −1,446.5 (1988) and −1,698.6 (1991). The model correctly predicted 68 percent of the cases in both samples. $N = 2,406$ (1988) and 2,765 (1991).
$* = p < .05$. $** = p < .01$.

tions (e.g., "it does not matter who wins an election, because all politicians are alike once they are elected") have no effect on voter turnout. Ordinarily, we would expect a high correlation between the variable that measures views of the behavior of politicians and the variable that asks whether voting decides how the country is run. In many democratic countries both variables measure forms of political alienation, and they are therefore highly correlated. In Mexico, in both 1988 and 1991 the correlation between these two variables is below .05; the question on candidates is never significant, while the question on the decisiveness of elections always is.

We believe that this low correlation between those two variables occurs in Mexico because voter responses to the question on the decisiveness of elections tap their attitudes about electoral fraud, which is not how the question is answered in most democratic countries. Consequently, in the United States and other democratic countries these two questions may be measuring the same dimension of political alienation; in Mexico, in contrast, the decisiveness of elections uncovers concerns about fraud while the expected policy reliability of candidates once elected focuses on different concerns. Only the concern about fraud depresses electoral turnout.

It is also noteworthy that respondents who consistently favored or consistently opposed neoliberal economic policies did not participate in the elections in significantly greater numbers than those with a mixed set of preferences. This suggests that politicians, parties, and social movements may fail to increase the likelihood of voter turnout if they simply stress ideological economic factors.

Other factors help to explain electoral turnout, but just for one of these elections, not for the other. In 1988 older voters and well-educated voters were much more likely to plan to vote. In 1991 neither age nor education was statistically related to the likelihood of voting. In 1991 churchgoers and females were much more likely to vote; workers were also more likely to vote. In 1988 neither religiosity, nor gender, nor social class was statistically related to the likelihood of voting.

The last point worth noting about table 6-5 is that the belief that the PRI had a lock on the 1988 election did not lead respondents to abstain in greater numbers in that election. This contradicts the overwhelming view of two-thirds of the 1991 poll respondents reported in table 6-4.

What would happen if Mexico were to have an election and all citizens believed that "voting decides how things are run in this country," so that only apathy, a low level of formal education, or other demographic factors would keep individuals from participating? Would the distribution of partisan preferences be different? Of course, such questions are not answerable in a specific or falsifiable way, but it is possible to use the regressions developed in chapters 4 and 5 to infer candidate preferences for those self-identified nonvoters whose turnout was depressed because they were suspicious about electoral fraud. These are the steps we followed in this exercise:

We focused on the 1988 presidential election because of its obvious importance and because respondents that year were especially distrustful of the electoral process. Based on the logit coefficients in table 6-5 (first column), we computed for each respondent a predicted probability of voting in 1988. (The average of these predicted probabilities is .65, since 65 percent of the respondents were classified as "likely voters.") Next, we computed an alternative set of probabilities of voting based on the (admittedly im-

Table 6-6.   Imputing the Presidential Preferences of 1988 Nonvoters

	Self-Identified Likely Voters		A Subset of Nonvoters		Total Hypothetical Distribution	
	%	N	%	N	%	N
Salinas	57	1,061	36	109	54	1,170
Clouthier	21	384	27	82	21	466
Cárdenas	23	427	37	112	25	539
Total	100	1,872	100	303	100	2,175

Source: IMOP S.A. (Gallup) poll, May 1988.
Note: Supporters of the many smaller parties in 1988 (2 percent of the sample) were dropped from this analysis. The preferences of 721 nonvoters could not be imputed because of missing data.

plausible) assumption that all respondents would have voiced total confidence in the voting process.[14] Next, we subtracted the second set of hypothetical probability estimates from the first set in order to select out those respondents who would have been significantly more inclined to participate if they had had full confidence in the electoral process. The self-identified nonvoters in this group became the subsample for whom a presidential preference was imputed. In total, 303 out of the 2,960 respondents in the 1988 survey were included in this subsample.

How would these likely abstainers have voted if they had gone to the polls? Does fraud-induced nonvoting bias the electoral system in favor of one of the parties? Using the earlier regression model from table 4-15, we inferred a probable vote choice based on a three-candidate race.[15] This distribution appears in table 6-6.

The hypothetical presidential choices for the abstainers strongly favored the opposition. Among the nonvoters, the race would have been very close, but Cárdenas had the edge, beating Salinas by 1 percentage point. The probable support for Clouthier also rises. If we combine these inferred vote choices with the partisan preferences that were actually stated, the PRI's margin drops by 3 percentage points, while Cárdenas gains 2 points and Clouthier less than 1.

How important might that shift have been? If the election had been held when the poll was taken in May 1988, the resulting changes would not matter much. But that is not the whole story. Given the very substantial increase in the votes recorded for Cárdenas from late May until election day on July 6, 1988, and given that the actual election results were probably much closer than the recorded results because of the fraud actually committed, it would not have taken much of a drop in support to push the PRI's vote below the symbolically important 50 percent mark. Perhaps a "free and fair election" would have been quite a close contest. Thus our calculation in table 6-6 suggests that well-founded suspicions regarding the electoral system have helped the PRI maintain its privileged position.[16]

From the perspective of Mexico's opposition, these findings ought to be disconcerting. The opposition seeks votes by persuading voters, among other things, that the system is corrupt and that the elections are fraudulent. A significant number of voters believe the opposition's claims about the pervasiveness of electoral fraud and consequently stay home on election day, making it easier for the PRI to win—which is exactly contrary to the intention of the opposition leaders and those whom they have persuaded. Moreover, recall that we showed in chapters 4 and 5 that the opposition had not been able to mobilize new blocs of voters. Now we have some insights into why this may have been the case: such citizens might have heard the opposition appeals, but they responded by abstaining rather than by participating.

MONITORING ELECTORAL IRREGULARITIES: ELECTION DAY 1991

Gallup conducted a large nationwide exit poll for the August 1991 elections (see appendix 2 for details). Polltakers were instructed to code whether anything out of the ordinary was occurring at the voting precincts where they were posted. Before beginning each interview with a respondent, the pollster had to prerecord on each questionnaire whether precinct officers, police officers, or anyone else was in any way seeking to pressure or intimidate the respondent; whether the respondent seemed to be part of a large group of voters who had been ferried to the voting place; and whether the respondent seemed unusually nervous during the interview.

Then the pollster asked various demographic questions. These were followed by two "secret ballot" questions (see discussion of this procedure in appendix 2) answered in writing by the respondent: in one the respondent reported the vote, and in the other, the reasons for the vote. The pollster did not see the completed "secret ballot" questionnaire; instead, the respondent directly deposited it in the "secret ballot box."

Therefore, the information concerning voting-place irregularities was recorded separately for each respondent in a double-blind format: the respondent did not know how the ballot had been precoded by the pollster, and the pollster did not change the report on irregularities after the respondent had marked the voting preferences through the "secret ballot" procedure. This is the database for the subsequent analysis.

Table 6-7.   Conditions at the Voting Booth in 1991 (percent)

	People Were Bothering Voters	People Arrived and Voted in Groups	Respondent Was Nervous	N
National sample	7	2	4	25,529
Guanajuato	10	4	3	3,291
San Luis Potosí	6	1	4	3,285

Source: IMOP S.A. (Gallup) exit poll, August 18, 1991.

Two of the most closely contested elections were held in the states of Guanajuato and San Luis Potosí. Gallup drew very large samples in both states; we focus this discussion on their gubernatorial contests.[17] In the state of Guanajuato, Ramón Aguirre Velázquez, former mayor of Mexico City, was the gubernatorial candidate of the PRI and the Frente Cardenista Nacional Renovation Party (PFCRN), the latter being one of the small parties that in 1988 had supported Cárdenas and that in 1991 was contesting the PRI in other races. Vicente Fox Quesada was the candidate of the National Action Party (PAN). Porfirio Muñoz Ledo, former PRI national party president and one of the leaders of the Cardenista defection in 1988, had been elected Cardenista senator in 1988 from the Federal District of Mexico City for three years; in 1991 he ran for governor of Guanajuato as the candidate of Cárdenas's Party of the Democratic Revolution (PRD) and of the People's Socialist Party (PPS), another small party that had supported Cárdenas in 1988 but was for the most part running its own independent campaign in 1991. In the state of San Luis Potosí the PRI's candidate for governor was Fausto Zapata Loredo. In a quite unusual turn of events, the PAN, the PRD, and the small Mexican Democratic Party (PDM) joined to support Salvador Nava for governor.[18]

The evidence in table 6-7 indicates that irregularities at voting places were infrequent and thus were not likely to affect the outcome. Only 7 percent of the respondents in the national sample were in circumstances where "people were bothering the voters," for example. Even fewer, less than 5 percent nationally, were thought to have arrived to vote in a group or seemed especially nervous while being interviewed. The reported irregularities in Guanajuato and San Luis Potosí were equally modest and not markedly different from the national pattern. (In a separate analysis, not shown here, we also found that education, age, and gender had little bearing on these findings.)

Immediately after the August 1991 elections, however, massive protests broke out concerning fraud in both Guanajuato and San Luis Potosí. The

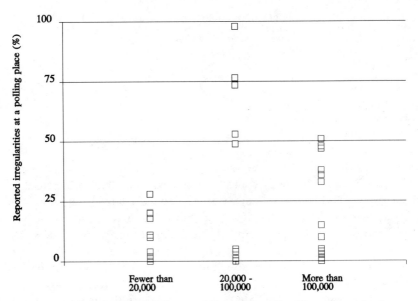

Figure 6-1. Likelihood of Electoral Fraud, by City Size: Guanajuato

Source: IMOP S.A. (Gallup) exit poll, August 18, 1991.

Note: In total, forty-six polling places are represented here. The average N within a polling place is 71. $F = 5.2$ ($p < .01$).

parties of the opposition and many voters believed that the opposition had won the governorship in each of these two states, but the official results proclaimed a PRI victory in both races. Was the opposition wrong about its impressions that widespread fraud had occurred?

The opposition was better organized in the larger cities and towns; its own observers as well as other national and international observers were therefore better able to examine conditions in urban areas. Their perceptions of electoral fraud reflected mainly what happened in cities and towns. Thus we consider whether place of residence made a difference in the reporting of fraud. These results appear in figures 6-1 and 6-2; each plots, by the size of the surrounding community, the proportion of respondents within a polling place for whom Gallup's pollsters had prerecorded evidence of electoral irregularities.

Population size is quite significantly related to voting irregularities.[19] In the state of Guanajuato, voting irregularities were important in the city of Guanajuato but especially in midsized cities and large towns. In the state of San Luis Potosí, voting irregularities were serious, especially in the city

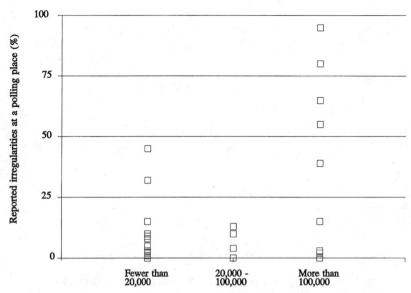

Figure 6-2. Likelihood of Electoral Fraud, by City Size: San Luis Potosí
Source: IMOP S.A. (Gallup) exit poll, August 18, 1991.
Note: In total, forty-nine polling places are represented here. The average N within a polling place is 70. $F = 6.5$ ($p < .01$).

of San Luis Potosí itself. Concentrated in cities, the election observers probably "saw" many more electoral irregularities than in fact occurred throughout the state. This does not in any way minimize the gravity of the violations, but it helps to explain the intense conviction of the opposition that the elections had been stolen.

In his classic 1949 study of politics in the southern states of the United States, V. O. Key argued that the likelihood of electoral discrimination increased as a district became more competitive.[20] For example, the dominant Democratic Party in Mississippi was more likely to disenfranchise blacks in districts where whites made up less than 50 percent of the population. Mississippi, and much of the southern United States, was at the time characterized by de facto one-party politics. For this hypothesis to apply in Mexico, we would expect that electoral fraud should increase as a district becomes more competitive: the more threatened the PRI felt, the greater the likelihood that its operatives would commit fraud.

Figures 6-3 and 6-4 plot, by the proportion of votes going to the PRI candidate in each polling place, the proportion of respondents on whose

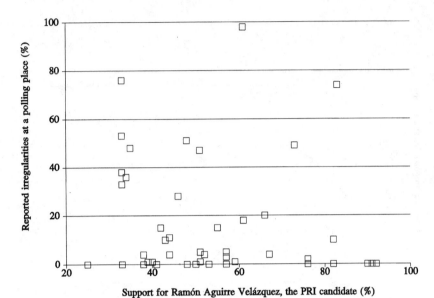

Figure 6-3. Likelihood of Electoral Fraud, by the Competitiveness of the PRI: Guanajuato Gubernatorial Race

Source: IMOP S.A. (Gallup) exit poll, August 18, 1991.

Note: In total, forty-six polling places are represented here. The average N within a polling place is 71. $\beta = -.14$ ($p > .25$). Dropping two statistically significant outliers yields a β of $-.34$ ($p < .05$).

questionnaires Gallup's pollsters had prerecorded evidence of electoral irregularities that affected the particular respondent. In both states the percentage of respondents vulnerable to electoral irregularities was higher in districts where there was less support for the PRI. For both states a regression line drawn through the points would have a negative slope. For San Luis Potosí the coefficient would be strongly significant.[21] In Guanajuato, if one removed the two "outlier" voting places in the upper-right part of the scatter plot (figure 6-3), then its regression line would also become statistically significant.[22]

One important difference between Mississippi in the 1940s and Mexico in the 1990s is that U.S. blacks lacked the resources to defend their political rights whereas the Mexican opposition, though weak, had at least the power to voice loud complaints. Therefore, the geography of PRI electoral fraud was especially inept. By concentrating efforts to commit electoral fraud in urban districts where the opposition was strong, the PRI's fraud

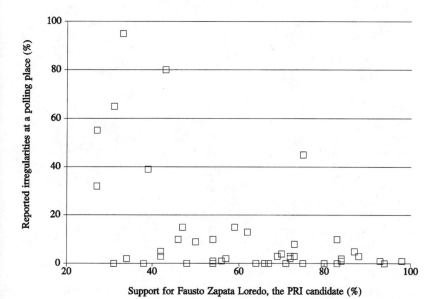

Figure 6-4. Likelihood of Electoral Fraud, by the Competitiveness of the PRI: San Luis Potosí Gubernatorial Race

Source: IMOP S.A. (Gallup) exit poll, August 18, 1991.
Note: In total, forty-nine polling places are represented here. The average N within a polling place is 70. $\beta = -.54$ ($p < .01$).

was as publicly evident as it was infuriating. The ruling party shot itself in the foot.

Despite the incidence of fraud, however, it is likely that the PRI candidates won the governorships in Guanajuato and San Luis Potosí, as the evidence in table 6-8 shows. The margin of victory is too large, and the incidence of fraud too modest (table 6-7), to give credence to the claim that the opposition won these governorships on election day.

Suppose we were to look just at voters in the "honest precincts" in Guanajuato and San Luis Potosí in order to understand how the "untainted" election turned out. The result (not shown here) is that the PRI would actually do better. The reason should be evident from figures 6-3 and 6-4, namely, the attempts to rig a precinct's ballot count were much more prevalent in precincts where the opposition was strong and the PRI was weak; removing such precincts, therefore, reduces the opposition's vote share and increases the PRI's.

Any level of fraud is the enemy of democracy. We believe that Mexico's

Table 6-8.   Official Vote Tallies Compared with Respondent Preferences
in 1991 (percent)

	Official Results	Exit Polls
Legislative elections		
PRI	61.5	62.1
PAN	17.7	16.9
PRD	8.3	6.0
Other	12.6	9.5
Annulled	—	1.0
Blank	—	4.6
Guanajuato gubernatorial election		
Ramón Aguirre Velázquez (PRI, PFCRN)	53.1	54.0
Vincente Fox Quesada (PAN)	35.5	27.6
Porfirio Muñoz Ledo (PRD, PPS)	7.7	6.2
Other	3.7	2.9
Annulled	—	9.2
San Luis Potosí gubernatorial election		
Fausto Zapata Loredo (PRI)	61.0	61.7
Salvador Nava (PAN, PRD, PDM)	31.7	26.7
Other	3.8	2.7
Annulled	3.6	8.7
Blank	—	0.1

Source: Mexico's Federal Elections Institute (IFE); IMOP S.A. (Gallup) exit poll, August 18, 1991.

Note: N = 25,529 (whole sample), 3,291 (Guanajuato), and 3,285 (San Luis Potosí).

1991 elections were marred by fraud; such fraud may well have seriously distorted the outcome of a fair number of local contests. We lack the evidence to render judgment on most of the elections held on August 18, 1991, but we do not believe that the final outcome of the gubernatorial elections in Guanajuato and San Luis Potosí was fraudulent: damnable as the evidence of fraud was in those two contests, the PRI probably won them.

THE AFTERMATH OF THE 1991 ELECTIONS

As noted above, the opposition parties believed that they had won the governorships of Guanajuato and San Luis Potosí and launched massive protests to make their case. Three days after the August 18 elections, President Salinas acknowledged that the opposition parties had protested loudly but that "until now the claims have been general and the proof very, very scarce."[23]

Nonetheless, in response to Salinas's personal involvement, on August 29 the PRI's Ramón Aguirre announced that he would not accept his election as governor of Guanajuato.[24] In protest, about a hundred PRI militants occupied the building of the Guanajuato state legislature and held it for thirty-six hours. On September 1, urged on by the national government's leaders, with fifteen of its twenty-eight members present—and with only six of those fifteen being members of the PRI—the Guanajuato state legislature by a vote of nine to six appointed PAN member Carlos Medina Plascencia as interim governor.[25]

On September 3 the PRI national party president, Luis Donaldo Colosio, explained these decisions to a stunned PRI National Executive Committee. He claimed that the PRI lawfully won the gubernatorial election in Guanajuato but that the "peculiar conditions of the contest in that state required us to balance the triumph with our moral principles in politics." Colosio argued that this concession was not a "pay-off in the context of an alleged generalized fraud." Instead, he said, the PRI decided to forgo "claiming its legitimate electoral victory" in Guanajuato for reasons of state and in deference to national party interests: "We took that decision because we are committed to democracy in its fullest sense." Colosio argued that democracy should "aggregate the society, not divide it." Guanajuato, he concluded, was "an exception"; the PRI did not intend to give up its victories elsewhere.[26]

Writing in the PRI's official magazine, Francisco Gil Villegas gave a blunter explanation of the outcome in Guanajuato. The decision to turn over the governorship to the PAN was justified by the need to save a national parliamentary agreement between the PRI and the PAN, which in turn was necessary in order to manage the country's politics and the process of economic change. Gil Villegas also recognized that the PRI in Guanajuato was "regressive" and characterized by "political underdevelopment." Under those circumstances, he argued, presidential intervention was required to save local democratic practices.[27]

Not surprisingly, the outcome in Guanajuato fueled protests in San Luis Potosí despite the claims of PRI governor-elect Fausto Zapata that the two cases were "qualitatively different and utterly unrelated." On September 26 President Salinas attended the inaugurations of the governor of Guanajuato, the PAN's Carlos Medina (most of the members of Medina's cabinet were also PAN leaders), and the governor of San Luis Potosí, the PRI's Fausto Zapata. Presumably referring to the opposition protests still under way, in his speech at Zapata's inauguration Salinas emphatically asserted that the national government would take "no decisions under the pressure of groups acting outside the law."[28] Even such a scholar as Francisco Gil Villegas accused the opposition in San Luis Potosí of "proto-fascist" behavior because some of its supporters among a group of housewives physically attacked some public officials with pots and pans.[29]

On October 9, however, Fausto Zapata resigned as governor of San Luis Potosí in order to restore "public tranquility." About fifty PRI party members seized the building of the state legislature to prevent Zapata's resignation from being accepted. Nonetheless, the state legislature elected PRI leader Gonzalo Martínez Corbalá as interim governor but also called for new gubernatorial elections to be held in April 1993.[30] (Those elections were held on April 18, 1993; the PRI was declared the victor, claiming a share of the vote approximately the same as in August 1991. Once again the opposition complained loudly of fraud, but this time the results stood.)[31]

The pattern begun in Guanajuato did not end in 1991. On July 12, 1992, the PAN won the governorship of the state of Chihuahua outright. On that same day gubernatorial elections were also held in the state of Michoacán, of which Cárdenas had once been governor and which had long been his family's regional political base. The PRI's candidate, Eduardo Villaseñor, was declared the victor. Once again massive protests broke out claiming electoral fraud; some Cardenistas took over government buildings in various parts of Michoacán.

Though Villaseñor took office—as Fausto Zapata had done—he resigned the governorship three weeks after his inauguration, a ceremony that Salinas had also attended. Faced with the choice of public disorder, the use of repressive force, or the removal of the incumbent governor, the PRI chose the latter in exchange for peace. The Michoacán state legislature accepted Villaseñor's "request for leave" on October 7 by a vote of eighteen to one, with two abstentions; PRD legislators boycotted the session. The state legislature named a veteran PRI state leader, Ausencio Chávez, as interim governor.[32]

In many other state and local elections, protests concerning electoral fraud have been common, at times intense, and occasionally violent. In many municipal elections too the PRI has agreed to overturn the apparent outcomes when they seemed marred by fraud.

The experiences in the gubernatorial elections in Guanajuato and San Luis Potosí in 1991 and in Michoacán in 1992, and the similar experiences in various municipal elections, however, raise a problem of a different sort. Elections in democracies must be not just free and fair but also decisive. The winner of the election must be allowed to take and remain in office. In

Mexico the elections have been insufficiently free and fair, and therefore the opposition quite understandably has taken to the streets and the back rooms to overturn the official results. The Salinas government agreed to such overturns motivated by the need to maintain local public order, ensure the PAN's cooperation at the national level in bringing about important policy changes, secure approval of the North American Free Trade Agreement by the United States and Canada, and genuinely foster some dimensions of political pluralism in Mexico. One result of fraud and the overturning of the outcomes of tainted elections was, however, to render the elections nondecisive.

The cure for Mexico's electoral ills, of course, is to eliminate fraud in order to conduct free and fair elections. The concession of state and municipal posts to the opposition at the discretion of the incumbent president, while well motivated, invites additional protests and violence, fails to address the incidence of fraud, reduces the efficacy of elections as the only means for citizens to choose their rulers in a democracy, and therefore has made a transition to a democratic Mexico more difficult.

CONCLUSION

Mexican elections have long been marred by fraud; the national, state, and local elections held in the late 1980s and early 1990s were no exception. The novelty in the late 1980s was the existence of much stronger and better-organized civic and partisan oppositions that publicized the fraud, protested it, and sought appropriate remedies.

In this chapter we did not seek to document the frequency and magnitude of electoral fraud in Mexico because, except for the gubernatorial elections in two states in 1991, our data do not permit such analysis. Instead, we have called attention to several of the less evident consequences of fraud in recent Mexican elections:

1. Mexicans were much more worried about various economic and social issues than about corruption and electoral fraud.
2. The perception of electoral fraud was nonetheless widespread, and it lowered voting turnout.
3. Fraud-induced nonvoters were disproportionately likely to support the opposition, thereby distorting the election results.
4. Opposition campaigns against fraud, however justified, backfired because one result was that many opposition supporters did not vote.
5. In 1991 the PRI was most likely to commit fraud against the opposition where the opposition was strongest, which was typically in urban areas.

6. Because opposition and other election observers were concentrated in urban areas, the geography of PRI-induced fraud backfired as well because it increased the perceived magnitude of fraud in the entire election.
7. Voters were not deterred from voting by the belief that the PRI was likely to win the election, nor were they mobilized to vote in response to economic ideological appeals. The first finding should encourage the opposition to persevere; the second finding should refocus opposition campaigns to increase turnout away from an emphasis on class-based issues.
8. Damnable as any electoral fraud is, the PRI probably won the two most highly contested gubernatorial races in 1991, which it nevertheless surrendered shortly after the elections.

These findings pose, in stark terms, a dilemma for Mexican democrats. On the one hand, they and their supporters have been motivated to oppose the PRI in order to eliminate the practice of electoral fraud. Nonetheless, the more attention opposition politicians call to the potential for fraud, the more likely it is that many opposition voters will believe such statements and stay home on election day; as a consequence, the PRI could win even by committing less fraud. On the other hand, the issue of fraud is one of the best and most important rallying points for the opposition; opposition politicians must rely on this issue to gather support. Their most sensible strategy would still raise questions about the possibility of fraud, but it would also urge the voters to turn out on election day; to be sure, in practice it would be very difficult to carry out this suggestion.

The Salinas presidency took some important and constructive steps to reduce the incidence of electoral fraud (see also discussion in the previous chapter). One of its well-meaning strategies was counterproductive, however. The decisions to overturn several electoral outcomes in response to protests rendered elections nondecisive and made Mexican politics less stable while failing to increase the credibility of elections or to foster the nation's democratization.

Political democratization is easiest when elections are free, fair, and decisive. That was characteristic of opposition victories time and again throughout the 1980s and early 1990s in South America and Eastern Europe: a key election defeated the incumbents, ended the authoritarian regime, and began a democratic regime governed by the hitherto political opposition. In these instances elections are agencies of democratization.

Political democratization is much more difficult when voters, political leaders, and parties have reason to distrust the outcome or believe that the conditions necessary for participation in a free and fair election do not exist. That kind of environment characterized elections in much of Central America and Mexico for many decades. These countries exemplified undemocratic electoralism: elections were held and opposition parties mounted campaigns, but the election's procedures and count were unfair and fraudulent. Such elections were a barrier to democratization. Far from fostering a transition to democracy, the holding of elections in these political systems deepens authoritarian rule and public mistrust.

Until 1991, however, in Mexico the declared election victor took power despite the often quite credible allegations of unfairness and fraud. The 1991 Mexican innovation was to render the elections but one stop along a dimension of power contestation that would no longer be settled for sure by an election itself—joining such cases as the Philippines at the end of Ferdinand Marcos's rule and Nigeria in 1993. The task of democratizing Mexico, therefore, requires making elections at long last free and fair—as well as decisive once again—in order to put an end to undemocratic electoralism.

Mexico must extirpate electoral fraud. Only electoral transparency can ensure the credibility of elections; only then would the PRI's claims to electoral victory become credible. The opposition should have the right to govern only in those instances when it has won an election, not just when it is convenient for the incumbent president to let them govern a state or a municipality. The computers must work unhampered, and the lights must shine brightly on all electoral processes in order to construct a stable democracy in Mexico, with free and fair contestation and full citizen participation in elections that accurately record and report the will of the majority.

EPILOGUE:
THE 1994 PRESIDENTIAL
CAMPAIGN

Mexico's presidential elections had been held amid economic crisis or political turmoil (or both) in 1970, 1976, 1982, and 1988. Throughout his term Carlos Salinas de Gortari worked tirelessly to prevent the pattern from being repeated during his last year in office. Above all, he wanted to pass on the presidency of a prosperous and politically stable Mexico to a candidate from his own Institutional Revolutionary Party (PRI), who would win the August 21, 1994, presidential elections freely and fairly; would be recognized as the legitimate winner by the opposition; and would go on to continue the program of economic change that Salinas had done so much to formulate, adopt, and implement. Alas, matters did not prove so simple. In this Epilogue we examine the 1994 presidential election campaign in the light of our findings in the previous chapters.

We argue that the 1994 national election was fairer and more equitable than earlier ones, thanks to important electoral reforms that were adopted belatedly, mainly in response to the insurgency that broke out in the state of Chiapas in January 1994. In the 1994 election Mexico took a giant step toward democratization. Nonetheless, the circumstances of the election campaign and of the election itself remained heavily weighted to favor the PRI. Mexico's full transition to democracy is not yet complete.

During the election itself the behavior of the candidates and the parties took cognizance of many of the factors we have examined in this book. For the most part the presidential candidates "hugged" the political center. The National Action Party (PAN) and its candidate, Diego Fernández de Cevallos, for the most part had endorsed the Salinas administration's economic program. In 1994 Cuauhtémoc Cárdenas ran for president once again as the candidate of the Party of the Democratic Revolution (PRD); this time he pledged, if elected, to implement the North American Free Trade Agreement (NAFTA), respect the independence of the central bank, and cut taxes on individuals and businesses. In turn, Ernesto Zedillo Ponce de León, the candidate of the PRI, presented himself as the candidate who could most be trusted to bring about change within the framework of order. As a result, the differences among the candidates on the issues were blurred much more than in previous elections: all three promised changes, all three promised continuities.

As in past elections, in 1994 the opposition emphasized the need to pass judgment on, and put an end to, the longstanding rule of the PRI, which in this election fielded first Luis Donaldo Colosio and then, upon Colosio's assassination, Ernesto Zedillo Ponce de León. Thus Cárdenas and Fernández de Cevallos hammered on the need for democracy and the reduction of corruption and fraud. Also as in the past, the PRI played its strong card: we know how to govern, witness how well the incumbent president has done. The key factors that shaped voter choice in 1994 were political and institutional considerations—party loyalty, the president's standing—as had been the case in 1991 and 1988.

The 1994 election witnessed once again the pervasiveness of the tactical opposition voter who "floats" between opposition candidates looking for the most effective vehicle to defeat the PRI. For these voters the first, one, and only presidential debate sealed the decision: they voted for the PAN, for the PAN seemed to have the best chance of defeating the PRI.

This election reconfirmed that the Cárdenas "phenomenon" of the 1988 election was not easily replicable. In 1991 the PAN reasserted itself as the second largest political force. In 1994 the same rank order of parties developed, even though Cárdenas this time headed the PRD ticket. The PAN was a stronger, better-organized, more coherent party—and it showed.

ECONOMIC PERFORMANCE

The Mexican economy did not boom during Salinas's years. The rate of growth in gross domestic product per capita (in constant 1980 prices) peaked at 2.5 percent in 1990; slowed to 1.7 percent in 1991 and 0.9 percent in 1992; dropped to -1.2 percent in 1993; and rose to 1.3 percent in 1994. Therefore, as Mexicans first turned their sights on the 1994 elections, the nation's economy was once again in a recession. Urban unemployment rose steadily every year from 1991 to 1994. The urban minimum salary in real terms dropped each year of the Salinas presidency; in 1993 it amounted to 41.6 percent of its 1980 level. At the macroeconomic level, the deficit in the balance-of-payments current account jumped from nearly $14 billion in 1991 to over $23 billion in 1993 and to over $28 billion in 1994.[1] This out-of-control current account deficit set the stage for the December 1994 financial panic and collapse of the peso, followed by the recession begun in 1995. In the run-up to the 1994 elections, however, Mexico's chances of better economic performance in the future were excellent, Salinas economists argued.

And yet did the large numbers of poor Mexicans believe it enough to vote for the PRI one more time?

As we have seen (especially in chapters 4 and 5), a key electoral concern is how Mexicans answer the question, Would the country's economy be better off if a party other than the PRI were to win the presidential elections? The PRI has run in the past as the party most likely to manage the economy effectively. Under Salinas, impressive economic policy changes were enacted, but the material conditions of most Mexicans improved only slightly. And for some Mexicans the standard of living did not improve at all during the Salinas years. The recession during 1993 compounded these politically sensitive economic woes.

Would the rational partisan and economic expectations of Mexicans at long last turn them away from the PRI? Would they believe that only a party from the opposition could help the nation's economy improve the conditions of their lives?

THE REFORM OF ELECTORAL PROCEDURES: ROUND I

Another question was whether the August 1994 elections would be perceived as free and fair, thus helping to legitimize the transfer of presidential power (see chapter 6). In response to extensive criticism of electoral law and practice, in mid-1993 President Salinas launched yet another reform of the Constitution and the electoral law.

The number of senators per state was increased from two to four; three would be elected by simple pluralities, and one would be allocated to the party obtaining the second highest number of votes in the state. Therefore, the opposition would be guaranteed no fewer than one-quarter of the Senate seats (it held fewer than 5 percent of the seats at the time of the reform). In the Chamber of Deputies the object of the reform was to prevent one party by itself from reforming the Constitution. The new rules would bar any party from holding more than 315 seats in the 500-member chamber; 325 votes would be needed to amend the Constitution, requiring thereby some interparty collaboration to that end.

With regard to the electoral process, the changes adopted were welcome and important but less impressive. Good work was undertaken to improve the quality of the voter registration list and to prevent "ghosts" from voting, but procedures were not adopted for an independent audit of the electoral registry. Limits on campaign spending were imposed, but they were excessively high (the equivalent of over $600,000 for an individual campaign contribution), permitting the PRI to raise vast funds.[2] The independence of the Federal Elections Institute (IFE) and the professionalism of its staff were enhanced, but the PRI and the government could still control key

IFE decisions. The law formally recognized the role of independent Mexican election observers (though not of international election observers).

The Council of Freely Elected Heads of Government provided an apt summary: "While positive, the electoral reforms taken as a group fell short of establishing a foundation that would give all parties and all the people of Mexico confidence that a genuinely free and fair election would occur in August 1994."[3] Founded and led by former U.S. president Jimmy Carter, the council has acquired great credibility throughout the Americas for its impartiality in election monitoring. Its judgment on these partial reforms proved all too accurate.

On November 28, 1993, the very day when President Salinas's choice for the PRI presidential nomination for the August 1994 election became public, the lights literally went out for an hour in the state of Yucatán, as PRI party militants allegedly doctored the results of state and local elections in a process reminiscent of the presidential election evening in 1988.

Protests broke out as the PAN claimed victory in the elections for governor and for mayor of the city of Mérida (the capital of the state of Yucatán); PRI supporters threatened violence to defend their own claims to victory. When President Salinas and other national leaders sought to address the Yucatán political crisis, the state's PRI governor, Dulce María Saurí, and her entire cabinet resigned, accusing Salinas of meddling. In the end the PRI retained the governorship of Yucatán, but the "victorious" PRI candidate for mayor of Mérida, Orlando Paredes Lara, resigned in order to maintain the peace. The Yucatán electoral college then chose the PAN's candidate, Luis Correa Mena, as mayor of Mérida. These results were consistent with the findings of a large group of Mexican election observers, who concluded that the PRI had won the governorship but that the PAN had won the Mérida mayoralty.[4]

The practice of after-the-fact negotiations about the election results was also consistent with similar cases examined in chapter 6. Since 1991, elections had ceased to be decisive; they had become instead one more moment in the struggle for power. Elections could not answer the important democratic question, Who has the legitimate right to govern? In many cases the identity of office holders came to be determined through back-room negotiations. These problems continued to cast doubt on the credibility of Mexico's electoral process even after the 1993 electoral law reforms. At stake was not just democracy but also political stability.

THE SELECTION OF THE PRI'S NOMINEE: ROUND I

On November 28, 1993, President Salinas tapped Luis Donaldo Colosio as his choice for the PRI presidential nominee for the August 1994 elections;

no election primaries were held. Over the years, the party's deliberative organs have routinely ratified every incumbent president's choice of successor, and this was no exception. This practice is known as the *destape*, or unveiling—as well as the *dedazo*, or "heavy thumb"—used to impose the president's decision. Colosio had long been associated with Salinas, at whose request he had served as PRI party president and, since 1992, as secretary for social development, in charge of the government's National Solidarity Program (PRONASOL)—an antipoverty program that many in the PRI wanted to use to build up political support for their party (see chapters 5 and 6).

The longstanding norms of Mexican politics call for all other presidential aspirants immediately to close ranks behind the president's choice. This time the first runner-up, Mexico City mayor Manuel Camacho, called a press conference to announce his disappointment and his resignation from the mayoralty (the mayor of Mexico City is appointed by the president of the republic). To prevent a party schism, Salinas reshuffled his cabinet and made Camacho the new foreign minister.

The timing of Colosio's *destape*, coinciding with the Yucatán election scandal, and Camacho's reaction, forced Colosio to dedicate much of his early campaign to the theme of democratizing Mexico. Soon enough Colosio took some steps to enhance the credibility of the electoral process. He pledged to issue regular reports on his campaign's funding sources and expenditures, a first for a PRI presidential campaign. Though he opposed a formal role for foreign election monitors, Colosio said that he would propose a wider role for Mexican-born election observers and noted that he would accept an independent audit of the voter rolls. To be sure, all of these issues would generate contention, but they signaled the ongoing movement, however limited, toward greater electoral openness and transparency.[5]

THE CHIAPAS UPRISING

On January 1, 1994, the North American Free Trade Agreement went into effect. The capstone of years of effort, NAFTA symbolized and embodied the Salinas presidency. It was a bold move to realign Mexico with the United States, despite so many historical problems and suspicions. NAFTA would open markets in the United States and Canada to Mexican trade and protect Mexico from trade protectionism in its two northern neighbors. NAFTA also promised to "lock in" most of Salinas's economic reforms for years to come.

On that very same day a revolt broke out in the southernmost state of Chiapas in protest against political, economic, and social conditions; many of the rebels were indigenous peoples from the region.[6] They called them-selves Zapatistas, invoking the name of Mexican revolutionary general Emiliano Zapata, known for his commitment to land reform and other means of assistance for peasants. Among their many demands, the Zapatis-tas claimed that NAFTA promised further decline for the standard of living of poor people in their region.

The revolt shocked the Mexican political establishment.[7] At first the Mexican Army responded with force; there were incidents of brutality.[8] Within two weeks, however, President Salinas had changed course. He de-clared a cease-fire. He asked for, and received, the resignation of Secretary of Government José Patrocinio González—who was also the immediate past governor of Chiapas—and replaced him with Jorge Carpizo, long prominent in the defense of human rights in Mexico. Salinas asked Foreign Minister Manuel Camacho to give up his ministry and to take up the task of negotiating with the insurgents to pacify Chiapas once again.[9]

The Chiapas uprising worried or enthralled most Mexicans and much of the world. U.S. Embassy personnel arrived in San Cristóbal, Chiapas, on January 2 within hours of the beginning of the uprising.[10] Television, radio, and print media journalists from all over the world converged on Chiapas. The public leader of the insurgency, known as Subcomandante Marcos, proved to be media-savvy and extraordinarily effective. His intelligence, articulate expression, and sense of humor captured wide support for his movement's objectives. During this mass media romance focused on re-dressing grievances, many forgot Marcos's use of violence and his breaking of the law, and the Zapatista army's violations of human rights. The Zapa-tista uprising was the first post–Cold War insurgency in the Americas.[11]

The Chiapas negotiations between Camacho on behalf of the government and Marcos on behalf of the insurgency led to an agreement on March 2, 1994, which, though comprehensive, dealt mainly with local and regional issues.[12] After months of discussion within their ranks, on June 12 the Za-patista insurgents rejected the peace agreement, allegedly by a vote of 98 percent against (not unlike the majorities the PRI used to claim in past elections in Chiapas). Zedillo blamed Camacho for the failure of the agree-ment; on June 16 Camacho resigned as the government's negotiator and pulled out of politics for the remainder of the election campaign.[13] The gov-ernment pledged to continue the negotiations. The Zapatistas called a con-vention, which met in Chiapas August 6–9, 1994; seven thousand delegates attended from all over Mexico. The convention agreed to urge Mexicans to vote against the PRI and the PAN. On election day the Zapatistas gave the order to hold their fire.[14] In fact, after the signing of the preliminary agree-ment in March, the Zapatistas receded to the background during the remainder of the election campaign. (In December 1994 the Zapatistas reactivated their insurgency; in response, the Mexican Army escalated its military actions.)

The Chiapas insurgency, however, had a profound impact well beyond the boundaries of that state. The insurgency had sought to affect the balance of national politics and indeed had direct and indirect effects on the evolving presidential campaign. As we have seen, the PRI's strong suit over the years had been its claim to stable governance. Suddenly the Salinas administration's economic policies stood accused of undermining the nation's social peace. To reclaim the banner of the guardian of order, the government and the PRI would be forced to revamp the electoral procedures to guarantee a much fairer process. Before examining those important changes, however, we need to focus on the presidential candidates and their evolving campaign.

THE COLOSIO ASSASSINATION AND THE SELECTION OF THE PRI'S NOMINEE: ROUND II

The Chiapas uprising had other political effects. Manuel Camacho's mediation minuet with Subcomandante Marcos gripped the nation's imagination. Reports of the negotiations dominated the front page of newspapers and the lead stories on the television evening news. The campaign for the presidency receded in significance: Colosio *who?* Marcos praised Camacho and suggested that the government's negotiator had become an indispensable personal guarantor of social peace. For his part, Camacho told a *Wall Street Journal* editorialist that he had not ruled out running for president in the August 1994 elections.[15] Under Mexico's electoral law, any party could replace its presidential candidate until one month before the election.

Would Camacho run? Would he run as the candidate of a small opposition party, a "party for rent?" Or would Salinas and the PRI leadership ask Colosio to give up his apparently foundering candidacy in favor of Camacho? After all, Colosio had been the PRI party president who along with Salinas had introduced a controversial practice into Mexican election outcomes in the aftermath of the 1991 elections: even PRI candidates who had seemingly won their elections as state governor were sometimes asked to resign for the sake of the presumed greater good, political and social peace. Colosio could be asked to swallow his own medicine: resign the nomination in favor of Camacho in order for the PRI to win the presidency in a free election. On March 22, however, Camacho took his name out of consideration for the forthcoming elections and threw his support to Colosio.[16]

The next day, on March 23, Luis Donaldo Colosio was assassinated while campaigning in the city of Tijuana. Not since the assassination of president-elect Alvaro Obregón in 1928 had anything similar occurred in Mexican politics. The Colosio assassination thus combined with the Chiapas uprising to raise the specter of a genuine danger to the country's political stability.

The investigation into the Colosio assassination was inconclusive. In an address to the nation on April 4 government prosecutor Miguel Montes García argued that a conspiracy had been organized to murder Colosio; it seemed that six men were directly involved, three of whom had been jailed, some of whom had connections with the PRI in the State of Baja California Norte. In early May Attorney General Diego Valadés was forced to resign, accused in part of obstructing the investigation into the murder. In late May all five members of a commission appointed by President Salinas to oversee the investigation resigned, claiming that they had been denied the resources to do their job and had never been allowed to read court files on the case. On June 3 prosecutor Montes reversed himself and announced that he had concluded that Mario Aburto Martínez was the sole and unassisted assassin; in October 1994 Aburto was convicted of the crime and sentenced to forty-two years in prison.[17]

Many Mexicans widely disbelieved this conclusion, blaming the murder on high-ranking PRI members who had been offended by some of Colosio's past and planned reforms; or on PRI politicians in the state of Baja California Norte, where Tijuana is located, who resented the fact that Colosio, as PRI national party president, in 1989 had recognized the PAN's victory in that state's gubernatorial elections; or on drug traffickers acting jointly with corrupt officials; or on some combination. Though the evidence is missing, the inconclusive and contradictory investigation undermined the government's credibility and tainted the PRI's already tarnished reputation. In February 1995 the Mexican government reopened this investigation and arrested a former PRI employee as the second gunman in the shooting. Othón Cortés Vázquez had long worked for the PRI in Baja California Norte.[18]

On March 29, 1994, twenty-seven of the PRI's twenty-eight state governors arrived at the presidential palace to discuss who should replace Colosio as the party's standard-bearer. The scene has been best described by Andrés Oppenheimer.[19] A majority seemed to lean toward PRI party president Fernando Ortiz Arana, a veteran politician with little background in economics; most party leaders wanted to participate effectively in making the selection in order to choose a consensus candidate to overcome the campaign's many troubles. Early in the meeting Manlio Fabio Beltrones, governor of the state of Sonora, and one of the governors closest to Salinas, stated that he spoke as the governor of the home state of the slain candidate;

he wanted to make a proposal that he thought would best represent Colosio's wishes. He gave a videotape to Salinas, who put it in a videocassette machine and turned it on. It was a recording of Colosio's November 29 press conference, in which he had appointed Ernesto Zedillo as his campaign manager and had praised him as a true patriot. Beltrones argued that Colosio himself had made the proposal. Salinas nodded. All the governors and other party leaders closed ranks. The announcement was made "unanimously and wholeheartedly." Salinas's *dedazo* of Colosio had been replaced by Salinas's, and allegedly Colosio's, *dedillo* (little finger) of Zedillo.

THE ZEDILLO CAMPAIGN: ITS FOUR PILLARS

Mexican society claimed the need for further democratization, Zedillo argued, but democracy meant much more than free elections: "The enemies of democracy are not in the PRI; they are among those who, in a throwback to the past, choose violence or are unwilling to accept the rules of competition."[20] On bumper stickers and in solemn speeches, time and again Zedillo sought to reclaim for the PRI its winning argument from past elections, namely, that it was the best defender of social peace. The PRI and the government, he suggested, should not be blamed for the violence in Chiapas or the murder of Colosio or other instances of public disorder; those who engaged in such violence are the guilty ones—and, he claimed, they seemed to be associated with the opposition. As a consequence, Zedillo's platform emphasized the need for law and order and the fight against violent crime to an extent unprecedented in previous presidential campaigns. On the positive side, he committed his government to improving the administration of justice and pledged to make police officers reliable enforcers of the law, not vultures preying on law-abiding citizens.

"I know that I am the youngest of the presidential candidates," the forty-two-year-old Zedillo noted, "but I am also the one with the longest experience in government." He had begun his career in public service as a teenager and rose to become secretary of planning and budget, and later secretary of public education: "Thus I know better than any other candidate the complexities of the daily work in government."[21] Zedillo appealed to voters on the basis of his youth (openness to innovation) even as he sought to reassure those who in elections past had feared that the economy would suffer were a party other than the PRI to govern Mexico. These were the PRI's most faithful voters; Zedillo wanted them to know about his experience and competence. This was the second pillar of his campaign. Indeed, Zedillo came to be known as "Doctor Zedillo"—reminding everyone that he had a Ph.D. in economics from Yale University. (Salinas had a Ph.D. in political economy and government from Harvard University, but he did not use the title in his political career.)

The third anchor of the Zedillo campaign was the party. Much more than Salinas in 1988, Zedillo ran "with" the PRI. He heaped praise on the party: "The PRI is the party of the Mexican Revolution and the Querétaro Constitution; the PRI is the party of the agrarian reform, of the achievements of workers, of economic growth and of Mexico's modernization, of women's right to equality and of the educational accomplishments of teachers throughout the nation. Our party has been at the center of our modern history, and it has participated—step by step—in the peaceful construction and reform of today's Mexico. And that is our greatest source of pride."[22]

Zedillo sought out the support of everyone within the PRI, including the party's old guard, sometimes known as the "dinosaurs." At a turning point during the campaign it became known that Agriculture Secretary Carlos Hank González, a metaphorical PRI *Tyrannosaurus rex*, had coordinated a paid announcement in support of Zedillo on behalf of fifty-seven former cabinet ministers and had ordered his subordinates to support the Zedillo campaign—deploying government fax machines, telephones, and personnel for partisan purposes; contravening the interparty agreements to prevent public officials from active participation in the campaign; and, some argued, breaking the law. The surrounding fury led to no indictments; it had been just a simple misunderstanding, said Attorney General Diego Valadés. Shortly thereafter Zedillo appointed one of Hank's key allies, Ignacio Pichardo, as PRI party president to run the campaign.[23] In many ways Zedillo had relatively few choices but to turn to the party establishment; he had not planned to run for president in 1994 and had not put together his own team. Nonetheless, these alliances cast a pall over Zedillo's professed commitment to cleansing Mexican politics and to separating the government from the governing party.[24]

Finally, Zedillo ran on President Salinas's record: "The current administration's achievements have enormous significance. With regard to the economy, they set the bases for a sustained economic recovery that will permit an improvement in the standards of living of Mexican families. With regard to politics, changes were made to the law and the necessary administrative steps were taken to guarantee absolute respect to every citizen's vote and to ensure full compliance with democratic procedures."[25] Zedillo owed his own selection to the outgoing president, and he understood that Salinas remained extraordinarily popular despite the terrible events of 1994. Zedillo's claim to "experience" could only be validated if he were to run on the Salinas administration's record. The PRI's opening campaign statement described Zedillo as an "architect of a modern Mexico."[26]

Changes would be made under a Zedillo presidency, claimed the candidate in order not to surrender the theme of "change" to his opponents, but these changes would unfold within the framework set by Salinas.

These four emphases are wholly consistent with the bases for public support for the PRI in recent elections. As we showed in chapters 4 and 5, voters who had indicated in elections past that they intended to vote for the PRI were particularly motivated by their partisan loyalty, their approval of the incumbent president's performance, and their fear about what would happen to the economy and to social peace if a party other than the PRI were to win. Zedillo ran a textbook campaign.

THE OPPOSITION

The Cárdenas Candidacy

In 1993 Cuauhtémoc Cárdenas once again launched his presidential candidacy. Supported by the party he had founded after the 1988 presidential elections, the Party of the Democratic Revolution, Cárdenas learned one important lesson each from the 1988 and the 1991 elections (see chapters 4 and 5). From 1988 he learned that would-be supporters cared most about defeating the PRI, and not so much about his predilections on economic policy issues; in 1994 Cárdenas stressed electoral, political, and economic fairness far more than specific economic policy proposals to set himself apart from the PRI candidate.

Specifically, Cárdenas modified his position on the North American Free Trade Agreement. Still acknowledging his earlier, strong criticism of NAFTA (see chapter 5), during the 1994 campaign he declared, "It is now the law of the country. If I am elected I intend to enforce it and assume full responsibility for the implementation of this trilateral commitment of my country." He reasserted that he still believed that "we are capable of a better deal," but he proposed to pursue his objectives "working within the existing framework of NAFTA towards that end." Indeed, he asserted that a "democratic government, legitimately elected in Mexico, respectful of the rule of law, would be a better, more responsible trading partner for the U.S. and Canada than the Salinas regime." His remaining critiques of NAFTA were remarkably similar to those of much of the Democratic Party majority in the U.S. Congress: the need for stronger protections for labor and the environment, better compensatory financial assistance to ease labor and community adjustment to trade-originated economic disruptions, and a more democratic Mexico.[27]

This "born again" Cárdenas endorsed and praised the new formal independence attained by Mexico's central bank on April 1, 1994; supported the international monetary cooperation agreement that Mexico signed in 1994 with the U.S. and Canadian central banks; pledged "to provide relief to business by reducing tax rates and simplifying other fiscal regulations"; and set a high priority on the enforcement of antitrust policies to combat the private monopolies that he claimed had been built up during the Salinas administration.[28]

In fact, ordinary voters would find it increasingly difficult to tell Cárdenas's economic policy proposals apart from those of the other candidates— all of whom advocated changes of some sort. Issues had had little impact on the electorate's choice of candidates in 1988 and 1991; in 1994 Cárdenas made it even more difficult for the voters to decide on the basis of economic issue differences.[29]

From the 1991 electoral debacle Cárdenas learned that one reason for the PRI's runaway victory was the division among the parties of the left; in 1994, therefore, he forged a coalition of small parties ranging from the political left to the center-right. Why forge an alliance that would bridge such a broad ideological spectrum? We have shown in chapters 4 and 5 that Mexican voters focus above all on the fate of the ruling party and its incumbents; only a minority of Mexican voters reach a second, more ideological stage in their electoral decision-making process. We have also shown that a fair proportion of Mexico's anti-PRI voters behave strategically; that is, they vote for the candidates most likely to defeat the PRI even if such voters have ideological or policy differences with those candidates.

In early November 1993 the Foro Democrático, a PAN breakaway (see chapter 5), endorsed the Cárdenas candidacy for president because at the time Cárdenas seemed the best bet for defeating the PRI. As former long-time PAN leader Bernardo Bátiz explained, the purpose of this cross-ideological alliance was "not to divide the vote in opposition to the system; by concentrating votes in favor of the strongest opposition candidate, it becomes possible to defeat the regime and thus to achieve a positive and definitive change toward the country's democratization." These ex-PAN members were also attracted to Cárdenas's emphasis on the search for democracy, the protection of human rights, the curtailment of the excessive powers of the presidency, and the struggle against corruption.[30] This alliance signaled a process of strategic learning among Mexican politicians, including Cárdenas, who at long last began to match the sophistication of many Mexican voters.

Ultimately, in this as in earlier elections, Cárdenas's principal appeal was his sense of personal dignity and his courage in taking on the "establishment." He was widely seen as the regime's key opponent—more so than any other political leader or party—and, for this reason, as the dominant force for Mexico's democratization.[31]

The Small Parties

Nonetheless, the opposition—especially on the left—remained divided enough as it moved toward the 1994 presidential elections. The following six small parties also nominated presidential candidates: the Workers' Party (PT), the Mexican Green Ecologist Party (PVEM), the Frente Cardenista National Renovation Party (PFCRN), the Authentic Party of the Mexican Revolution (PARM), the Mexican Democratic Party (PDM), and the People's Socialist Party (PPS). If they were to be as successful in 1994 as they had been in 1991 in splitting the opposition vote, their presence in the race would contribute to a PRI victory in a fair presidential election, even if the PRI were to win just a minority of the votes cast.

The PAN

In preparation for the 1994 elections the National Action Party nominated its congressional leader, Diego Fernández de Cevallos, to run for the presidency. His campaign emphasized the PAN's longstanding commitment to democratic politics as an alternative to the governing PRI's inability to effect a full transition to democracy. The single most effective campaign slogan was Fernández de Cevallos's "For a Mexico without lies."

Our research has shown (chapter 6) that those voters who believed in the high likelihood of electoral fraud were also those most likely to abstain from voting; such abstainers, moreover, were disproportionately opposition supporters. Belief that the votes would really count could therefore increase electoral turnout as well as the opposition's share of the vote. The reform of the electoral laws might persuade citizens that this time the election would be honest and fair. For this reason the PAN and Fernández de Cevallos devoted much of their energy to the reform of the electoral laws (see chapter 5 and other sections in this Epilogue). Once important reforms were in place in 1994, Fernández de Cevallos deliberately eschewed talk that the election would be fraudulent.[32] He did not want to foster voter apathy; he relied on voter engagement.

The PAN also sought to reassure the electorate on two broad issues. First, it endorsed the broad direction of the Salinas administration's opening toward a market economy, though it criticized certain specific policies. Second, the PAN argued that it had demonstrated that its partisans could do an effective job in running state governments in Baja California Norte, Chihuahua, and Guanajuato as well as many municipal governments.

By 1994 over fifteen million Mexicans lived in communities under PAN government.

In these ways the PAN sought support from an electorate that, as we have shown, in principle favors the possibility of parties other than the PRI winning elections (chapter 2) but is also concerned about the capacity of parties other than the PRI to govern the economy and maintain social peace (chapters 4 and 5). In effect the PAN stood for a more democratic, still stable and competent, and persistingly market-oriented Mexico.

As seen in chapters 4 and 5, the PAN derived much of its continuing strength from the steady loyalty of its voters. In the late 1980s and early 1990s, moreover, it expanded its formal membership. In 1986 the PAN had approximately twenty thousand members. That number had doubled by the 1988 presidential election and had doubled again by the 1991 congressional elections. In May 1994 the PAN's membership reached 134,000.[33]

In 1994, in addition, the personal traits of the PAN's presidential candidate became an important factor during the campaign. In contrast to the other major candidates, Fernández de Cevallos insisted on being called by his first name, Diego, but otherwise he portrayed a conservative image on certain social issues.[34] He was the only major presidential candidate to describe himself as a practicing Roman Catholic (Cárdenas was the only one to describe himself as an agnostic). Fernández de Cevallos had been married only in a church wedding, refusing to inscribe the marriage in the civil registry. He was also the only candidate to oppose abortion outright. During the campaign he referred to women as "el viejerío" (a bunch of old wives). And he was the only presidential candidate to admit that he disliked rock music.[35]

In November 1993, in the newspaper *Excélsior*, Francisco Garfias best described Fernández de Cevallos:

> God, the family, and the fatherland are the fundamental values for Diego Fernández de Cevallos, a well known lawyer and PAN member, bearer of a noteworthy beard on the style of [Emperor] Maximilian, unabashed admirer of Don Quixote, Hernán Cortés . . . a radical in his youth, a pragmatist and deal-maker in his adulthood. Emotional and of pleasant conversation . . . an excellent negotiator, he has a temper and is frank no matter what the consequences. . . . Intelligent, acerbic, and temperamental, and twice the champion debater at the University . . . he provokes admiration as well as opposition.[36]

THE PRESIDENTIAL DEBATE

For the first time ever, nearly all the presidential candidates—including the three principal ones—agreed to participate in a televised presidential debate. The candidates of the small parties had a first debate just among themselves. The three main candidates held their debate on May 12, 1994. The word *debate* is a slight exaggeration; the agreed-upon format basically called for sequential speeches before the same television cameras.

Champion school debater Fernández de Cevallos showed his mettle. As an experienced legislator and litigator by profession, he clearly outclassed his two rivals.[37] Early on in the debate he turned to face Cárdenas and told him, "You do not represent the democratic alternative." Fernández de Cevallos proceeded to recite a long list of antidemocratic actions allegedly committed by Cárdenas during his term as governor of the state of Michoacán: an authoritarian state electoral law, violations of academic freedom in the schools, and the use of government funds to support the PRI (at the time, still Cárdenas's party). When the television cameras turned to Cárdenas, he seemed stunned; instead of replying to these charges, he spoke of electoral fraud in 1988.

A few minutes later Fernández de Cevallos turned to face Zedillo to tell him, "You have been a good boy who got good grades but, with regard to democracy, frankly you do not pass." In particular, Fernández de Cevallos contrasted his own selection through democratic means within the PAN with Salinas's hand-picking of Zedillo. But he went on to tackle Zedillo's economic record in government, quoting from documents issued by Zedillo during his term as planning and budget minister. Zedillo had erred by billions of dollars, argued Fernández de Cevallos, in his forecast of the balance-of-payments current account deficit; he had also forecast a 6 percent rate of economic growth for 1993, when in fact the economy slipped into recession. And if Zedillo wanted to claim credit for the Salinas administration's economic accomplishments, he should also take responsibility for the persistent poverty plaguing forty million Mexicans. Like Cárdenas before him, Zedillo too chose not to respond.

Eloquent, articulate, impressive, and aggressive in his demeanor,[38] Fernández de Cevallos was the unquestioned winner of the debate. Nearly every week during the 1994 campaign, Miguel Basáñez, on behalf of MORI de México and the magazine *Este país*, had surveyed public opinion in five of Mexico's largest cities (including Mexico City). His polls had been showing Colosio, and then Zedillo, well ahead of the opposition, with Cárdenas and Fernández de Cevallos running neck and neck for the second spot. On the day after the debate, May 13, Basáñez's poll showed that Zedillo's support had plummeted and Cárdenas's had dipped, with Fernández de Cevallos leading the race for the presidency (the number of undecided voters also increased sharply). Basáñez's surveys would show Fernández de Cevallos and Zedillo disputing the lead in these five cities for the remainder of May and June.[39]

Other larger public-opinion polls reflected a similar trend, though with Zedillo remaining in the lead. An internal poll conducted for the PRI reportedly showed Zedillo with 39 percent and Fernández de Cevallos with 40 percent in the week after the debate, with Cárdenas far behind.[40] In early June a national poll sponsored by *El Norte* and *Reforma* showed Zedillo with 41 percent of the preferences, Fernández de Cevallos with 29 percent, and Cárdenas with just 9 percent.[41] The INDEMERC Louis Harris team polled in February, April, and early July. The replacement of Colosio by Zedillo did not seem likely to cost the PRI any votes; in February Colosio had led with 59 percent of the votes, while in April Zedillo led with 58 percent. In the February poll Fernández de Cevallos had been slightly ahead of Cárdenas, but by April Cárdenas had pulled clearly into second place with 22 percent, while Fernández de Cevallos settled at 15 percent. By early July Zedillo's support was at 50 percent—below the April figure, but higher than the early-June *Reforma* poll—while Fernández de Cevallos had risen to 32 percent and Cárdenas had dropped to 13 percent.[42]

Poised perhaps for a presidential election victory for the first time since the PAN's founding in 1939, Fernández de Cevallos failed to build on his impressive debate performance. In June he limited his public appearances, and he virtually stopped campaigning during the first half of July. In the five campaign months before the debate, Fernández de Cevallos had no official campaign activity during sixteen days; in the three months following the debate, he had no official campaign activity during thirty-four days. On July 9 the PAN's National Executive Committee asked the candidate to explain his inactivity; the results were inconclusive.[43] Whether more vigorous campaigning would have elected Diego Fernández de Cevallos president of Mexico will never be known; given the PRI's considerable strength, the answer is probably no. Nonetheless, the absence of vigorous campaigning certainly doomed him to defeat.

THE REFORM OF ELECTORAL PROCEDURES: ROUND II

As the presidential election campaign unfolded, so did a new, deeper, and more important process of changing the electoral law. This second round of electoral reform was a direct response to some of the demands articulated during the Chiapas uprising. On January 27, 1994, the new secretary of government, Jorge Carpizo, concluded the first successful round of negotiations with the political parties, an important early step in fulfilling his commitment to leading Mexico toward much fairer elections. All the presidential candidates and parties—except the small People's Socialist Party—agreed to a package of new electoral reforms. Among other changes, there would be an effort to increase the impartiality of the authorities in charge of the election. All parties would have full access to the electoral registry. The government-owned media were to give fair coverage to all parties. Public resources could not be used to favor one party over another. This was the first time Cárdenas signed on to an electoral reform agreement with the PRI.[44]

Within a week Mexico's Federal Elections Institute had announced new campaign spending limits for the August presidential election, cutting the maximum permitted expenditure for each political party from $220 million to $42 million. While the change demonstrated good faith in honoring the electoral agreements that had just been reached, the new limit—roughly $1 per registered voter—still remained far beyond the campaign-financing capabilities of all parties but the PRI.[45]

On February 14 PRI presidential candidate Colosio reiterated his willingness to accept further electoral reforms. On February 28 Secretary Carpizo announced that the political parties had reached seven specific agreements, which he pledged to implement: (1) to establish guidelines for the accreditation and activities of those Mexican citizens who would serve as election observers; (2) to create a special attorney's office to prosecute electoral crimes; (3) to contract with private firms or academic institutions to conduct an independent external audit of the electoral registry; (4) to create a technical council to supervise that external audit; (5) to increase public financing for the political parties; (6) to change the ballot to permit more accurate monitoring of the voting procedures; and (7) to adopt uniform standards for the presentation of candidacies.[46] At about the same time, the Mexican government quietly called off its opposition to international election observers; on March 6 Colosio announced that he too favored accepting foreign "visitors" who would be present during the elections.[47]

The electoral reform process ended three months later. On June 3 Carpizo summarized the important changes.[48] The electoral registry, the lists of voters, and the voter identification cards would be subject to external audits. Every month each party would receive a copy of the electoral registry on magnetic tapes. A new Office of the Special Prosecutor for electoral crimes was established, and penalties for such crimes became stiffer.

The PRD's proposal for the selection of officials at the polling booths was adopted; these officials would be chosen through a double random lottery based on their month of birth and the first letter of their last name. That is, the local polling-booth officials would be ordinary citizens chosen independently of their known partisan affiliations, if any. Electoral ballots would have numbered slips to prevent the stuffing of ballots while preserving the secrecy of the vote. Upon casting their ballots, voters would have their fingers marked with indelible ink, to be manufactured especially for this purpose by scientists at the National Polytechnic Institute. Each voter would have a new voter card, with that person's name and address, voter identification number, photograph, signature, and fingerprint. To prevent the swift destruction of ballots that had occurred after the 1988 elections, no electoral lists or ballots could be destroyed during the six months following the election.

Mexican citizens could be accredited as election observers, and formally designated "international visitors" would also be accredited to be present during the elections (but not to "observe" the elections as such—a fine legal technicality that would be ignored in practice on election day). A United Nations technical mission would provide assistance both to the election officials and to designated groups of Mexican election observers.

The General Council of the Federal Elections Institute (IFE) was overhauled. It would have eleven voting members. Six "citizen counselors" would be nominated by the political parties and elected by a two-thirds vote of the Chamber of Deputies (thus preventing any one party from imposing its will). The other five IFE members would be the secretary of government (who chaired it), two senators, and two deputies; among the latter four, one from each chamber had to come from the largest party and one from each chamber from the largest opposition party represented in that chamber. In the past the PRI had in effect controlled the General Council;[49] this power was suddenly gone. This depoliticization of the IFE's General Council was perhaps the single most important change in the electoral law. In addition, no government official, and no government office, could work for or against a political party (though, as we have seen, this rule was broken in some important instances).

Each party would be allotted one full hour on radio on the three Sundays prior to election day. In addition, no partisan propaganda would be allowed on radio and television during the ten days before election day. Similarly, government propaganda for the PRONASOL (see analysis in chapter 5) and PROCAMPO (rural development agency) programs would be suspended for the twenty days before the election.

Assessing the Significance of the Electoral Reforms

These electoral reforms were very important and created the conditions, for the first time in Mexican history, for a fair election. This was the main conclusion of the technical mission sent by the United Nations.[50] The Civic Alliance—an important nongovernmental organization that received funding and training from the United Nations, and funding from other international sources as well—came to apparently different conclusions, which deserve analysis.

Generally critical of the government throughout the electoral process as befits a nongovernmental organization, the Civic Alliance published a report on the eve of the election stating that the 1994 electoral process could not be called "fair or reliable." Nonetheless, the Civic Alliance acknowledged that advances had been made that made it possible that the forthcoming elections would be "relatively credible." Beyond these general and somewhat contradictory comments, in fact the Civic Alliance's analysis helps us to assess the improvements and limitations in the environment surrounding the 1994 elections.[51]

The Civic Alliance praised the reforms made to the nation's Constitution to guarantee opposition party representation in the Senate; to eliminate aspects of PRI overrepresentation in the Chamber of Deputies; to prevent a single party by itself from having the votes to amend the Constitution; to permit native-born Mexicans of foreign parentage to be elected president; and to shift the authority to pass judgment on the validity of congressional elections away from the Congress toward the General Council of the Federal Elections Institute.

Another important advance was the improved quality and reliability of the electoral registry. Over forty external audits were performed, most of them by private firms contracted by the electoral authorities but also some by the political parties; all reached the conclusion that the registry had been developed within statistically acceptable margins of error (typically below 5 percent). The last audit sponsored by the IFE on the eve of the election showed a 96.72 percent reliability rate.[52] Whatever errors were found revealed no pattern of intention to commit fraud. The Civic Alliance could not conduct a full audit, but it did carry out a partial audit in six cities; the margin of error ranged between 2.2 percent and 5.9 percent. Though the Civic Alliance understandably expressed worry over these error rates, such numbers represent stunning advances over previous Mexican electoral registries. The IFE notes that Mexico's new electoral registry has wider voter coverage than similar instruments in the United States, Canada, France, Spain, Italy, or Australia.[53]

The Civic Alliance also praised the new voter identification card and other improvements in the administration of the election. To be sure, the Civic Alliance was pleased that the conception of election observers had been fully incorporated into the new electoral process.

In two other areas the Civic Alliance celebrated the changes in the legal framework for the election but quite rightly faulted their implementation.

The new rules sought to establish election authorities who would be fair and impartial. The government and the PRI lost their majority on the IFE; citizen counselors constituted a majority of the IFE's General Council. On the other hand, the shift toward citizen authorities lagged greatly at the state and local levels, in part because the changes in the electoral law were adopted just three months before the election and in part because of resistance by local PRI leaders.[54] Moreover, the PRD voted against the appointment of Arturo Núñez as director-general of the IFE because he had held various important positions within the PRI (though in itself this does not rule out impartiality in his new post). A second laudable change in the electoral law that went largely unenforced concerns the creation of a special prosecutor for electoral crimes. One was appointed, but his office was not given adequate resources to carry out the job; on the eve of the election 218 formal complaints had been lodged with the special prosecutor, but only two of these had been addressed.[55] The task of correcting these two flaws in implementation—insufficient numbers of citizen electoral authorities and inadequate funding for the Special Prosecutor's Office—remains on the agenda; the new government should proceed to improve the implementation of the law forthwith.

With good reason, the Civic Alliance also sharply criticized the legal framework of the financing of campaigns. The law fails to make it possible for the press or nongovernmental organizations to verify partisan campaign expenditures; nor does it require the publication of the names of those who make individual campaign donations (however large), or of the amounts they have given. There are no effective and meaningful controls on campaign spending and finance. In the context of contemporary Mexican politics, the law permits a level of campaign expenditures so high as to tilt the election overwhelmingly toward the PRI; only the PRI can raise such vast sums.

Similarly, the Civic Alliance criticized the now banned but significant vestigial instances of the use of government resources to support the PRI. Prior to the election the Civic Alliance had gathered evidence of such practices in 215 cases in twenty-seven of the thirty-two states.

Finally, and justifiably, the Civic Alliance criticized the strong pro-PRI bias of most of the means of communication, and especially television news programs, which are the main source of political information for Mexicans.[56] The potential importance of television was highlighted during and after the May 12 presidential debate, which on its own made the Fernández de Cevallos candidacy a credible challenge to Zedillo. Mexico has three kinds of television stations: the huge privately owned TELEVISA; the much smaller Televisión Azteca, a former state enterprise privatized in 1993; and some small government-owned television stations.[57] Some advances were registered to improve opposition access to television. The government bought television air time for spots to be presented by all the parties; the TV stations were obligated to sell air time to all the parties at commercial rates. TELEVISA and Televisión Azteca voluntarily donated some air time to all the parties, and they transmitted live both the presidential debate and each candidate's closing public rallies (the *cierres de campaña*). Nonetheless, the Civic Alliance (and other organizations) documented the strong pro-PRI bias of the main news programs of both TELEVISA (*24 Horas*) and Televisión Azteca (*Hechos*). The bias was most marked during the first quarter of 1994, was less blatant in June (especially in Televisión Azteca), but reappeared in August.[58] Unfortunately, the desire to equalize the mass communications opportunities for the parties is limited by the equally important principle that the state should not censor the privately owned mass media or mandate the content of their news programs.

In a more partisan vein, the PRD put some distance between itself and the package of electoral reforms. Though Cárdenas signed the electoral reform agreements reached in January and February, by late March he had dissented from the process. On March 18 PRD legislators voted for a special congressional session to approve the reform laws agreed to in weeks of negotiations. The PRD party president, Senator Porfirio Muñoz Ledo, had been the PRD's chief negotiator; he described these reforms as "what we have been demanding since 1989." Nonetheless, hours later Cárdenas announced that he rejected the changes as insufficient.[59] PRD legislators subsequently divided, some still supporting the reforms while others opposed them.

In particular, the PRD objected to the electoral registry. The PRD did not conduct an audit of the registry, though it did carry out ancillary studies;[60] but on its behalf, IFE General Council member Senator Porfirio Muñoz Ledo cast the lone dissenting vote against accepting the registry as accurate. When pressed, the PRD seemed to suggest that the registry's margin of error exceeded 10 percent and perhaps reached 20 percent.[61]

On July 18 all the presidential candidates but Cárdenas signed an Agreement for Civility, Amity, and Justice in Democracy, pledging to accept the election results.[62] A month before the election Luis Javier Garrido published a sharp assault on the electoral process, claiming that the PRI was preparing the "perfect fraud"—sophisticated technical manipulations of the electoral registry, the subtle rigging of electoral rules, and some old-fashioned abuse of power in order to foster the likelihood that its fraudulent electoral victory would be widely recognized as an honest win at home and abroad.[63]

Nonetheless, for the first time since its foundation, in our judgment, the PRI now faced the "threat" of honest presidential elections at the national level as well as the opportunity for an election victory that would be genuinely legitimate. In many respects the reforms were impressive and effective. And yet the many resources at the PRI's disposal, the continuing informal practice of government resources being available in various ways for the PRI's election campaigns, the bias of the mass media, and the flawed implementation of aspects of the electoral law remained formidable assets serving PRI candidates at all levels and an obstacle to Mexico's full democratization.[64]

Moreover, fraud in Mexican elections is often highly decentralized at the local level. At times, pro-PRI election-day fraud has been "inefficient." Local activists have sought to cut the opposition's lawful share of the votes in districts where the opposition is strong and where it can therefore discover and protest the fraud (see chapter 6). At best it remained unclear whether national agreements could ensure transparency and fairness at the local level throughout Mexico when the national legal framework remained deficient.

The Public's View of the Electoral Reforms

The Mexican public overwhelmingly believed that important and positive changes had been made to improve the electoral process. In late July 1994, 55 percent of Mexicans indicated in a large nationwide poll that the electoral system had improved compared with three years earlier, whereas only 9 percent thought that it had deteriorated (26 percent thought that it had remained the same, while the remainder did not know or did not answer).[65] The respondents were far more positive in this regard than in their assessment of education, public safety, or the economy. Consequently, a majority of Mexicans believed that an opposition party could defeat the PRI in 1994.

Such improvements did not mean, however, that Mexicans thought all was well. In the same July 1994 poll only 41 percent of respondents thought that the elections would be clean, though this was up from just 30 percent in 1991 (see table 6-2); 17 percent thought that the elections would be reasonably clean, while 30 percent thought that the amount of electoral fraud would range from considerable to great, with the balance not knowing. Half of all Mexicans thought that there would be some scattered violence in response to the elections, but only 15 percent thought that the violence would be significant. Though concerns clearly remained, this was a rather more positive attitude toward the elections than had prevailed in years past.

THE OFFICIAL RESULTS OF THE 1994 ELECTIONS

On August 21, 1994, Ernesto Zedillo was elected president of Mexico with 48.8 percent of the officially recorded votes. Fernández de Cevallos came in second, with 25.9 percent, and Cárdenas third, with 16.6 percent; the minor parties garnered 5.9 percent of the votes, and 2.8 percent of the votes were annulled.[66] The PAN and the PRD had improved considerably over their 1991 electoral performance, while the PRI had lost much ground since that election. In 1994 the Chamber of Deputies would have 300 deputies from the PRI,[67] 119 from the PAN, 71 from the PRD, and 10 from the PT (Workers' Party). The Senate would have 96 members from the PRI, 24 from the PAN, and 8 from the PRD. Compared with 1991, the PRI vote totals increased the most in the three states with PAN governors (Chihuahua, Baja California Norte, and Guanajuato). The opposition's competitiveness returned to the 1988 level, greatly improving on its performance in 1991. Of the 300 congressional districts, the winner's margin of victory was below 15 percent in 127 districts in 1988 and was only 26 in 1991, rising to 108 in 1994.[68]

The minor parties fared quite badly compared with both 1988, when they backed Cárdenas, and 1991. Only the PT—led by an effective campaigner, Cecilia Soto, though allegedly with covert PRI funding to take votes away from Cárdenas—qualified for membership in Congress. The PPS, the PARM, and the PFCRN would lose their seats in Congress for the first time in many years. The turnout was the highest in Mexican history: 77.7 percent of registered voters.[69]

A novel feature of this election was the IFE's authorization of fourteen different "quick counts" or, more accurately, quick samplings of the results of precincts throughout the country. They were remarkably consistent among themselves and with the final results. All fourteen gave the PRI between 43 and 52 percent of the votes; Civic Alliance accorded the PRI 47.8 percent of the votes recorded.[70] These quick counts served to validate the official results.

There were, however, many election irregularities. The Civic Alliance gave the most detailed account.[71] According to their observers, the vote was in fact not secret in 39 percent of the polling places, rising to 51 percent in the rural areas. In addition, in 7 percent of the precincts some persons whose names were not on the electoral registry were allowed to vote, more so also in the rural areas. In 70 percent of the polling places, moreover, some voters with voter credentials were not able to vote because their names did not appear on the list of voters. In 25 percent of the precincts attempts were made to coerce voters; this happened in 36 percent of the precincts in the most rural areas. There were also problems with the application of the indelible ink: the ink was not applied in 8 percent of the polling places, while in 4 percent of the polling places, persons who arrived with ink on a finger were allowed to vote. Despite these worrisome irregularities, the Civic Alliance also concluded that Zedillo won the election because his margin of victory was well ahead of the likely sum of the effects of these irregularities.

To put these Civic Alliance findings in perspective, we should distinguish between the number of *polling places* where difficulties occurred and the number of *people* affected by such difficulties, the latter being ultimately the major concern. The Civic Alliance itself has calculated that although in 70 percent of the voting places some people with voting credentials were not allowed to vote because their names were not on the list of voters, the actual number of people so affected averaged just above four per precinct, comprising less than 1 percent of the registered voters.[72]

Consistent with this finding, a major international observer group—constituted by the National Democratic Institute for International Affairs and the International Republican Institute, representing the Democratic and Republican parties of the United States, respectively—reported that on election day, "delegation members noted a number of minor irregularities and isolated instances of intimidation of voters. In addition, delegation members received a number of allegations of partisan behavior by some local election officials."[73] The magnitude of the irregularities at the individual level was far smaller than at the polling-place level. In the same vein, veteran journalist Andrés Oppenheimer has written that "foreign reporters visiting polling places in Mexico City on election day found that, in most cases, the number of people who couldn't vote because their names didn't show on the lists was less than 1 percent of the voters registered in those polling places."[74] Given that the IFE's final audited error rate (noted earlier) in the electoral registry was 3.3 percent, it was to be expected that about 1.5 million Mexicans may have been disenfranchised on election day. (See also the next section's discussion of attempts at voter intimidation.)

The response of the two main political parties was quite different. Within hours of the closing of the polls, Diego Fernández de Cevallos and PAN party president Carlos Castillo recognized, in effect, Zedillo's election. The PAN's "quick count" justified that judgment. Fernández de Cevallos noted, however, that he would await the formal resolution of the various challenges of possible instances of electoral fraud before fully accepting Zedillo's victory. With bitterness, moreover, he called attention to what he labeled the "unfair and inequitable" set of conditions leading up to the election.[75] In the days that followed, the PAN challenged the results of over thirteen thousand of the approximately ninety-six thousand precincts. Moreover, Vicente Fox, PAN candidate for governor of the state of Guanajuato in 1991 and a likely PAN contender for the presidency in the year 2000, broke with his party's national leadership and called for selected acts of civil resistance to electoral fraud.[76] For the most part, however, the PAN accepted the results of the election.

On the day after the election Cárdenas gathered with tens of thousands of supporters at the Zócalo, Mexico City's main public square, and declared that the election had been marked by "massive fraud." Within hours he further argued that the only viable choices were to clean up or to annul the elections.[77] One reason why Cárdenas may have believed that massive fraud had been committed against him was the size of the crowds he had been able to draw to his public rallies; in particular, his campaign's closing public rally filled the huge Zócalo area, leading him and his supporters to believe that they were on the road to victory.[78]

Consequently, on August 22 and the days that followed, thousands of PRD supporters in many states of Mexico engaged in acts of protest and, in about a half-dozen states, in acts of violence such as the seizure of city halls or civil resistance such as street blockades; in some cases, as in the city of Guadalajara, hundreds of PAN supporters also committed acts of civil resistance.[79] By far the most severe conflict emerged, not surprisingly, in the state of Chiapas. Both the PRI and the PRD claimed victory in the gubernatorial election; the IFE's results backed the PRI. National and international observers reported substantial levels of fraud in Chiapas. The PRI candidate, Eduardo Robledo, took office in early December. Major protests ensued. Two months later, prodded by Zedillo, Robledo resigned and was replaced by another PRI official. In this fashion the indecisiveness of elections continued from the Salinas to the Zedillo presidency, all in order to safeguard social peace.[80]

In the weeks that followed the August election, Cárdenas repeated his charge that massive fraud had been committed, and he held Secretary of Government Jorge Carpizo personally responsible. On September 12 Carpizo refuted these and other allegations, defending his personal integrity and that of the elections.[81]

As the electoral courts began to hear specific complaints about fraud, it became evident that electoral irregularities had in fact had a decisive impact on some closely contested races, though not on the presidential election. For example, electoral courts overturned the preliminary results for two seats in the federal legislature from the states of Michoacán and Jalisco, and those for the mayoralty election in Monterrey; in each case the PRI was shown to have benefited from the electoral irregularities, and it lost the seat.[82]

On November 9, 1994, the newly elected Chamber of Deputies, according to law, voted to confirm Ernesto Zedillo's election. Only the 300 PRI deputies and 4 PT deputies voted to confirm, however. The 119 PAN deputies abstained, while the 71 PRD deputies and 6 PT deputies voted against. The negotiations with the PAN to gain bipartisan support for Zedillo had failed.[83]

Considering all of these factors as well as those bearing on the significance of the electoral reforms, we concur with three key judgments shared by some of Mexico's most distinguished intellectuals who have been important critics or opponents of the PRI:[84]

1. Ernesto Zedillo was elected president of Mexico.
2. This was Mexico's fairest election ever.
3. Many of the circumstances prior to the election campaign remained "unfair and inequitable" (as Fernández de Cevallos phrased it in his concession speech), heavily tilting the election to favor the PRI, while many of the irregularities on election day were quite worrisome.

Mexico took a giant step toward democratization, but the Mexican political system is not yet fully democratic. A day after the election, Guadalupe Loaeza devilishly wondered, "What could be worse, that there be fraud or that millions of Mexicans would vote for the PRI?"[85] Surely it would be better if the winner of the election could do so fairly and without blemish. Days after the election, President Salinas himself put it well: "There is still a lot of progress to be made" on the road to political reform.[86]

VOTER INTENTIONS AND BEHAVIOR

During 1994, as prior to past elections, there was considerable debate about the validity and reliability of public-opinion polling. In fact, as the election neared, the findings of the better, professionally conducted and nonpartisan polls converged, not surprisingly, and proved to be remarkably accurate. The polls identified clearly the final rank order of the candidates, and they forecast that Zedillo would get approximately the share of the vote that he eventually received. As many pollsters suspected and noted, the undecided vote broke in the end mainly for the opposition.[87]

The most thorough pre-election poll was conducted by Belden and Russonello between July 23 and August 1 among 1,526 Mexicans throughout the country.[88] Consistent with our findings in chapters 4 and 5, the PRI's share of the vote increased as the size of the city or community became smaller; the PRI won 38 percent of the votes in cities larger than one million but 55 percent of the votes in communities smaller than twenty-five hundred. Conversely—and as was already notable in 1991—the PAN had become principally an urban party. The PAN made some strides to break out from being just a northern regional party; the PRD's strength remained concentrated in Mexico City and its surroundings and in southern Mexico.[89]

Consistent with our findings in chapter 2, the democratization of the Mexican public proceeded apace. Asked in 1994 about their interest in the current presidential election, 41 percent of likely voters said that they were very interested, up from 34 percent in 1988 and 30 percent in 1991. In addition, 38 percent stated that people in Mexico feel free to say what they think about politics and government; though the question was worded differently, in 1991 the comparable statistic was just 27 percent (see table 2-4). Moreover, though 55 percent of Mexicans thought it possible that an opposition party could beat the PRI in 1994, only 45 percent believed that the government would recognize such an opposition victory.[90] As in elections past, Mexicans were readier than their government or the PRI for the practice of democratic politics.

The public's assessment of the state of the nation was grim, however. In 1994, 39 percent believed that the nation's economy had worsened during the preceding three years (24 percent thought it had improved), while 30 percent believed that their own personal economic situation had worsened (27 percent thought it had improved). This suggests a more negative perspective than in 1988, when 23 percent believed that the nation's economy was doing well and 57 percent believed that they themselves were doing well in financial terms (table 3-9). The objective facts are probably different; we simply note that Mexicans *believed* that times were tougher.

In 1994, moreover, 46 percent of Mexicans thought that public safety had worsened during the preceding three years (only 19 percent thought it had improved); 64 percent believed that poverty had grown during that time period (only 8 percent thought it had declined); 62 percent were convinced that there was more pollution than in 1991 (13 percent said there was less); and 49 percent stated that the level of governmental corruption had grown during the second half of the Salinas administration (7 percent declared that it had dropped).[91] Mexican voters approached the voting booth in a foul mood.

On election day, August 21, 1994, a large exit poll was carried out by Mitofsky International and BIMSA under the auspices of the Mexican Chamber for Radio and Television. (For the actual wording of the questions, see appendix 1; for the technical description, see appendix 2.) The pertinent results are summarized in tables E-1, E-2, and E-3.

As in 1988 (table 4-10), so in 1994 (table E-1): the lower the level of edu-

Table E-1.   Demographic and Social Determinants of Candidate Choice
             in 1994 (percent)

	Zedillo (PRI)	Fernández de Cevallos (PAN)	Cárdenas (PRD)
Education			
None	64	18	12
Primary	58	23	15
Secondary	49	30	15
Preparatory	40	36	18
University	41	36	18
Age			
18–23	48	32	13
24–29	49	30	16
30–44	52	26	17
45–59	53	25	16
60+	55	25	16
Gender			
Female	53	27	14
Male	49	29	17
Monthly family income (new pesos)			
Less than 1,375	54	25	16
1,375–2,291	45	33	15
2,292–4,581	45	34	16
4,582–13,743	49	33	14
More than 13,743	45	44	7

Source: Exit poll conducted by Mitofsky International, Inc., and
BIMSA, August 21, 1994.
   Note: N = 5,635.

cation, the larger the vote for the PRI and the smaller the vote for the PAN.
More than in 1988, women seemed to lean more toward the PRI than toward either of the two main opposition parties. But the results in table E-1
suggest three noteworthy changes since 1988. In 1994, demographic factors
explain little about the vote for Cárdenas (except that Cárdenas does markedly less well among wealthier Mexicans); the motivation to vote for Cárdenas must instead be found in political commitments. Second, whereas in
1988 Cárdenas did better than the PAN among the youngest voters, in 1994
the PAN beat the PRD by better than two to one among such voters. Third,
the social-class dimensions of the PAN voter had become more pronounced
than in 1988; in 1994 support for the PAN was strongest among the well

Table E-2.   Economic Perceptions and Candidate Choice in 1994 (percent)

	Zedillo (PRI)	Fernández de Cevallos (PAN)	Cárdenas (PRD)
Under Salinas, the economy has:			
Gotten better	68	21	7
Stayed the same	42	34	18
Gotten worse	20	39	34
Under Salinas, your personal/ family economic situation has:			
Gotten better	71	18	8
Stayed the same	47	31	16
Gotten worse	21	42	29
Concerning Salinas's economic policies, the next president should:			
Continue them	75	17	5
Change them	38	35	21

Source: Exit poll conducted by Mitofsky International, Inc., and BIMSA, August 21, 1994.
Note: N = 5,635.

educated and well-off. On balance, however, in 1994 as in elections past, demographic factors do not appear to be the main explanations for voter behavior.

Given the grim outlook of many voters, what was the relationship between attitudes toward the economy and candidate choice? In 1994 as in 1988 the PRI won two-thirds of the votes among those who believed that the Mexican economy was performing well (in the exit poll, these voters represented 53 percent of the total). But whereas in 1988 the PRI also won among those voters who thought that the economy was performing badly, in 1994 those voters overwhelmingly supported the opposition; Fernández de Cevallos came out ahead among them (table E-2).

In 1988 the PRI won among those voters who declared that their current financial situation was good; in 1994 the PRI ran away to victory with these voters (these were only 40 percent of the total, however—the first time we have found that optimism about the economy is higher than optimism about personal finances). In 1988 the PRI had won even among voters whose personal finances were doing badly, but in 1994 these voted overwhelmingly for the opposition, especially for Fernández de Cevallos.

One question evoked the public's pessimism very well: 64 percent of all Mexicans wanted the next president of Mexico to change Salinas's economic policies in important ways. Nonetheless, Zedillo won among these change-oriented voters. (To be sure, he carried three-quarters of the minority of voters who wanted a continuation of Salinas's policies.) This suggests that Zedillo succeeded in positioning himself as a candidate for change and therefore undercut the campaigns of his opponents.

On the whole, these findings lend support to the proposition that in 1994, perhaps much more than in 1988 or 1991, Mexicans engaged in "retrospective voting" (for discussion, see chapters 4 and 5). That is, they rewarded or punished the PRI depending on their estimation of the performance of the nation's economy and their own personal finances.[92] And, in a separate analysis, Julio Madrazo and Diana Owen suggest that retrospective voting was far more important than prospective voting in 1994; that is, voters were more likely to reward or to punish the PRI on the basis of their assessment of past economic performance than on the basis of their expectations about the future course of the economy or their own finances.[93]

Finally, we turn to institutional and political factors, which, we have argued, are especially important to understanding the electoral behavior of Mexicans (table E-3). In 1988 a majority of Mexicans approved of how Miguel de la Madrid had governed Mexico (table 4-11), even if they thought that the country's economy was in bad shape. In 1994 the circumstances were identical. Despite the public's general pessimism, 67 percent of Mexicans fully approved of Salinas's performance. Among these, Zedillo ran away with the election. Among those who disapproved of Salinas's performance, Fernández de Cevallos barely edged out Cárdenas. Among those who gave only conditional approval to Salinas's performance as president, Fernández de Cevallos won big, exactly as would be expected from the PAN's position during the preceding six years: criticizing the government politically but supporting many of its economic policies.

Partisan loyalty in election after election has been a determining feature of Mexican electoral behavior (see chapters 4 and 5). In 1991, voter loyalty explained much of the vote for the PAN, the PRI, and the parties heir to the 1988 Cárdenas insurgency. The PRI's loyalists stayed with Salinas in 1988 and in 1991. As in elections past, in 1994 we again observe stunning partisan loyalty (table E-3). Zedillo retained three-quarters of Salinas's 1988 voters; Fernández de Cevallos got 73 percent of Clouthier's; and Cárdenas kept almost two-thirds of his own earlier supporters (the Cárdenas retention share rises if one adds to his 1994 total the vote for the smaller parties that had supported him in 1988 but not in 1994).

The strength of partisanship is evident as well in the other questions included in table E-3. About 51 percent of Mexicans always vote for the same party; among these, Zedillo got almost two-thirds of the votes. Moreover,

Table E-3. Perceptions of the PRI's Viability and Candidate Choice in 1994 (percent)

	Zedillo (PRI)	Fernández de Cevallos (PAN)	Cárdenas (PRD)
Do you approve or disapprove of how President Salinas has governed?			
Approve	67	20	8
Approve, in part	34	42	17
Disapprove	14	40	39
Vote choice in 1988			
Salinas	75	16	6
Clouthier	15	73	7
Cárdenas	9	20	64
When did you decide to vote for your preferred party or candidate?			
Always vote for same party	65	19	12
Once candidates were known	40	32	21
After the debate	29	50	15
In the past few days	39	28	23
You voted as you did because you:			
Like the party	58	24	14
Like the candidate	45	31	17
Don't like the others	49	28	17
You preferred your candidate because he:			
Has the experience to govern	62	22	13
Has the personality to govern	44	37	12
Is honest	45	35	15
Is closer to the people	46	24	23

Source: Exit poll conducted by Mitofsky International, Inc., and BIMSA, August 21, 1994.

Note: N = 5,635.

we can discern whether those who voted for Zedillo were motivated more by party loyalty or by candidate appeal; in table E-3 it is evident that Zedillo ran 13 percentage points behind his party.

In elections past, the PRI had won electoral support because voters believed in its continued viability and in its social, economic, and political effectiveness. Our research indicates strongly that voters could turn to an opposition party if they come to doubt the PRI's institutional and policy effectiveness. The events and processes discussed in this Epilogue suggest that the PRI was vulnerable to such voter movements along these lines. Though the voters thought better of the PRI than they did of Zedillo, his campaign succeeded in preventing major defections. Note that Zedillo did quite well among voters who chose him because they did not like the other candidates (table E-3). Some of the most useful questions were not asked in 1994, but a proxy for what might happen if a party other than the PRI were to win is the question about "experience" for governing. Zedillo won big (table E-3), far better than he did when voters were asked about other candidate traits, such as personality, honesty, or closeness to the people.

We argued in chapters 4 and 5 that these political and institutional factors—the reverence for the presidency even in perceived bad times, and sturdy party loyalty—are the main factors that explain the voting behavior of Mexicans. In 1994 too these factors (table E-3) seemed to carry more weight than demographic features or economic attitudes (tables E-1 and E-2).

It is also possible to observe the behavior of the swing or tactical voter. The key campaign event in 1994 was the presidential debate. Only 13 percent of the voters decided on the basis of the debate. Among them, however, Fernández de Cevallos won half the votes. Interestingly, Cárdenas's share of the votes among those who decided according to their perception of the debate is almost the same as his apparent final vote share in the election itself; nonetheless, the debate probably cost Cárdenas the support of the swing voter. The debate's big loser was Zedillo: his vote share among the debate-influenced voters lagged 20 percentage points behind his eventual vote share. Cárdenas and Zedillo were protected from the ill effects of the debate by the loyalties of their partisans, who backed them however badly they performed.

As for opposition voters who simply wanted to beat the PRI and were prepared to sacrifice their ideological predilections accordingly, the debate may have swung them to Fernández de Cevallos over Cárdenas. That is, the debate may have made it possible for the PAN vote to grow much more than the PRD vote. Observe (table E-3) that Fernández de Cevallos was able to get 20 percent of the 1988 Cárdenas voters whereas Cárdenas was able to get only 7 percent of the 1988 PAN voters. Fernández de Cevallos's better than two-to-one edge over Cárdenas among the youngest first-time voters may also have been influenced by the televised debate.

In sum, though we lack the same battery of questions for the 1994 elections that we had for the previous elections, we believe that the results available confirm our earlier findings that political and institutional factors are particularly significant in understanding Mexican electoral behavior.

Our research also shows that much of the electorate could be mobilized politically, either by the PRI or by the opposition. Mexicans are able to take political stands and to back parties that have the necessary organizational resources and expertise (chapters 2 and 3). In 1994 the electoral turnout was very large, the largest ever in a Mexican election. Mexicans were ready for democracy, and in 1994 the PRI showed that it could get a very large share of their votes.

Indeed, our faith in the growing sophistication and independence of the Mexican voter has been reaffirmed by one of the findings of the exit poll. Recall that the Civic Alliance observed that attempts had been made to coerce voters in 25 percent of the precincts. In the exit poll, individual voters were asked whether anyone had tried to coerce them into voting for a specific party or candidate. Only 7 percent said yes. We then compared the distribution of reported votes between those individuals who had been victims of attempts at coercion and those who had not. The victims of intimidation voted 52 percent for Zedillo, 30 percent for Fernández de Cevallos, and 12 percent for Cárdenas. Those who indicated that they had not suffered such attempts at coercion went 50 percent for Zedillo, 29 percent for Fernández de Cevallos, and 16 percent for Cárdenas. We conclude that the effort at voter coercion failed; the differences are minor.

This finding is, of course, not inconsistent with the Civic Alliance's, but it calls attention to the need to distinguish among three levels: the intention of some local bosses to commit fraud (observable in one out of every four precincts); the proportion of citizens affected in some way by such intentions (7 percent); and the success of such attempts (negligible). Those feeling pressured were only slightly less likely to back Cárdenas, while preferences for Fernández de Cevallos went virtually unchanged in the face of intimidation. This analysis also underscores one of our recurring themes: Mexican citizens are readier for democracy than are some of those who still seek to rule them.

CONCLUSION

Carlos Salinas de Gortari had once looked on the August 1994 presidential election as the guarantee that his policies and his party would continue to prevail. Leading up to the 1994 election, political circumstances looked reminiscent of the July 1988 elections. In the immediate aftermath of the 1988 elections Salinas proclaimed, "The age of what is practically a one-party system is over. We are at the beginning of a new political era."[94]

In the 1994 election, Mexican politics changed significantly. Ernesto Zedillo is the first president of Mexico who can claim to have been elected in a competitive and free enough election, with his victory accepted by the public, by national and international observers and "visitors," and by all but one of the opposition presidential candidates—and even many important Cárdenas supporters also acknowledge that Zedillo won.

In the 1994 election, the democratization of Mexico's electoral procedures finally motivated over three-quarters of the nation's citizens to turn out to vote, at long last taking steps to align the citizenry's readiness for democracy with the electoral institutions that would make it possible.

But democracy in a fuller sense had not yet arrived in Mexico even after the 1994 election. The electoral procedures remained unfair in important respects. In other instances the procedures are formally fair but have yet to be implemented. Ernesto Zedillo agrees. In his inaugural address he pledged to "resolve . . . each and every one of the issues still causing dissatisfaction in terms of democracy," including "party funding, ceilings for campaign expenditures, access to the media, and the autonomy of the electoral authorities."[95] On January 17, 1995, the four parties represented in Congress signed a National Political Accord to bring about yet another round of electoral reform to improve the prospects for electoral democracy.[96] Beyond the elections, moreover, democracy is but a distant gleam in the eye in the workplace, in the labor movement, in rural Mexico, and especially among indigenous peoples.

Mexico's democratization moved forward during the 1988, 1991, and 1994 national elections. The task for the second half of the 1990s remains to complete the democratic transition now clearly begun.

APPENDIX 1
LIST OF VARIABLES

This appendix lists all the questionnaire items from the various surveys that we have used in the book to construct our own tables or figures. Each table or figure in the text refers to particular questions in specified surveys; this appendix reports the phrasing of each question. The question items are presented in the sequence of the original survey. The number of each question refers to the question's location in the codebooks available at the Inter-University Consortium for Political and Social Research (ICPSR) in Ann Arbor, Michigan, or at the Roper Center for Public Opinion Research in Storrs, Connecticut.

1959 SURVEY
From Gabriel Almond and Sidney Verba, *The Civic Culture Revisited: Political Attitudes and Democracy in Five Nations* (Princeton: Princeton University Press, 1963), ICPSR 7201.

6. What was the size of the town where you were born?

27. If you wanted to discuss political and governmental affairs, are there some people definitely you would not turn to, that is, people with whom you feel it is better not to discuss such topics? About how many people would you say there are with whom you would avoid discussing politics? [Coded: never talk about politics; many people with whom I can't talk politics; some, few, or one or two with whom I can't talk politics; talk politics with anyone.]

52. Speaking generally, what are the things about this country that you are most proud of as a Mexican?

81. What about the campaigning that goes on at the time of a national election: do you pay much attention to what goes on, just a little, or none at all?

112. We would like to find out something about your education. How far did you get with your education? [Coded for years in school.]

127, 129. Here are things that people say, and we want to find out how other people feel on these things. I will read them one at a time and you just tell me off-hand whether you agree or disagree:

127. "The way people vote is the main thing that decides how things are run in this country."

129. "A few strong leaders would do more for this country than all the laws and talk."

154. About how often do you attend church services? [Coded: every week, nearly every week, one or two times a month, sometimes during the year, or never.]

155. How old are you?

161. Gender

163. Interviewer rating of respondent's socioeconomic class

165. Attitude of respondent toward interview: friendly or eager, cooperative but not eager, indifferent or bored, hostile

1983 SURVEY

From Miguel Basáñez, "Public Opinion on Political Parties in Mexico," Roper Center Archive no. MXBASANEZ83-ENPOL83.

1. Gender

2. Age

3. What was the last grade that you completed in school?

27. Which political party do you support?

29. Do you attend events organized by your party, such as conferences or meetings—always, nearly always, at times, never?

42. In your view, should the Church participate in politics?

43. In your view, should the military participate in government?

Column 17. Place of work

Column 18. Monthly income received

1986 SURVEY

From the *New York Times* Mexico survey, 1986, ICPSR 8666.

1. In general and given what you know, would you say that things in Mexico are headed on the right track or headed on the wrong track?

2. What would you say is the main problem that we have in the country today?

3. How would you rate the current condition of the national economy? Would you say that it is very good, good, bad, or very bad?

4. And how would you rate your own current economic situation? Would you say that it is very good, good, bad, or very bad?

11. From the choices on this card [show card], please tell me how much interest would you say you have in politics? [Choices: none, little, some, or great interest.]

12. [In the midst of a sequence of questions on politics:] In your way of thinking, do you lean toward the right, the center, or the left?

13. Which political party do you prefer?

16. Please tell me which of these two phrases best describes your own opinion:
    "The Mexican political system should be changed so that candidates of other parties will be able to win more often."
    "The existing system works well and should be left as it is."

54. Please tell me how often do you attend church services? Would you say that you attend every week, nearly every week, one or two times a month, sometimes during the year, or never?

59. What was the last grade you completed in school?

61. Gender
62. Age
65. Interviewer rating of respondent's socioeconomic class

1988 SURVEY
From "The Gallup Poll, 1988," The Gallup Organization, Princeton, N.J.

1. Age
2. Could you tell me which of the following means of communication that appear on this card do you use to learn about current affairs? [show card]
    talking with other people
    Mexican newspapers and magazines
    foreign newspapers and magazines
    radio programs
    television programs
    cable or satellite television programs
    foreign radio or television programs
    other (SPECIFY)
4. From the choices on this card [show card], please tell me how much interest would you say you have in politics? [Choices shown on card: none, little, some, or great interest.]
5. How much thought have you given to the coming election this July, a lot, or a little?
7. Now, just for the sake of this study, let us imagine that today is election day and you are going to vote for the next President of the Republic. What you indicate will be completely confidential and will only be used for this poll. On this sheet [a sheet is handed out featuring the pictorial symbols for each of the political parties running candidates for president, with the name of the candidate placed immediately below the corresponding party symbol] please mark the party for which you intend to vote for President of the Republic and deposit it in this box [a box is given]. If you do not intend to vote, or if you are not yet sure if you are going to vote, or if you are not yet sure for which party you are going to vote, please mark any of these options on the sheet but, please, mark also which is the candidate whom you like best at this time and for whom you would vote if you would so decide. [The listed candidates were: Manuel Clouthier (PAN), Gumersindo Magaña (PDM), Heberto Castillo (PMS), Rosario Ibarra (PRT), Carlos Salinas de Gortari (PRI), and Cuauhté-moc Cárdenas S.—Cárdenas appeared separately under the symbols for PFCRN, PARM, and PPS. The sheet also featured five circles for the following voter choices: Another candidate, with a line below it to write in the name; not yet sure for which party I will vote; I am going to vote but I will annul my vote or vote blank; I am not yet sure if I am going to vote or if I am not going to vote; I am sure that I am not going to vote.]
12. Using a scale from 1 to 10, how would you rate the performance of Miguel de la Madrid as President? On this scale a rating of "1" is the least favorable that you can give and "10" is the most favorable.

13. In general and given what you know, would you say that things in Mexico are headed on the right track or headed on the wrong track?

15. How would you rate the current conditions of the national economy? Would you say that the national economy is doing very well, well, badly, or very badly?

16. And how would you rate your own personal economic situation? Would you say that your personal economic situation is very good, good, bad, or very bad?

18. Now I want to ask you some questions about Mexico's future. Would you say that at the end of the next six-year term Mexico's economic situation will be better than it is now, will be the same, or will be worse than now?

19. And how do you think inflation will be during the next six-year term? Will it be higher, will it be the same, or will it be less than now?

20. And how do you think the next six-year term will be with regard to unemployment? Will it be higher, will it be the same, or will it be less than now?

23. Now speaking about yourself, compared to a year ago, would you say that in economic terms you are better off, a bit better, a bit worse, or much worse than then?

24. And how do you expect that your economic situation would be within one year? Much better, a bit better, a bit worse, or much worse than it is currently?

26. Considering all the consequences, the good and the bad, in your judgment is investment in Mexico on the part of foreign companies positive or negative for this country?

27. In your view, should the next government continue to pay the country's foreign debt, or should it stop paying it?

28. In your view, should the death penalty be used to punish certain crimes, or are you opposed to the death penalty under any conditions?

30. Regarding state enterprises, what do you think that the next government should do? Should it keep most of them or should it sell the majority of them to private enterprises?

31. With regard to the importation of foreign products into Mexico, should the next government make easier the importation of these goods or limit their importation?

34. Now I am going to read you some phrases and I ask you please to tell me which of the three candidates whom I have mentioned [in the immediately previous question—which we are not using—the interviewer had asked respondents to rate Cuauhtémoc Cárdenas, Manuel Clouthier, and Carlos Salinas de Gortari] is best described by each phrase. Tell me first which of these candidates seems to you [phrases were rotated; we have used only the phrases listed below]:

has the best leadership qualities

is honest

is intelligent

cares about people like you

35. Which of these three candidates would you say best represents the interests of [interviewer mentions many groups, of which we have used only the ones listed below; the three candidates remain Cárdenas, Clouthier, and Salinas; interviewer rotates the questions]:

peasants
the working class
the bureaucrats
the United States
rich people

38. Which of these two phrases best describes your own opinion?

a) The Mexican political system should change so that candidates of parties other than the PRI could win elections more often; or

b) The existing system works well and should be left as it is.

39. In ten years do you expect that the PRI will be a stronger party than it is now, a weaker party than it is now, or more or less as strong as it is now?

40. How would you prefer that the PRI should select its presidential candidate? The PRI presidential candidate should be selected just by the president, or by a PRI national assembly in which all the leaders from this party from the entire country participate, or by means of an internal election in which all the party members could vote.

41. When do you think that a PRI candidate will lose the presidential elections to a candidate from the opposition? Could this happen in these elections, or within the next two to three elections, or after the next three elections, or never?

42. If a party other than the PRI were to reach power, do you think that Mexico's economic conditions would improve, would remain the same, or would worsen?

43. If another party were to reach power, do you think that there would be problems with the country's social peace or do you think that there would not be problems with social peace?

47. Now I am going to read you some phrases that surely you have heard that we Mexicans sometimes say. Please tell me whether you agree completely, agree, disagree, or disagree completely with each of them.

"I am very proud of my country."

"The way people vote is the main thing that decides how things are run in this country."

"The speeches of all the candidates sound good, but one never knows what they will do after being elected."

"A few strong leaders would do more for Mexico than all the laws and talk."

48. How often do you attend church services? More than once a week, every week, two or three times a month, once a month, from time to time, or never?

50. Please tell me which of these kinds of jobs [show card] best describes the work that you perform? [Choices are: professional such as lawyer, doctor, professor or engineer; professional such as nurse, accountant, programmer, systems analyst, or musician; manager, executive, or official in firms, in the government, in agencies, or in other organizations; owner or manager in a firm, store, factory, etc.; employee or clerk in firms, government or other kind of organization, secretary, postal worker, bank clerk, etc.; sales worker in a store, door to door, etc.; factory agent, generally in sales; employed in services such as police officer, fire fighter, waiting on tables, household employee, barber, hair dresser, pharmacist, etc.; skilled worker such as

painter, electrician, mechanic, plumber, etc.; semi-skilled worker such as machine operator, car driver, taxi driver, etc.; worker such as plumber's assistant, factory worker, any physical work; worker in agriculture, fishing, or lumber; something else.]

53. Which was your last grade in school?

56. Do you or your spouse belong to a labor union or any other workers' association? If so, which?

58. Could you mark on this sheet [sheet is given], without my seeing it, the political party that you prefer? When you have done so, please deposit the sheet in this box [box is given; the list is the same as for question 7 but without the names of presidential candidates or other election choices].

59. Did you vote in the last presidential elections?

60. [Of those who replied yes to question 59:] Could you please tell me, for which candidate did you vote in those elections? [A box and a sheet are given. The sheet featured the pictorial symbols for each of the four political parties that ran candidates for President. The name of the presidential candidate was placed immediately below the corresponding party symbol. They were as follows: PAN, Pablo Emilio Madero; PDM, Ignacio González Gollaz; PRI, Miguel de la Madrid; and PRT, Rosario Ibarra. The sheet also featured two circles for the following voter choices: Another candidate, with a line below it to write in the name; or none.]

Card 3, column 58. Gender

Card 3, column 59. Interviewer rating of respondent's socioeconomic class

Card 3, column 64. Region

Card 3, column 65. Interviewer records size of town.

1991 PRE-ELECTION SURVEY
From "The Gallup Poll, 1991," The Gallup Organization, Princeton, N.J.

1. Age

2. Speaking generally, what are the things about this country that you are most proud of as a Mexican?

3. What would you say are the three main problems that we have in the country today?

4. In general and given what you know, would you say that things in Mexico are headed on the right track or headed on the wrong track?

5. From the choices on this card [show card], please tell me how much interest would you say you have in politics? [Choices shown on card: none, little, some, or great interest.]

6. Now I want to ask you some questions about Mexico's future. Would you say that within three years Mexico's economic situation will be better than it is now, will be the same, or will be worse than now?

7. How would you rate the current conditions of the national economy? Would you say that the national economy is doing very well, well, badly, or very badly?

8. With regard to you, personally, how would you rate your personal economic situation? Would you say that it is very good, good, bad, or very bad?

9. Compared to three years ago, would you say that in economic terms you are better off, a bit better, a bit worse, or much worse than then?

10. And how do you expect that your economic situation would be within three years? Much better, a bit better, a bit worse, or much worse than it is currently?

12. Thinking about all the issues in which the government must invest money and effort, such as education, road construction, agricultural production, and so on, how much importance should be given to the protection and improvement of the environment? Would you say that improving the quality of the air and water should be the government's most important priority, should be an important priority but not the most important, should have a moderate or routine level of priority, or should not have any priority?

13. Considering all the consequences, the good and the bad, in your judgment is investment in Mexico on the part of foreign companies basically positive or basically negative for our country?

14. With regard to the importation of foreign products into Mexico, in your view is the policy of making easier the importation of these products basically a good policy or a bad policy?

18a. We are also interested in knowing your opinion about the reasons that people might have *not* to vote. As I read you some phrases, tell me, following this card [show card] how many people do you think would agree with this reason for not voting. In your opinion [phrases are read in rotation] is a reason believed by many people, is a reason believed by some but not many people, or is a reason that only a few people believe for not voting?

"It does not matter who wins the elections because all politicians are alike once they are elected."

"It does not matter whether one votes or not, because the same party always wins anyway."

"People are too lazy to vote or they have other things to do on election day."

"People do not believe that the elections would be honest or clean."

"People are not interested in politics."

19. I am going to read you some phrases that surely you have heard that we Mexicans sometimes say. Please tell me whether you agree completely, agree, disagree, or disagree completely with each of them.

"I am very proud of my country."

"The way people vote is the main thing that decides how things are run in this country."

"The speeches of all the candidates sound good, but one never knows what they will do after being elected."

"A few strong leaders would do more for Mexico than all the laws and talk."

20. Which of these two phrases best describes your own opinion?

a) The Mexican political system should change so that candidates of parties other than the PRI could win elections more often; or

b) The existing system works well and should be left as it is.

21. Now I am going to read the names of some of the most important political

parties and, as I mention each, I am going to ask you if you think that within ten years that party will be stronger than it is now, will be weaker than it is now, or will be more or less as strong as it is now. First, how do you think that the [parties are read in rotation] will be in ten years? [Question is repeated for the PRI, the PAN, and the PRD.]

22. If a party other than the PRI were to reach power, do you think that Mexico's economic conditions would improve, would remain the same, or would worsen?

23. If another party were to reach power, do you think that there would be problems with the country's social peace or do you think that there would not be problems with social peace?

24. I am going to read you some phrases and I would like you to tell me please which of them best represents your feeling about what will happen in the federal elections that will take place next month [the phrases are always read in the same sequence]:

"The elections will be clean and the results will be respected."

"There will be some fraud and minor problems that will not affect the national, state, or local results."

"There will be some fraud and serious problems that will affect some state or local results but that will not affect the results at the national level."

"There will be major problems and fraud and the final results will be a real falsehood at every level."

25. How often do you attend church services? More than once a week, every week, two or three times a month, once a month, from time to time, or never?

27. Please tell me which of these kinds of jobs that appear on this card [show card] best describes the work that you perform? [Choices are: professional such as lawyer, doctor, professor or engineer; professional such as nurse, accountant, programmer, or musician; manager, executive, or official in firms, in the government, in agencies, or in other organizations; owner or manager in a firm, store, factory, etc.; employee or clerk in firms, government or other kind of organization, secretary, postal worker, bank clerk, etc.; sales worker in a store, door to door, etc.; factory agent, generally in sales; employed in services such as police officer, fire fighter, waiting on tables, household employee, barber, hair dresser, pharmacist, pollster, etc.; skilled worker such as painter, electrician, mechanic, plumber, etc.; semi-skilled worker such as machine operator, car driver, taxi driver, etc.; worker such as plumber's assistant, factory worker, any physical work; worker in agriculture, fishing, or lumber; something else.]

30. What was your last year in school?

33. Do you or your spouse belong to a labor union or any other workers' association? If so, which?

36. How much thought have you given to the coming election this August, a lot or a little?

39. Now, just for the sake of this study, let us imagine that today is election day and you are going to vote. To do that, I am going to give you a ballot where you will

mark your preference without my seeing it and then you will deposit it in this closed box. What you indicate on the sheet will be completely confidential and will only be used for statistical purposes. On this sheet [a sheet is handed out] please mark the party for which you intend to vote and then fold it and deposit it in the box. If you do not intend to vote, are unsure if you are going to vote or not, or do not yet know for which party you are going to vote, please mark any of these options on the sheet but, please, mark also which is the party that you currently prefer and for which you would vote if you would so decide. [The sheet featured the pictorial symbols and acronyms for each of the ten political parties that were running candidates in the election, that is: PAN, PDM, PFCRN, PRD, PRI, PARM, PRT, PPS, PT, PEM. The sheet also featured five circles for the following voter choices: Another candidate; don't know for which party I will vote; will vote but will annul or cancel my vote; I am sure that I am not going to vote; or I am not yet sure if I am going to vote or not going to vote.]

41. Did you vote in the last elections in 1988?

42. Following the same procedure that we have just used for your voting intentions in the forthcoming elections, could you please tell me on this other sheet [sheet given] the candidate for whom you voted in 1988? When you are done, fold the sheet and deposit it in the box. [The sheet featured the pictorial symbols for each of the eight political parties that ran candidates for President. The name of the presidential candidate was placed immediately below the corresponding party symbol. They were as follows: PAN, Manuel J. Clouthier; PDM, Gumersindo Magaña; PARM, PFCRN, PPS, and PMS, Cuauhtémoc Cárdenas Solórzano; PRI, Carlos Salinas de Gortari; PRT, Rosario Ibarra. Another space was given to indicate another candidate.]

43. Now, using a scale from 1 to 10, please rate on this sheet [sheet is given], without my seeing it, the performance of Carlos Salinas de Gortari as President of the Republic. Remember than on this scale a rating of "1" is the least favorable that you can give and that "10" is the most favorable.

44. In your view, what has been the main achievement to date of the government of Salinas de Gortari?

46. We are interested in knowing how honest do you think the answers of other people will be when we ask them the same questions in this survey. On this sheet [give sheet] please indicate without my seeing it if you think that other people will be very honest, somewhat honest, somewhat dishonest, or very dishonest when they share their opinions with us.

47. Now I would like to know how much confidence do you have in the promise that I made that your answers will be held in complete confidence. On this sheet [give sheet] please mark, without my seeing it, how much confidence do you have in this promise. Are you very confident, somewhat confident, not very confident, or not at all confident in this regard. When you are done, please fold the sheet and deposit it in this box [give box].

48. Independent of this survey, please tell me which of the phrases that I am go-

ing to read is the one that best represents what you normally think about sharing your political opinions with other people in daily life:

"I feel good when I discuss with anyone my true political opinions."

"I like to discuss my true political opinions with other people, but not with just anybody."

"I discuss my true political opinions only with people I know very well."

"I do not like to talk about my true political opinions with anyone, not even with my close friends."

Card 1, column 17. Region

Card 1, column 18. Interviewer records size of town.

Card 1, column 19. Gender

Card 1, column 20. Interviewer rating of respondent's socioeconomic class

1991 ELECTION EXIT SURVEY

From "National Electoral Poll, Gallup-TELEVISA, August 18, 1991," The Gallup Organization, Princeton, N.J.

01–04. Interviewer codes the spot, noting the state, the town, and its size.

05. Interviewer three-level coding of environment in voting and poll area: quite good (voting is free and precinct officers facilitate the exit poll); more or less normal (voting is free, while precinct officers are neutral toward the exit poll); problematic (interviewees are reticent, or suspicious, or their honesty might be questionable).

06. Interviewer marks whether voting booth personnel or police are intimidating or pressuring the interviewees as they try to answer the poll.

07. Interviewer marks if the interviewee seems to be part of a large group of voters who had been transported to vote as a coordinated endeavor to affect the vote massively.

08. Interviewer marks if the interviewee seems nervous.

A. Gender

B. Age

F. What was your last year in school?

I. When did you decide to vote? [Choices: between yesterday and today; during the week; during the month; since I knew who were the candidates; I always vote for the same party]

J and K. Now I am going to ask you that you answer all by yourself, without my seeing it, the second part of this questionnaire. Your answers will be completely anonymous, confidential, and secret. The first question is: For what party did you vote for Deputy? And you can answer it by marking with an X. [The ballot given to the interviewees has the symbols and acronyms of the ten political parties running candidates for Deputy, that is, PAN, PRI, PPS, PFCRN, PARM, PRD, PDM, PRT, PEM, and PT; it also has a space to write in the name of another party.] Then, please write the reason why you voted for that party. When you are done, fold your questionnaire and deposit it in the box [box is given].

M. The same procedure used in questions J and K was repeated in the States of Guanajuato and San Luis Potosí in the races for Governor.

1994 ELECTION EXIT SURVEY
From Cámara de la Industria de la Radio y la Televisión, "Mexican Elections 1994," conducted by Mitofsky International, Inc., and BIMSA.

c. Sex

d. How old are you?

e. What is the highest level of education that you have achieved? None, primary school, secondary school, and university or more.

f. In general, do you approve or disapprove of the way President Salinas has governed the country? Approve, to some extent, disapprove.

g. Do you think that the economic situation has improved or deteriorated since President Salinas took office? Improved, remained the same, deteriorated.

h. Compared with the situation before President Salinas' term, how would you describe your current economic situation? Better, same, worse.

j. When did you make up your mind to vote for the candidate or party you chose today? Always vote for the same party, since I knew who the candidates were, since the televised debate, in the last few days.

l. Would you prefer that the next President continue with President Salinas' economic policies, or would you rather see some important changes?

m. In regards to who you voted for, why did you vote for this candidate or party? Like the party, like the candidate, don't like the others.

n. Which of the following is closer to your reason for voting for your candidate? Has experience to govern, has the personality to govern, is honest, is closest to the people.

o. What is your family's total monthly family income? In "new pesos," 0–1374, 1375–2291, 2292–4581, 4582–13743, 13744+.

p. For which candidate or party did you vote for president of the nation today? [A sheet is handed out with the pictorial symbol and acronym of each party and with the name of each candidate below the corresponding symbol as follows: PAN, Diego Fernández de Cevallos; PRI, Ernesto Zedillo Ponce de León; PPS, Marcela Lombardo Otero; PRD, Cuauhtémoc Cárdenas Solórzano; PFCRN, Rafael Aguilar Talamantes; PARM, Alvaro Pérez Treviño; PDM, Pablo Emilio Madero Belden; PT, Cecilia Soto Gonzalez; PVEM, Jorge González Torres.]

r. In the 1988 presidential elections, which candidate did you vote for? [A sheet is handed out with the following options: Manuel Clouthier, Carlos Salinas de Gortari, Cuauhtémoc Cárdenas Solórzano, Rosario Ibarra de Piedra, other, couldn't vote.]

t. Did anyone try to coerce you into voting for a specific party or candidate? [A sheet is handed out with following options: yes, no.]

APPENDIX 2
THE PUBLIC-OPINION SURVEYS

This book studies Mexican public opinion principally through analyses of nation-wide surveys. The first three of these surveys were conducted by others in 1959, 1983, and 1986. The next three, one conducted in 1988 and two in 1991, were carried out by the Gallup Organization with the active participation of one of us (Domín-guez) in the design of their polls. Additionally, our Epilogue on the 1994 election includes some findings from an exit poll conducted by Mitofsky International, Inc., and BIMSA; this was the only exit poll done that year. Appendix 1 lists the questions actually used in each survey.

In her history of survey research in the United States, Jean Converse described three essential ingredients for the advancement of scientific opinion polling in the 1950s and 1960s: developments in machine technology, such as mainframe comput-ers and high-speed communications; publicly accessible archives for easy dissemi-nation of polling information; and funding from the federal government and other sources to help develop an independent survey research infrastructure for the country.[1]

In Mexico these conditions have not been present to the same degree. The com-puter revolution arrived much later, and there are still no survey research archives in Mexico comparable to the Inter-University Consortium for Political and Social Research (Ann Arbor, Michigan) or the Roper Center for Public Opinion Research (Storrs, Connecticut). Up until the 1980s, moreover, the vast majority of polls taken in Mexico were either small and just regional in scope, or larger but also partisan. Often, questionnaires are not as comparable over time in Mexico as they are in public-opinion research in other countries. The seven polls we analyze in chapters 2 through 6 and in the Epilogue are the best selection available to us.

TECHNICAL DESCRIPTION OF THE SURVEYS

One baseline for our study is the 1959 survey conducted as part of Gabriel Al-mond and Sidney Verba's five-nation project, which led eventually to their book *The Civic Culture*.[2] The interviews were conducted by International Research Associates of Mexico, based in Mexico City, using a multistage stratified random sample. Mexico's three largest cities, Mexico City, Guadalajara, and Monterrey, were auto-matically placed in the sample. Urban centers of over ten thousand population were divided into five strata. Twenty-seven other cities randomly selected within the strata were chosen with a probability proportionate to size. Calculation of the proportion of interviews that should derive from each stratum was made in accordance with census data. In the end, thirty cities were selected to represent five regions of Mexico as then defined by the Mexican census. Altogether, 1,008 structured, personal interviews, each lasting from about forty-five to sixty minutes, were completed in June and July 1959; that was equal to 60 percent of the total sample. After weighting in order to better represent Mexico City, the sample size became 1,295, which is what we have used.[3]

Some may worry about how Mexicans might have responded to this first nationwide public-opinion poll designed to ask about their political views. The *Civic Culture* research team shared this concern and instructed its interviewers to code each respondent's demeanor during the interview. The results appear in table A2-1.

Mexicans responded to the interview situation in 1959 about as well as U.S. and Italian citizens did in the late 1950s. Only 5 percent of Mexicans were hostile to the interviewer, and only 12 percent were indifferent or bored. Over four-fifths of Mexican respondents were friendly or eager or at least cooperative during the interview. In short, we believe that this 1959 Mexican poll met rigorous international scholarly standards and received ample cooperation from Mexican citizens. In our own polls we have typically found Mexican respondents to be cooperative during interviews; Mexicans like to be asked their views and are pleased when someone listens to them.

In April 1983 Dr. Miguel Basáñez, a well-regarded Mexican scholar, conducted a nationwide survey among 7,051 respondents, all above age eighteen (Mexico's voting age). Called "Public Opinion on Political Parties in Mexico," this study monitored attitudes toward Mexico's political system and its parties. Basáñez also measured levels of political involvement within each partisan bloc. We make use of these data in chapters 2 through 4. In total, Basáñez sampled from fifteen occupational strata in all thirty-two Mexican states;[4] 66 percent of the respondents were men. His interviews were short, averaging roughly fifteen to twenty minutes; the poll asked forty-six structured questions. Overall, the margin of error for this study attributable to sampling error is comparable to large academic polls in the United States (approximately 2 percentage points). This study was commissioned by the Institutional Revolutionary Party (PRI), though respondents were not made aware of this.[5]

In 1986 the *New York Times* contracted with Gallup México, known as IMOP S.A., for a national probability sample of 1,576 adult respondents who lived in communities of 2,500 or larger and a smaller representative sample of 299 individuals living in communities with 1,000 to 2,499 inhabitants. The weighted N for this study is 1,899. Interviews occurred between October 28 and November 4, 1986, with the results weighted to make sure that each community in Mexico was represented in proportion to its share of the population. Individual subjects were chosen according to quotas designed to reflect the country's population in terms of gender, age, and socioeconomic status.[6]

In 1988 and 1991 three nationwide public-opinion polls were conducted by the U.S. Gallup Organization (Princeton, New Jersey) in collaboration with its Mexican

Table A2-1. Mexican Reactions to Opinion Polling, in Comparative Perspective
(percent)

	Mexico	United States	United Kingdom	West Germany	Italy
Friendly or eager	42	44	67	59	45
Cooperative	41	47	29	23	35
Indifferent or bored	12	6	4	9	15
Hostile	5	2	—	5	5

Source: The Civic Culture study.
Note: N = 1,295 (weighted, Mexico), 970 (United States), 963 (United Kingdom), 955 (West Germany), and 995 (Italy).

affiliate, Gallup México (IMOP S.A.).[7] Sampling, questionnaire design, and overall direction were U.S. Gallup's responsibility. IMOP's personnel, long experienced in polling Mexicans, had the direct responsibility for the fieldwork. The 1988 poll was conducted from May 12 until June 1, 1988, carrying out a total of 2,960 personal interviews.[8] The 1991 poll was conducted from July 15 through July 28, 1991, carrying out a total of 3,053 interviews.

In both instances, on average each interview lasted about forty minutes. The interviewees were all eighteen years old or older. Mexico was divided into four regions (north, south, Mexico City Federal District, and the remainder of central Mexico minus the Federal District). The distribution of interviews was proportionate to each region's population. Designated polling locations from cities, towns, and villages (with at least one thousand residents) were chosen randomly within each of the four regions; there were 78 such locations in 1988 and 270 in 1991. Within each polling location, blocks, households, and respondents in the household were selected at random, with about equal numbers of men and women. The margin of error attributable to sampling error is plus or minus 3 percentage points in 1988 and 2 percentage points in 1991.

On August 18, 1991, Mexico's nationwide election day for members of Congress, Gallup conducted an exit poll; voters were interviewed as they came out of the voting area. The exit poll relied on a multistage area probability sample, with each geographic entity having the same probability of falling into the sample according to its weight in the electoral registry. There were 350 sampling sites throughout the country. The statistical margin of error attributable to sampling error was plus or minus 1 percentage point. (For the sake of clarity and consistency, we refer to the 1991 exit poll as the "exit poll"; references to the 1991 "poll" refer to the poll conducted in July 1991.)

Ten of the exit poll's sampling sites provided no information. In fifteen other sampling sites, it was impossible to conduct the interviews at the originally chosen site; thus it was necessary to fall back on a preselected alternative site. Gallup interviewers encountered various forms of harassment at twenty-six sites where interviews were conducted; eight Gallup interviewers were arrested temporarily. We discuss the effects of some of these problems in chapter 6.

In 1994 Mitofsky International, Inc., and BIMSA conducted a nationwide exit poll on election day, August 21; the poll was sponsored by the Chamber for the Radio and Television Industry, which gathered the funds from its member stations. All polling places were divided into one of five regions; within each region, polling places were divided into two strata according to the percentage urban of the district that contained the polling place. This process resulted in ten strata defined by geographic criteria. Within each stratum, systematic samples were selected with probability proportional to the size of the 1991 total vote in each polling place. At each polling place, respondents were selected systematically throughout the election day; approximately one hundred voters would be interviewed at each polling place. The initial goal was to receive reports from 250 precincts; on election day that number had dropped by one. In fact, reports were received from 241 sites.[9]

THE POLITICAL CONTEXT OF THE GALLUP SURVEYS

The 1988 Gallup poll ended five weeks before the presidential election. Instantly upon the publication of its results in mid-June, the poll became a major source of contention in the presidential campaign. Clouthier and Cárdenas, each separately, denounced the Gallup poll as part of the PRI's evolving strategy to prepare an election fraud.[10] This was false, of course, but understandably, neither candidate wished to acknowledge the prospects of a PRI electoral victory in the absence of fraud.

Thoughtful critics were right to point out, however, that Mexicans were unfamiliar with polling and were therefore likely to be skeptical of pollsters; they might not always have responded truthfully. (For the Gallup poll's attempt to cope with this problem, see below.) Moreover, Mexico's largest private television network, TELEVISA, which paid for the Gallup poll through its Los Angeles subsidiary, had a close relationship with the PRI and the Salinas candidacy. TELEVISA displayed the Gallup poll's results not as mere news about the state of the election race at a given moment but as virtual anticipatory ratification of Salinas's "certain" election to the presidency. Critics of the Gallup poll rightly noted that its financial backing was needlessly obscured in early reporting of the poll's results, and they were also right to object to the manner of TELEVISA's presentation of the results.[11]

In June and early July 1988 the support for Cárdenas grew dramatically (see 1988 Gallup poll and official results at table A2-2). The parties of the left rallied around Cárdenas. Heberto Castillo, presidential candidate of the Mexican Socialist Party (PMS)—which included the old Mexican Communist Party—terminated his own campaign; he and the PMS endorsed Cárdenas. This step occurred just as Gallup was finishing the poll, and therefore it was mostly unrecorded by the poll. Cárdenas campaigned effectively in varied settings, whether in the countryside or at the National University (UNAM) in Mexico City. He toned down some of his early, more radical campaign rhetoric and stood principally as a symbol of change.

Gallup's and other polls[12] probably helped Cárdenas to gain votes. All the reliable polls placed the Cárdenas coalition in second place, ahead of the PAN, hitherto the

Table A2-2. Partisan Preferences in 1988 and 1991: Two National
Gallup Polls and Official Results (percent)

	Gallup Polls		Official Results	
	1988	1991	1988	1991
PRI	55	68	50	61
PAN	20	15	17	18
Cardenista/PRD	22	7	32	8
Other	2	9	1	13

Source: IMOP S.A. (Gallup) polls, May 1988 and July 1991; Embassy
of Mexico to the United States.

Note: Respondents who did not have a clear partisan preference have
been dropped from this table. N = 1,914 (65 percent of the total sample) in
1988 and 2,029 (66 percent) in 1991.

only credible opposition party. Suddenly Cárdenas became the most credible opposition candidate for the presidency and, alas, even one with a chance to win.[13] Strategic voters whose main interest was to defeat the PRI, not necessarily to elect the PAN's Clouthier, switched to back Cárdenas (see discussion of such strategic behavior in chapters 4 and 5).

Many observers believe that the vote for Cárdenas was in fact higher (the final result of the "real" election is neither known nor knowable). This discrepancy does not mean that the Gallup poll was in error. The poll probably reflected accurately the state of opinion in the second half of May. What happened is that the state of opinion changed.[14]

The 1991 Gallup poll ended three weeks before the congressional elections. In the official results the PRI was credited with less support than the Gallup poll had found (table A2-2). The results for the PAN, the PRD (the party founded by Cárdenas and his associates after the 1988 elections), and the minor parties are fairly close between the Gallup poll and the recorded votes.

As we saw in chapter 5, there was a surge of support for the minor parties in the days just before the election. The fact that Mexico had a "floating voter" population in 1991 suggests that such voters may also have existed in 1988 and "broken late" in favor Cárdenas in the 1988 election. We cannot test this hypothesis for 1988, however, because the Mexican government banned all exit polls on the eve of that election, including the exit poll that Gallup had expected to conduct (see discussion in chapter 6).

For the 1991 pre-election poll and for the exit poll, Gallup took special steps to make certain that its operation was not only transparent in its honesty and professionalism, as it had been in 1988, but also publicly evident, in order to avoid some of the confusion that had surrounded its 1988 poll. In 1991 Gallup's funding contract was directly with TELEVISA; there was no obscuring TELEVISA's sponsorship of the surveys. At the exit poll sites, Gallup pollsters were instructed to wear an identification label noting that they represented "Gallup-TELEVISA." They were also instructed on other sensitive details, such as not wearing a combination of colors that might suggest affiliation with any political party.[15]

COPING WITH UNTRUTHFUL RESPONSES: THE NATURE OF THE PROBLEM

The concern about the potential untruthfulness of Mexican respondents has been raised most forcefully by some of the research conducted by Miguel Basáñez in the run-up to the 1994 presidential election. On March 4–6, 1994, Basáñez sampled 466 Mexico City residents face to face on the street. He divided the sample into four segments, though the same questionnaire was used for all segments. In the first three segments, interviewers introduced themselves to the respondents pretending to be polling for the PRI, the PAN, or the PRD, respectively (each segment had about one hundred respondents). For the fourth segment ($N = 162$), interviewers presented themselves as polling for the respected weekly newsmagazine *Este país*.[16]

On average, support for a given candidate doubled—as compared with the null base, the *Este país* segment of the poll—when the interviewer reported to be polling for the candidate nominated by the party that was allegedly sponsoring the poll. Thus, for example, 36 percent of respondents told the alleged *Este país* pollsters that they would vote for the PRI presidential candidate, but 60 percent told the alleged PRI pollsters that they would vote PRI. The same distortion appeared when citizens were asked whether the elections would be clean and, to a lesser extent, in their rating of the president's performance. Interestingly, however, there were no significant distortions by the identity of the pollster when other questions were asked, such as what one's personal financial situation was.

On May 4–8, 1994, Basáñez conducted another experiment sampling 351 Mexico City respondents in face-to-face interviews on the street. This time half the sample was asked about its voting intentions orally, while the other half was asked through the simulated ballot box method (described in greater detail for the Gallup polls in the next section). Support for the opposition parties dropped when the question was asked orally. In the ballot box, the PRD got 24 percent; orally, it got 13 percent. In the ballot box, the PAN got 18 percent; orally, it got 15 percent. The small parties got 12 percent when the question was asked through the ballot box but only 3 percent when it was asked orally. The proportion of undeclared voters rose from 4 percent to 34 percent when the question was asked orally.

In the May 1994 poll Basáñez also divided the simulated ballot box portion of the sample ($N = 174$) into two segments; in one segment the question on voting intention was asked at the beginning of the interview, and in the other segment it was asked at the end. (The length of the questionnaire was eleven questions.) Asking the question at the end reduced the PRI's share of the vote by 8 percentage points and boosted the PRD's share of the vote by 21 percentage points.

Basáñez prefers to poll on the street rather than at home because he believes that the anonymity of street interviews increases the likelihood of respondent candor. At home, interviewees may assume that the pollster has made a note of the address for purposes of reprisal if the response is deemed to be anti-PRI. In a poll done for the daily newspaper *Reforma* in March 1994, the sample was divided into two segments. For one segment, interviews were conducted on the street; for the other segment, at home. Support for the PRI was 10 percentage points higher when the survey was conducted at home.[17] On the other hand, in a poll conducted by Belden and Russonello in late July 1994, three hundred in-home interviews were matched with another three hundred on-street interviews; the experiment was carried out mainly in Mexico City.[18] The demographic profile was the same for the in-home and the on-street interviewees.[19] Overall, on-street and in-home interviewing yielded about the same voter preferences for presidential candidates and about the same proportion of voters who declared themselves undecided. We think that this concern merits further research.[20]

COPING WITH UNTRUTHFUL RESPONSES: THE POLLSTERS AT WORK
The 1988 and 1991 Gallup Polls

In the case of the May 1988, July 1991, and August 1991 Gallup polls, there is a likely overestimate of the support for the PRI beyond the formal comparison between the polls and the respective official results. Some who told Gallup's pollsters that they would vote for the PRI did not in fact do so. It is impossible to use the poll to discern who changed their minds or who may have lied. The effect of these difficulties on our analysis is that our measure of support for parties other than the PRI is quite conservative. It identifies those who did not fear to tell the pollsters about their preferences. In the case of Cardenistas in 1988, these were the coalition's founders.

The design of each of the three Gallup polls took into account the expectation that some voters would be reluctant to express their true preferences. In 1988, for example, the question with regard to presidential candidate preference was phrased as follows: "Now, just for the sake of this study, let us imagine that today is election day and you are going to vote for the next President of the Republic. What you indicate will be completely confidential and will only be used for this poll. On this sheet [a sheet is handed out] please mark the party for which you intend to vote for President of the Republic and deposit it in this box." Then a simulated ballot box was presented to attempt to convey the sense of confidentiality.

Almost half of those who said through this procedure that they would vote for Cárdenas or for the PAN in 1988 said something different when they were asked a similar question openly and directly. In the open question, which offered no promise of confidentiality, half of the opposition voters said that they would vote for Salinas, or reported that they did not know for whom they would vote, or simply refused to answer. Thus we confirmed that many voters were indeed afraid to be truthful unless steps were taken to ensure confidentiality, as we did. (And we anticipated Basáñez's 1994 findings.) Our findings underline the importance and utility of the 1988 poll's chosen methodology. In the 1991 polls the procedure was similarly designed to foster belief in, and to ensure, confidentiality in the relationship between interviewer and interviewee.

In all three Gallup polls conducted in 1988 and 1991, the same procedure that simulated a secret ballot was repeated for questions deemed to be potentially controversial. In 1988 this procedure was used for the following questions: choice of presidential candidate in 1988; rating the 1988 presidential candidates on a scale from 1 to 10; indicating party preference; and reporting the candidate for whom the respondent had voted in the previous (1982) presidential election. In the 1991 pre-election poll this procedure was used for the following questions: choice of party to be supported on election day; reporting the candidate for whom the respondent had voted in the previous (1988) presidential election; rating President Carlos Salinas de Gortari's performance in office on a scale from 1 to 10; belief in the honesty of other Mexicans in their responses to this survey; and belief in the promise made with regard to this survey that the answers would be held in confidence. In the 1991 exit poll this procedure was used to ask about the party the respondent supported in the races for Congress and governor and about the reasons for such votes.

In the Gallup polls conducted in 1988 and 1991, the problem of perceived interviewer partisan bias did not arise. Gallup interviewers introduced themselves, as noted above, as representing Gallup México (IMOP S.A.) and, in the 1991 exit poll, as representing Gallup-TELEVISA (not unlike the polling for a newsmagazine). We are pleased that Basáñez ascertained that distortions are insignificant for the bulk of the kinds of questions that constitute the Gallup 1988 and 1991 pre-election polls and that are the basis for our analysis.

In Gallup's 1988 and 1991 polls the question on voter intention was never asked at the beginning. The 1988 poll opened by asking respondents about those things that made them proud about Mexico, going on to questions on media exposure and then moving into political topics. The simulated ballot box question on voting intention was seventh; we doubt that asking the question in seventh place (our location) or eleventh place (Basáñez's location) would make much difference. Nor would there be much difference with Basáñez on question placement with regard to Gallup's 1991 exit poll, when the simulated ballot box question was asked tenth. The 1991 pre-election poll question on voting intention—also through the simulated ballot box—was thirty-ninth, after the general questioning on the analytical issues facing the nation. Question order, therefore, is not likely to elicit any pro-PRI bias in 1991; on the contrary, if Basáñez's findings were to hold all the time, there might be a slight pro-opposition bias.

Gallup's 1988 and 1991 pre-election polls were conducted at home. The reason is straightforward in the polling community: street polls offer no statistical reliability and no measurable margin of error. The usual demographic filters employed in house-to-house or telephone polls, which are designed to provide a representative sample, cannot be used with equal effectiveness in random street polls.

These various precautions undoubtedly increased the validity of the Gallup surveys, but, of course, in the end there is no way to tell if all survey participants were truthful. We can, however, probe the sources of invalidity through two indirect means. In 1991, individuals were asked to comment on the honesty of others in their responses to the pollsters (and thereby describe their own cynicism about polling).

Table A2-3. Attitudes toward Public-Opinion Surveys in 1991 (percent)

How Honest Do You Think the Other Respondents in This Survey Were?	
Very honest	32
Somewhat honest	44
Somewhat dishonest	17
Very dishonest	3

How Confident Are You That Your Responses Will Remain Anonymous?	
Very confident	42
Somewhat confident	39
Not very confident	14
Not at all confident	4

Source: IMOP S.A. (Gallup) poll, July 1991.
Note: N = 3,053.

They were also asked to state how confident they were that their responses would remain confidential. As reported above, these two questions used the more elaborate procedure that simulated a secret ballot in order to increase the likelihood of truthfulness. The results are presented in table A2-3.

Three-quarters of Mexicans believed that there would be substantial honesty in survey responses; four-fifths displayed substantial confidence in the confidentiality of the responses they gave to the pollsters. Only 20 percent of the sample believed that survey respondents were "somewhat" or "very" dishonest, and only 18 percent did not feel at least "somewhat" confident that their answers would be kept confidential.

Nonetheless, a reading of table A2-3 also shows that only between 32 percent and 42 percent of Mexicans were "very confident" about the honesty of their fellow citizens in their responses to this poll and about the pollster's willingness and ability to keep their responses entirely confidential. These perceptions are therefore both encouraging and cautionary; readers should keep them in mind.

Polling in 1994

The 1994 exit poll relied as well on the simulated ballot box procedure to ask about the vote for president in 1994 and in 1988, and also to inquire whether anyone had attempted to coerce the voter into supporting a specific party or candidate. The question concerning the vote for president in 1994 was asked thirteenth; the question on the 1988 vote was asked fifteenth; and the question on attempted coercion was asked seventeenth. These procedures and question-order guard against the problems Basáñez had noted.

QUALITATIVE INTERVIEWS AND PARTICIPANT OBSERVATION

In this book we also make use of several long, in-depth interviews with a number of Mexican leaders, including each of the three principal presidential candidates for the 1988 elections (see especially chapter 4).

These interviews come mainly from the WGBH-TV (Boston) Mexico project. In 1987, WGBH-TV organized a substantial research project in preparation for a three-part television special on Mexico that was broadcast over the U.S. Public Broadcasting System in late November and early December 1988. The specific dates varied from station to station, but the first broadcasts were on November 28, 29, and 30, 1988. Austin Hoyt was executive producer, Adriana Bosch was series editor, and Domínguez was the chief editorial adviser. Hundreds of hours of interviews were conducted on videotape; only some of this interview material was ever broadcast.[21]

Finally, Domínguez was in Mexico during both the 1988 and (more briefly) the 1991 elections. In 1988 he accompanied Carlos Salinas de Gortari during three full days of his presidential campaign in Mexico City and in the rural state of Hidalgo. He attended Salinas's presidential inauguration in December 1988 and has participated in group interviews and discussions with Salinas in Mexico and at Harvard University. (Materials from Domínguez's field notes appear mainly in chapters 1 and 6 and in the Epilogue.) In 1993 and 1994 Domínguez visited Mexico about once every three months and was present during and after the 1994 presidential election; he served as an adviser to Mexico's Televisión Azteca in the days before and after the election. In 1993 he hosted then–Minister of Education Ernesto Zedillo during a two-day visit to Harvard University.

NOTES

PREFACE

1. Carlos Salinas de Gortari, *Por la política moderna: Cien temas* (Mexico: Partido Revolucionario Institucional, 1987), 27.

CHAPTER 1. CHALLENGES TO MEXICO'S DEMOCRATIZATION

1. From Domínguez's field notes while accompanying Carlos Salinas de Gortari during the 1988 presidential campaign. This event occurred on Saturday, May 28, 1988.

2. Interview on the presidential candidate's bus on Sunday, May 29, 1988, conducted by Domínguez along with Delal Baer, William Schneider, and Cathryn Thorup.

3. Salinas earned three degrees from Harvard University. In 1973 he got a master of public administration; in 1976 he received a master's in political economy and government; and in 1978 he completed the Ph.D. in political economy and government.

4. For an important, historically based interpretation, see Lorenzo Meyer, "Historical Roots of the Authoritarian State in Mexico," in *Authoritarianism in Mexico*, ed. José Luis Reyna and Richard S. Weinert (Philadelphia: Institute for the Study of Human Issues, 1977).

5. Taken from Jorge I. Domínguez, "The Caribbean Question: Why Has Liberal Democracy (Surprisingly) Flourished?" in *Democracy in the Caribbean: Political, Economic, and Social Perspectives*, ed. J. I. Domínguez, R. A. Pastor, and R. D. Worrell (Baltimore: Johns Hopkins University Press, 1993), 2.

6. For two fine surveys of Mexican politics that shed light especially on the years from the 1960s to the 1990s, see Roderic Ai Camp, *Politics in Mexico* (Oxford: Oxford University Press, 1993); and Wayne A. Cornelius and Ann L. Craig, *The Mexican Political System in Transition*, Monograph Series no. 35 (La Jolla: Center for U.S.-Mexican Studies, University of California–San Diego, 1991).

7. Above all, José López Portillo fits this characterization. See his display of both traits in WGBH-TV Educational Foundation, "Mexico: From Boom to Bust, 1940–1982," first broadcast on November 29, 1988, U.S. Public Broadcasting System.

8. From 1938 to 1946 the official party was called the Party of the Mexican Revolution.

9. Pending more specific citations in later chapters, the following provide a general overview of politics in Mexico, with special attention to the 1980s and early 1990s: Carlos Bazdresch, Nisso Bucay, Soledad Loaeza, and Nora Lustig, eds., *México: Auge, crisis, y ajuste*, 3 vols. (Mexico: Fondo de Cultura Económica, 1992); Miguel Basáñez, *La lucha por la hegemonía, 1968–1990*, rev. ed. (Mexico: Siglo XXI, 1990); Soledad Loaeza and Rafael Segovia, *La vida política mexicana en la crisis* (Mexico: El Colegio de México, 1987); Pablo González Casanova, ed., *Las elecciones en México: Evolución y perspectivas* (Mexico: Siglo XXI, 1985); Carlos Martínez Assad, ed., *La sucesión presidencial en México, 1928–1988*, rev. ed. (Mexico: Nueva Imagen, 1992); Soledad Loaeza, *El llamado de las urnas* (Mexico: Cal y Arena, 1989); Juan Molinar, *El tiempo de la legitimidad: Elecciones, autoritarismo, y democracia en México* (Mexico: Cal y Arena, 1991); John J. Bailey, *Governing Mexico* (New York: St. Martin's, 1988); George W. Grayson, ed., *Prospects for Democracy in Mexico*, rev. ed. (New Brunswick: Transaction, 1990); and Wayne A. Cornelius, Judith Gentleman, and Peter H. Smith, eds., *Mexico's Alternative Political Futures*, Monograph Series no. 30 (La Jolla: Center for U.S.-Mexican Studies, University of California–San Diego, 1989).

10. The central text in the scholarly study of democracy in the past quarter-century has been Robert A. Dahl's *Polyarchy: Participation and Opposition* (New Haven: Yale University Press, 1971).

11. Samuel P. Huntington, *The Third Wave: Democratization in the Late Twentieth Century* (Norman: University of Oklahoma Press, 1991). On contestation, see chap. 3; on participation, see chap. 4.

12. Guillermo O'Donnell and Philippe Schmitter, *Transitions from Authoritarian Rule: Tentative Conclusions about Uncertain Democracies* (Baltimore: Johns Hopkins University Press, 1986).

13. From the 1950s to the end of the 1980s, two examples were voter support for Japan's Liberal Democratic Party and for Italy's Christian Democratic Party.

14. Douglas Rae, *The Political Consequences of Electoral Laws* (New Haven: Yale University Press, 1967).

15. Brazil has often been described in these ways. See Scott Mainwaring, "Political Parties and Democratization in Brazil and the Southern Cone," *Comparative Politics* 21 (1988): 91–120; and Frances Hagopian, "'Democracy by Undemocratic Means'?: Elites, Political Pacts, and Regime Transition in Brazil," *Comparative Political Studies* 23 (1990): 147–70. For a different view, see Kurt von Mettenheim, "The Brazilian Voter in Democratic Transition, 1974–1982," *Comparative Politics* 23 (1990): 23–44.

16. Larry Diamond and Juan J. Linz, "Introduction: Politics, Society, and Democracy in Latin America," in *Democracy in Developing Countries*, ed. Larry Diamond, Juan J. Linz, and Seymour Martin Lipset (Boulder: Lynne Rienner, 1989), 12–13.

17. Seymour Martin Lipset, "The Social Requisites of Democracy Revisited," *American Sociological Review* 59 (February 1994): 3.

18. Terry Lynn Karl, "Dilemmas of Democratization in Latin America," *Compara-*

tive Politics 23 (1990): 19; see also Terry Lynn Karl and Philippe C. Schmitter, "Modes of Transition in Latin America, Southern, and Eastern Europe," *International Social Science Journal* 43 (1991): 269–84.

19. Edward N. Muller and Mitchell A. Seligson, "Civic Culture and Democracy: The Question of Causal Relationships," *American Political Science Review* 88 (September 1994): 635–52.

20. Diamond and Linz, "Introduction: Politics, Society, and Democracy in Latin America," 10. Lipset too argues that the emergence and consolidation of democracy are "linked to probabilities associated with the presence or absence" of various requisites, including political culture. See his "Social Requisites of Democracy Revisited," 16.

21. Gabriel A. Almond, "The Intellectual History of the Civic Culture Concept," in *The Civic Culture Revisited,* ed. Gabriel A. Almond and Sidney Verba (Boston: Little, Brown, 1980), 29.

22. Seymour Martin Lipset and Stein Rokkan, "Cleavage Structures, Party Systems, and Voter Alignments," in *Party Systems and Voter Alignments: Cross-National Perspectives* (New York: Free Press, 1967).

23. Diamond and Linz, "Introduction: Politics, Society, and Democracy in Latin America."

24. For a review of the literature, see Norman H. Nie and Sidney Verba, "Political Participation," in *Handbook of Political Science,* vol. 4, ed. Fred I. Greenstein and Nelson W. Polsby (Reading, Mass.: Addison-Wesley, 1975).

25. John A. Booth, "Political Participation in Latin America: Levels, Structure, Context, Concentration, and Rationality," *Latin American Research Review* 14 (1979): 29–60; Enrique Baloyra, "Criticism, Cynicism, and Political Evaluation: A Venezuelan Example," *American Political Science Review* 73 (1979): 987–1002. For a fine though rare example of the use of public-opinion research to study a transition to democracy, see Edgardo Catterberg, "Attitudes towards Democracy in Argentina during the Transition Period," *International Journal of Public Opinion Research* 2 (1990): 155–68.

26. For a general discussion, see Russell J. Dalton, Scott C. Flanagan, and Paul Allen Beck, eds., *Electoral Change in Advanced Industrial Democracies* (Princeton: Princeton University Press, 1984).

27. For a general analysis, see James C. Scott, *Comparative Political Corruption* (Englewood Cliffs, N.J.: Prentice-Hall, 1972), esp. chaps. 6–7, 9.

28. Robert E. Scott, *Mexican Government in Transition,* rev. ed. (Urbana: University of Illinois Press, 1964), 299.

29. Ibid., 244–45.

30. The tendency toward increasing bureaucratic competence deepened in the 1980s and 1990s. See Miguel Angel Centeno, *Democracy within Reason: Technocratic Revolution in Mexico* (University Park: Pennsylvania State University Press, 1994).

31. Among others, see George Philip, *The Presidency in Mexican Politics* (New York: St. Martin's, 1992); Samuel Schmidt, *The Deterioration of the Mexican Presidency* (Tucson: University of Arizona Press, 1991); Rogelio Hernández Rodríguez, "Ines-

tabilidad política y presidencialismo en México," *Mexican Studies* 10 (Winter 1994): 187–216; Alicia Hernández Chávez, "Mexican Presidentialism: A Historical and Institutional Overview," *Mexican Studies* 10 (Winter 1994): 217–25; Meyer, "Historical Roots of the Authoritarian State in Mexico"; and Ann Craig and Wayne Cornelius, "Houses Divided: Parties and Political Reform in Mexico," in *Building Democratic Institutions: Parties and Party Systems in Latin America,* ed. Scott Mainwaring and Timothy Scully (Stanford: Stanford University Press, 1994).

32. During President Carlos Salinas's presidential term, about half of the state governors were removed from office.

33. For a comparative argument based on a different presidential system, see Nelson W. Polsby, "The Institutionalization of the U.S. House of Representatives," *American Political Science Review* 62 (March 1968): 145–46.

34. The Mexican Academy of Human Rights and Civic Alliance/Observation 94 published various reports, among them *The Media and the 1994 Federal Elections in Mexico: A Content Analysis of Television News Coverage of the Political Parties and Presidential Candidates* (Washington, D.C., May 19, 1994) and *Las elecciones federales en México según los noticieros "24 Horas" de TELEVISA y "Hechos" de Televisión Azteca, 30 de Mayo a 30 de Junio de 1994* (Mexico, July 1994).

35. Though warning against overstating the overlap between the government and the PRI, Victoria E. Rodríguez and Peter M. Ward nonetheless argue this point persuasively. See their "Disentangling the PRI from the Government in Mexico," *Mexican Studies* 10 (Winter 1994): 163–86.

36. Craig and Cornelius, "Houses Divided: Parties and Political Reform in Mexico."

37. Kevin J. Middlebrook, "Political Liberalization in an Authoritarian Regime: The Case of Mexico," in *Transitions from Authoritarian Rule: Latin America,* ed. Guillermo O'Donnell, Philippe C. Schmitter, and Laurence Whitehead (Baltimore: Johns Hopkins University Press, 1986), 128–30, 136–40; Silvia Gómez Tagle, "La dificultad de perder: El partido oficial en la coyuntura de 1988," *Revista mexicana de sociología* 51 (October–December 1989): 245–47.

38. Personal observation by Domínguez, seated in the chamber's gallery as an official guest.

39. In part this was a response to the televised disruption of President Miguel de la Madrid's last presidential report to the Congress in September 1988. The government did not wish a repetition on presidential inauguration day. See Jaime Sánchez Susarrey, "Informe y diálogos de sordos," *Vuelta,* no. 158 (January 1990): 51–53.

40. For subsequent confirmation that an array of negotiations occurred certainly between the PAN and the PRI, see statements by PAN president Luis H. Alvarez in *Excélsior,* January 22, 1993.

41. WGBH-TV Educational Foundation, "Mexico: End of An Era, 1982–1988," first broadcast on November 30, 1988, U.S. Public Broadcasting System.

42. Inter-American Development Bank, *Economic and Social Progress in Latin America: 1991 Report* (Washington, D.C., 1991), 273.

43. For a magisterial account of the relationship between the state and labor

unions, see Ilán Bizberg, *Estado y sindicalismo en México* (Mexico: El Colegio de México, 1990).

44. United Nations, Economic Commission for Latin America and the Caribbean, *Preliminary Overview of the Latin American Economy, 1988*, LC/G.1536 (New York, 1989), 17–18; ibid., *1992*, LC/G.1751 (New York, 1992), 43–45; ibid., *1994*, LC/G.1846 (New York, 1994), 41–42.

45. Peter Gourevitch, *Politics in Hard Times: Comparative Responses to International Economic Crises* (Ithaca: Cornell University Press, 1986).

46. See Jorge I. Domínguez, ed., *Mexico's Political Economy: Challenges at Home and Abroad* (Beverly Hills: Sage, 1982).

47. For a fine, detailed analysis, see Nora Lustig, *Mexico: The Remaking of an Economy* (Washington, D.C.: Brookings Institution, 1992).

48. United Nations, *Preliminary Overview, 1992*, 41, 43–45; ibid., *1994*, 41–42.

49. Ibid., *1994*, 39, 41–42; Naciones Unidas, Comisión Económica para América Latina y el Caribe, *Balance preliminar de la economía de América Latina y el Caribe, 1993*, LC/G.1794 (New York, December 1993), 33, 35, 36, 37.

CHAPTER 2. NORMS OF MEXICAN CITIZENSHIP: ARE MEXICANS "DEMOCRATS?"

1. Samuel P. Huntington, *The Third Wave: Democratization in the Late Twentieth Century* (Norman: University of Oklahoma Press, 1991), chap. 2; Larry Diamond, Juan J. Linz, and Seymour Martin Lipset, eds., *Democracy in Developing Countries*, 4 vols. (Boulder: Lynne Rienner, 1989); Claus Offe, *Contradictions of the Welfare State* (Cambridge: MIT Press, 1984).

2. This proposition is quite consistent with the arguments of Guillermo O'Donnell and Philippe C. Schmitter in *Transitions from Authoritarian Rule: Tentative Conclusions about Uncertain Democracies* (Baltimore: Johns Hopkins University Press, 1986), 4–5, 26, 48.

3. Daniel Cosío Villegas, "The Mexican Revolution Then and Now," in *Is the Mexican Revolution Dead?* ed. Stanley R. Ross (New York: Knopf, 1966), 123–24.

4. Gabriel Almond and Sidney Verba, *The Civic Culture: Political Attitudes and Democracy in Five Nations* (Princeton: Princeton University Press, 1963), 414.

5. Ibid., chap. 13.

6. Alberto Hernández Medina and Luis Narro Rodríguez, eds., *Cómo somos los mexicanos* (Mexico: Centro de Estudios Educativos, 1987), 10–12, 96–97. Their national survey ($N = 1,837$) was conducted between August and November 1982. The representation of Mexico's northern region is twice as great in this survey as in the 1980 census, while the representation of central Mexico is half as great. The southern region and the Federal District's share of the survey match well their share of the census. The representation of towns with a population below fifteen thousand is two-fifths as great as that of the census.

7. See, for example, Enrique Alduncín Abitia, *Los valores de los mexicanos: Mexico entre la tradición y la modernidad* (Mexico: Fondo Cultural Banamex, 1986); and Hernández Medina and Narro Rodríguez, *Cómo somos los mexicanos*, chaps. 6 and 8.

8. Richard R. Fagen and William S. Tuohy, *Politics and Privilege in a Mexican City* (Stanford: Stanford University Press, 1972), 122–27.

9. Seymour Martin Lipset, *Political Man* (Garden City, N.Y.: Anchor Books, 1960), chap. 4.

10. Rafael Segovia, *La politización del niño mexicano* (Mexico: El Colegio de México, 1975), 124–26, 130.

11. Wayne A. Cornelius, *Politics and the Migrant Poor in Mexico City* (Stanford: Stanford University Press, 1975), 96, 150.

12. Henry A. Landsberger and Bobby M. Gierisch, "Political and Economic Activism: Peasant Participation in the *Ejidos* of the Comarca Lagunera of Mexico," in *Political Participation in Latin America*, vol. 2, ed. Mitchell A. Seligson and John A. Booth (New York: Holmes and Meier, 1979), 96.

13. John A. Booth and Mitchell A. Seligson, "The Political Culture of Authoritarianism in Mexico: A Reexamination," *Latin American Research Review* 19, no. 1 (1984): 106–24.

14. On the unimportance of social class and religiosity and the importance of instrumental motivations in the context of electoral behavior, see Kenneth M. Coleman, "The Capital City Electorate and Mexico's Acción Nacional: Some Survey Evidence on Conventional Hypotheses," *Social Science Quarterly* 56 (December 1975): 502–9.

15. Miguel Basáñez, *El pulso de los sexenios: 20 años de crisis en México* (Mexico: Siglo XXI, 1990), part 3.

16. The Euro-Barometer Study, no. 31, was conducted in March–April 1989. The principal investigators were Karl Heinz Reif and Anna Melich. The data were made available through the Inter-University Consortium for Political and Social Research (ICPSR study no. 9322). Information on political interest is found on p. 191 of the study codebook. The United States General Social Survey Cumulative Codebook, 1972–91, was produced by the National Opinion Research Center of the University of Chicago. Its principal investigators are James A. Davis and Tom W. Smith. These data were also made available through ICPSR (study no. 9710). Information on political interest in 1987 (the latest year when the question was asked in the GSS) appears on p. 380 of the codebook.

17. In mid-1993 the Salinas government sold off two public television stations to a private consortium, partly in the hopes of generating some competition for TELEVISA.

18. Euro-Barometer Study, no. 31.

19. For a discussion of church-state relations in contemporary Mexico, see Soledad Loaeza, *El llamado de las urnas* (Mexico: Cal y Arena, 1989), part 3.

20. Alain Rouquié, *The Military and the State in Latin America*, trans. Paul E. Sigmund (Berkeley: University of California Press), 201–7, quotation from 204; see also David Ronfeldt, "The Modern Mexican Military," in *Armies and Politics in Latin America*, ed. Abraham F. Lowenthal and J. Samuel Fitch (New York: Holmes and Meier, 1986).

21. Basáñez, *El pulso de los sexenios*, 236–42.

22. The best description of the PRI nomination process remains Robert E. Scott's *Mexican Government in Transition,* rev. ed. (Urbana: University of Illinois Press, 1964), 197–223.

23. For a discussion of institutional obstacles to democratization at the local level, see Jonathan Fox, "The Difficult Transition from Clientelism to Citizenship: Lessons from Mexico," *World Politics* 46 (January 1994); and Jonathan Fox and Luis Hernández, "Mexico's Difficult Democracy: Grassroots Movements, NGOs, and Local Government," *Alternatives* 17 (1992): 165–208.

24. BANAMEX, *México social: 1990–91* (Mexico, 1991), 240, 247.

25. Huntington, *Third Wave,* 72–85.

26. As we shall see in chapter 4, the economic crisis of the 1980s hurt much of the nation, so much and so evenly that perceptions of Mexico's economic situation failed to distinguish well the attitudes of Mexicans on other issues. On the other hand, the severity of the economic crisis no doubt may have predisposed Mexicans to think more openly about their political alternatives.

27. E. E. Schattsneider, *The Semisovereign People: A Realist's View of Democracy in America* (Hinsdale, Ill.: Dryden, 1975), 1–18. The book was first published in 1960.

28. See, for example, Huntington, *Third Wave;* and Adam Przeworski, "Some Problems in the Study of the Transition to Democracy," in *Transitions from Authoritarian Rule: Comparative Perspectives,* ed. Guillermo O'Donnell, Philippe C. Schmitter, and Laurence Whitehead (Baltimore: Johns Hopkins University Press, 1986).

29. Scott Mainwaring, "Transitions to Democracy and Democratic Consolidation: Theoretical and Comparative Issues," in *Issues in Democratic Consolidation: The New South American Democracies in Comparative Perspective* (Notre Dame: University of Notre Dame Press, 1992), 308–10.

30. Vikram Chand, "Civil Society, Institutions, and Democratization in Mexico: The Politics of the State of Chihuahua in National Perspective" (Ph.D. diss., Harvard University, 1991).

31. Loaeza, *El llamado de las urnas.*

32. José Antonio Crespo, "PRI: De la hegemonía revolucionaria a la dominación democrática," *Política y gobierno* 1 (January–June 1994): 48.

33. On the ephemeral nature of mass mobilization in other cases, see O'Donnell and Schmitter, *Transitions from Authoritarian Rule: Tentative Conclusions,* 26.

34. Ronald Inglehart, "The Renaissance of Political Culture," *American Political Science Review* 82 (December 1988): 1219.

35. Robert Fishman, "Rethinking State and Regime: Southern Europe's Transition to Democracy," *World Politics* 42 (April 1990): 436–37; Huntington, *Third Wave,* 258–65.

CHAPTER 3. IDEOLOGY, ISSUE PREFERENCES, AND APPREHENSION: PUBLIC OPINION DURING THE 1988 PRESIDENTIAL ELECTION

1. Norman H. Nie, Sidney Verba, and John R. Petrocik, *The Changing American Voter* (Cambridge: Harvard University Press, 1976).

2. Luis Rubio, "Las dificultades de un sexenio," in *México: Auge, crisis, y ajuste,*

ed. Carlos Bazdresch, Nisso Bucay, Soledad Loaeza, and Nora Lustig (Mexico: Fondo de Cultura Económica, 1992), 76.

3. Adolfo Gilly, "The Mexican Regime in Its Dilemma," *Journal of International Affairs* 43 (Winter 1990): 278–79.

4. For a fuller account, see Nora Lustig, *Mexico: The Remaking of an Economy* (Washington, D.C.: Brookings Institution, 1992).

5. Lorenzo Meyer, "Las relaciones con Estados Unidos: Convergencia y conflicto," in *México: Auge, crisis, y ajuste,* 109.

6. United Nations, Economic Commission for Latin America and the Caribbean (hereafter ECLAC), *Preliminary Overview of the Economy of Latin America and the Caribbean, 1990,* LC/G.1646 (New York, 19 December 1990), 34–35.

7. Merilee S. Grindle, "Public Policy, Foreign Investment, and Implementation Style in Mexico," in *Economic Issues and Political Conflict: US–Latin American Relations,* ed. Jorge I. Domínguez (London: Butterworths, 1982).

8. Manuel Armendáriz Etchegaray, "New Forms of Foreign Investment and Technology Transfer," in *The Economics of Interdependence: Mexico and the United States,* ed. William Glade and Cassio Luiselli, papers prepared for the Bilateral Commission on the Future of United States–Mexican Relations (La Jolla: Center for U.S.-Mexican Studies, University of California–San Diego, 1989).

9. John J. Bailey, *Governing Mexico: The Statecraft of Crisis Management* (New York: St. Martin's, 1988), 86.

10. For a description of this long-lasting process, see Jorge I. Domínguez, "International Reverberations of a Dynamic Political Economy," in *Mexico's Political Economy: Challenges at Home and Abroad,* ed. Jorge I. Domínguez (Beverly Hills: Sage, 1982), 202–17.

11. The source for these paragraphs on trade is Glade and Luiselli, eds., *Economics of Interdependence.* See chapters by Luis Bravo Aguilera, "Mexico's Foreign Trade Policies and Commercial Relations with the United States"; Guy F. Erb and Joseph A. Greenwald, "U.S.-Mexican Trade Issues"; and B. Timothy Bennett, "Cooperation and Results in U.S.-Mexico Relations." See also ECLAC, *Preliminary Overview of the Economy of Latin America and the Caribbean, 1990,* 28–29.

12. BANAMEX, *México social: 1990–1991* (Mexico, 1991), 302, 309–10.

13. Nie, Verba, and Petrocik, *Changing American Voter,* 142, 370–71.

14. For U.S. evidence over time concerning the higher issue consistency among those who are better educated, as well as for discussions about the limitations of an education-based explanation for issue consistency, see Philip E. Converse, "Public Opinion and Voting Behavior," in *Handbook of Political Science,* vol. 4, ed. Fred I. Greenstein and Nelson W. Polsby (Reading, Mass.: Addison-Wesley, 1975), 104; and Nie, Verba, Petrocik, *Changing American Voter,* 148–50.

15. ECLAC, *Preliminary Overview of the Economy of Latin America and the Caribbean, 1990,* 25–27.

16. Ibid., 26–27.

17. Anthony Downs, *An Economic Theory of Democracy* (New York: Harper and Row, 1957), 96–113.

CHAPTER 4. THE PARTISAN CONSEQUENCES OF CITIZEN ATTITUDES: VOTING INTENTIONS IN THE 1988 ELECTION

1. For an excellent account of Mexico's political parties and elections, see Silvia Gómez Tagle, "Los partidos, las elecciones, y la crisis," in *Primer informe sobre la democracia: México 1988*, ed. Pablo González Casanova and Jorge Cadena Roa, 2d ed. (Mexico: Siglo XXI, 1989).

2. For an overview of the history of Mexican elections, see Pablo González Casanova, ed., *Las elecciones en México: Evolución y perspectivas* (Mexico: Siglo XXI, 1985). For an overview of the history of Mexican presidential successions, see Carlos Martínez Assad, ed., *La sucesión presidencial en México, 1928–1988*, 2d ed. (Mexico: Nueva Imagen, 1992). And for an overview of the more recent party competition in historical context, see Juan Molinar, *El tiempo de la legitimidad: Elecciones, autoritarismo, y democracia en México* (Mexico: Cal y Arena, 1991).

3. Russell J. Dalton, Scott C. Flanagan, and Paul Allen Beck, eds., *Electoral Change in Advanced Industrial Democracies* (Princeton: Princeton University Press, 1984), 13. See also Walter Dean Burnham, *Critical Elections and the Mainsprings of American Politics* (New York: Norton, 1970).

4. Anthony Downs, *An Economic Theory of Democracy* (New York: Harper and Row, 1957); Richard D. McKelvey and Peter C. Ordeshook, "A General Theory of the Calculus of Voting," in *Mathematical Applications in Political Science, VI*, ed. James F. Herndon and Joseph L. Bernd (Charlottesville: University Press of Virginia, 1972); Bruce E. Cain, "Strategic Voting in Britain," *American Journal of Political Science* 22, no. 3 (1978): 639–55; Walter J. Stone and Alan I. Abramowitz, "Winning May Not Be Everything, but It's More Than We Thought: Presidential Party Activists in 1980," *American Political Science Review* 77, no. 2 (1983): 945–56; Paul R. Abramson, John H. Aldrich, Phil Paolino, and David Rohde, "Sophisticated Voting in the 1988 Presidential Primaries," *American Political Science Review* 86, no. 1 (1992): 55–69.

5. John J. Bailey, *Governing Mexico: The Statecraft of Crisis Management* (New York: St. Martin's, 1988); Miguel Basáñez, "Encuestas de opinión en México," in *México: Auge, crisis, y ajuste*, ed. Carlos Bazdresch, Nisso Bucay, Soledad Loaeza, and Nora Lustig (Mexico: Fondo de Cultura Económica, 1992).

6. Samuel P. Huntington, *The Third Wave: Democratization in the Late Twentieth Century* (Norman: University of Oklahoma Press, 1991), 174–92. For a suggestive comparison with Mexico's 1988 election, see the discussion of Brazil's 1974 national elections in Bolivar Lamounier, *"Authoritarian Brazil* Revisited: The Impact of Elections on the *Abertura,"* in *Democratizing Brazil*, ed. Alfred Stepan (Princeton: Princeton University Press, 1989).

7. Michael Lewis-Beck, *Economics and Elections* (Ann Arbor: University of Michigan Press, 1988).

8. Silvia Gómez Tagle, "La dificultad de perder: El partido oficial en la coyuntura de 1988," *Revista mexicana de sociología* 51 (1989): 240–42.

9. For an excellent account of the political regime and the PRI's role within it, see Wayne A. Cornelius and Ann L. Craig, *The Mexican Political System in Transition,*

Monograph Series no. 35 (La Jolla: Center for U.S.-Mexican Studies, University of California–San Diego, 1991), esp. 23–44, 55–83.

10. Luis Javier Garrido, "Un partido sin militantes," in *La vida política en la crisis,* ed. Soledad Loaeza and Rafael Segovia (Mexico: El Colegio de México, 1987).

11. Kevin J. Middlebrook, ed., *Unions, Workers, and the State in Mexico* (La Jolla: Center for U.S.-Mexican Studies, University of California–San Diego, 1991).

12. Bailey, *Governing Mexico,* 30. For a discussion of the presidency and presidentialism, the presidency's formal and informal powers, and the strengths and limits of this institution, see George Philip, *The Presidency in Mexican Politics* (New York: St. Martin's, 1992); Luis Javier Garrido, "The Crisis of *Presidencialismo,*" in *Mexico's Alternative Political Futures,* ed. Wayne A. Cornelius, Judith Gentleman, and Peter H. Smith (La Jolla: Center for U.S.-Mexican Studies, University of California–San Diego, 1989); and Samuel Schmidt, *The Deterioration of the Mexican Presidency* (Tucson: University of Arizona Press, 1991).

13. WGBH-TV Educational Foundation, "Mexico: End of an Era, 1982–1988," first broadcast on November 30, 1988, U.S. Public Broadcasting System. A compilation of Cuauhtémoc Cárdenas's speeches during the 1988 presidential campaign is available in his *Nuestra lucha apenas comienza* (Mexico: Editorial Nuestro Tiempo, 1988).

14. WGBH-TV Educational Foundation, interview with Cuauhtémoc Cárdenas, November 4, 1987. The interview has been translated from the Spanish. The quotations in this paragraph were never broadcast but were given on the record.

15. Ibid.

16. WGBH-TV Educational Foundation, interview with Carlos Salinas de Gortari, June 11, 1988, conducted in English in Acapulco, Mexico. The quotations in this paragraph were never broadcast but were given on the record.

17. Interview with Carlos Salinas de Gortari, May 29, 1988, conducted in English by Domínguez along with Delal Baer, William Schneider, and Cathryn Thorup.

18. WGBH-TV, interview with Salinas, June 11, 1988. The quotations in this paragraph were never broadcast but were given on the record.

19. Ibid.

20. Interview with Salinas, May 29, 1988, conducted by Domínguez, Baer, Schneider, and Thorup.

21. WGBH-TV, interview with Salinas, June 11, 1988. The quotations in this paragraph were never broadcast but were given on the record.

22. WGBH-TV, interview with Cárdenas, November 4, 1987. The quotations in this paragraph were never broadcast but were given on the record.

23. WGBH-TV Educational Foundation, interview with Manuel Clouthier, June 4, 1988, conducted in English in Mexico City. The quotations in this paragraph were never broadcast but were given on the record.

24. WGBH-TV, interview with Salinas, June 11, 1988. The quotations in this paragraph were never broadcast but were given on the record.

25. Ibid.

26. Seymour Martin Lipset and Stein Rokkan, "Cleavage Structures, Party Sys-

tems, and Voter Alignments," in *Party Systems and Voter Alignments*, ed. S. M. Lipset and Stein Rokkan (New York: Free Press, 1967).

27. Joseph L. Klesner, "Modernization, Economic Crisis, and Electoral Alignment in Mexico," *Mexican Studies* 9, no. 2 (1993): 187–233; Dale Story, "The PAN, the Private Sector, and the Future of the Mexican Opposition," in *Mexican Politics in Transition*, ed. Judith Gentleman (Boulder: Westview, 1987); Barry Ames, "Bases of Support for Mexico's Dominant Party," *American Political Science Review* 64, no. 1 (1970): 153–67.

28. Vikram Chand, "Civil Society, Institutions, and Democratization in Mexico: The Politics of the State of Chihuahua in National Perspective" (Ph.D. diss., Harvard University, 1991).

29. Soledad Loaeza, *El llamado de las urnas* (Mexico: Cal y Arena, 1989), part 3; Gabriel Almond and Sidney Verba, *The Civic Culture* (Boston: Little, Brown, 1963), 130.

30. Edgar W. Butler, James B. Pick, and Glenda Jones, "Political Change in the Mexico Borderlands," in *Sucesión Presidencial: The 1988 Mexican Presidential Election*, ed. Edgar W. Butler and Jorge Bustamante (Boulder: Westview, 1991).

31. WGBH-TV, interview with Salinas, June 11, 1988. The quotations in this paragraph were never broadcast but were given on the record.

32. See also Guadalupe Pacheco Méndez, "Los sectores del PRI en las elecciones de 1988," *Mexican Studies* 7, no. 2 (1991): 253–82.

33. For an account of the 1988 campaign and election critical of the PRI, the government, and the Salinas candidacy, see Jaime González Graf, *Las elecciones de 1988 y la crisis del sistema político* (Mexico: Instituto Mexicano de Estudios Políticos/Diana, 1989). For an even more critical account, see Xorge del Campo, *Los días que despertaron a México* (Mexico: Red Ediciones y Servicios Redacta, 1989).

34. For an explanation of the importance of the opening, see Luis Rubio F., "The Presidential Nomination Process," in *Prospects for Democracy in Mexico*, ed. George W. Grayson (New Brunswick: Transaction, 1990).

35. See Silvia Gómez Tagle, "Los partidos, las elecciones y la crisis," 255–59; and Miguel Basáñez, *La lucha por la hegemonía en México, 1968–1990* (Mexico: Siglo XXI, 1990), 259–61.

36. For a few years in the mid-1980s, therefore, dealignment from the political parties was the dominant trend. Such dealignment was short-lived. For an argument and evidence that dealignment was the persisting and predominant trend, see Klesner, "Modernization, Economic Crisis, and Electoral Alignment in Mexico." Miguel Basáñez has made a similar point by linking political independence from parties to the lack of meaningful electoral conflict. According to Basáñez, Mexicans seem to distance themselves from parties between elections but to align with parties once again on election day. The proportion of Mexicans who expressed no party preference rose dramatically between the early 1980s and the early 1990s, provided one excludes all elections. See his "Is Mexico Headed toward Its Fifth Crisis?" in *Political and Economic Liberalization in Mexico*, ed. Riordan Roett (Boulder: Lynne Rienner, 1993), 106–7. There may be, therefore, powerful long-term dealigning forces that

nonetheless do not yet express themselves on election day. Our focus is on the relationship between public opinion and elections, and therefore we continue to note the very high voter loyalty to parties from election to election.

37. Cárdenas, *Nuestra lucha apenas comienza*, 37–45.

38. WGBH-TV, interview with Clouthier, June 4, 1988. The quotations in this paragraph were never broadcast but were given on the record.

39. WGBH-TV, interview with Salinas, June 11, 1988. The quotations in this paragraph were never broadcast but were given on the record.

40. Ronald Inglehart, "The Changing Structure of Political Cleavages in Western Society," in *Electoral Change in Advanced Industrial Democracies.*

41. For a superb account of the PAN's transformation, see Loaeza, *El llamado de las urnas,* 241–72. Other fine accounts are Carlos Salomón, *Parteaguas democrático en México* (Mexico: El Día, 1989), 30–35; and Leonor Ludlow, "El 'fenómeno panista': Rasgos y ritmos (1982–1988)," in *México: Auge, crisis y ajuste.*

42. Walter J. Stone and James A. McCann, "Delegates to State Nominating Conventions: How Representative Are They?" in *Encyclopedia of American Political Parties and Elections,* ed. L. Sandy Meisel (New York: Garland, 1991); Patrick Seyd and Paul Whiteley, *Labour's Grassroots: The Politics of Party Membership* (Oxford: Clarendon, 1992).

43. For comparative evidence and analysis, see Sidney Verba, Norman H. Nie, and Jae-on Kim, *Participation and Political Equality: A Seven-Nation Comparison* (Cambridge: Cambridge University Press, 1978); and Margaret Conway, *Political Participation in the United States* (Washington, D.C.: CQ Press, 1991).

44. Norman H. Nie, G. Bingham Powell, and Kenneth Prewitt, "Social Structure and Political Participation: Developmental Relationships. Parts 1 and 2," *American Political Science Review* 63 (1969): 361–78, 808–32. They point out, however, that organizational involvement worsens political inequality even more in the United States and the United Kingdom than in Mexico.

45. See Arthur H. Miller, Martin P. Wattenberg, and Oksana Malanchuk, "Schematic Assessments of Presidential Candidates," *American Political Science Review* 80 (1986): 521–40; Donald Kinder, "Presidential Character Revisited," in *Political Cognition,* ed. Richard Lau and David Sears (Hillsdale, N.J.: Lawrence Erlbaum, 1986); and James A. McCann, "Changing Electoral Contexts and Changing Candidate Images," *American Politics Quarterly* 18 (April 1990): 124–40.

46. The functional form of our logit equations may be written as follows. If we code a preference for the PRI as 1, PAN support as 2, and Cardenista as 3, the probability of an individual voting for each of the parties is:

$$\text{Prob(Vote PAN)} = \exp(x\beta_1) / [1 + \exp(x\beta_1) + \exp(x\beta_2)]$$

$$\text{Prob(Vote CARD)} = \exp(x\beta_2) / [1 + \exp(x\beta_1) + \exp(x\beta_2)]$$

$$\text{Prob(Vote PRI)} = 1 / [1 + \exp(x\beta_1) + \exp(x\beta_2)]$$

In these equations, exp refers to the exponential function, x stands for a vector of all independent variables, and β_1 and β_2 correspond to the logit regression coefficients computed via maximum likelihood for the equations. Coding the dependent variable in this way allows the probability of voting for the PRI to serve as our base alternative. See also Gary King, *Unifying Political Methodology: The Likelihood Theory of Statistical Inference* (Cambridge: Cambridge University Press, 1989), chap. 5.

47. For an analysis of the reconstruction of the political left as a coalition, see Alberto Aziz Nassif, "La izquierda: Un continente que se rehace," in *México: Auge, crisis y ajuste.*

48. Morris P. Fiorina, *Retrospective Voting in American Elections* (New Haven: Yale University Press, 1981).

49. It is possible, of course, that economic evaluations indirectly influenced voter choice through perceptions of the PRI's long-term viability and its future governing capabilities. To illustrate, consider the following multinomial logit coefficients (with standard errors in parentheses) based on the 1988 sample. The estimates in the first two columns are taken directly from table 4-15, while those in the second two columns come from an equation that did not include the three predictors related to the PRI as an institution ("PRI getting stronger," "Economy—Other Party," and "Unrest—Other Party").

	Including the Three "Institutional" Variables		Excluding the Three "Institutional" Variables	
	PAN	CARD	PAN	CARD
Current national economy	.09 (.12)	−.07 (.11)	−.11 (.14)	−.22 (.11)*
Future national economy	−.36 (.12)**	−.08 (.11)	−.39 (.14)**	−.09 (.11)

$* = p < .05, ** = p < .01$

When the three prospective judgments related to the PRI are left out of the equations, evaluations of Mexico's economic performance in 1988 are a bit more closely connected to voting choice. This suggests that attitudes toward the economy have some bearing on presidential preferences but that such effects are largely mediated by the more powerful items, which tap into the PRI's future viability and governing capabilities.

50. Of course, it is possible that judgments regarding the PRI's viability and capabilities were inferred or rationalized on the basis of the respondent's vote choice. Given all presently existing data sets, it remains impossible to model this potential dynamic thoroughly. Nevertheless, our findings from a series of regressions estimated via instrumental variables—which are available from the authors upon request—suggest that prospective evaluations of the PRI did indeed cause voters to support or oppose the party.

51. Scott Flanagan in *Electoral Change in Advanced Industrial Democracies,* 96.

52. Cornelius and Craig, *Mexican Political System in Transition,* 70. See also Klesner, "Modernization, Economic Crisis, and Electoral Alignment in Mexico," table 3 (p. 200).

53. Wayne A. Cornelius, "The Political Sociology of Cityward Migration in Latin America: Toward Empirical Theory," in *Latin American Urban Research,* vol. 1, ed. Francine Rabinovitz and Felicity Trueblood (Beverly Hills: Sage, 1971).

54. See Martin Harrop and William L. Miller, *Elections and Voters* (London: Macmillan, 1987), chaps. 6–7; and Edward G. Carmines and James L. Stimson, "The Two Faces of Issue Voting," *American Political Science Review* 74, no. 1 (1980): 78–91. For comparison with Western Europe, see Arend Lijphart, "Political Parties: Ideologies and Programs," in *Democracy at the Polls: A Comparative Study of Competitive National Elections,* ed. David Butler, Howard Penniman, and Austin Ranney (Washington, D.C.: American Enterprise Institute, 1981); Samuel H. Barnes, "Left, Right and the Italian Voter," *Comparative Political Studies* 4 (July 1971); and Hans D. Klingemann, "Measuring Ideological Conceptualizations," in *Political Action: Mass Participation in Five Western Democracies,* ed. Samuel H. Barnes, Max Kaase, and Klaus R. Allerbeck (Beverly Hills: Sage, 1979). On the Chilean electorate, see Carlos Huneeus, *Los chilenos y la política: Cambio y continuidad en el autoritarismo* (Santiago: Editorial CERC/ICHEH, 1987), 169.

55. Scott Mainwaring, "Politicians, Parties, and Electoral Systems: Brazil in Comparative Perspective," *Comparative Politics* 24 (October 1991): 21–41; Edgardo Catterberg, *Argentina Confronts Politics: Political Culture and Public Opinion in the Argentine Transition to Democracy* (Boulder: Lynne Rienner, 1991), 63–73.

56. See, for example, Stephan Haggard and Robert R. Kaufman, "Economic Adjustment in New Democracies," in *Fragile Coalitions: The Politics of Economic Adjustment,* ed. Joan Nelson (New Brunswick: Transaction, 1989), 70.

57. Vivienne Bennett, "The Evolution of Urban Popular Movements in Mexico between 1968 and 1988," in *The Making of Social Movements in Latin America,* ed. Arturo Escobar and Sonia E. Alvarez (Boulder: Westview, 1992).

58. For this expression and conceptual analysis, see Guillermo O'Donnell and Philippe Schmitter, *Transitions from Authoritarian Rule: Tentative Conclusions about Uncertain Democracies* (Baltimore: Johns Hopkins University Press, 1986), chap. 5.

59. Adam Przeworski, *Capitalism and Social Democracy* (Cambridge: Cambridge University Press, 1985), 99–101.

60. Thoughtful scholars have differing views on this point. Juan Molinar and Jeffrey Weldon believe that a realignment may have occurred; see their "Elecciones de 1988 en México: Crisis del autoritarismo," *Revista mexicana de sociología* 52 (October–December 1990): 229. Joseph Klesner believes that a realignment did not occur but that the dealignment evident—we think only briefly—in the mid-1980s continued; see his "Modernization, Economic Crisis, and Electoral Alignment in Mexico," 210–11, 215, 221.

61. Dalton, Flanagan, and Beck, *Electoral Change in Advanced Industrial Democracies*, passim, but esp. chaps. 4–7.

62. WGBH-TV Educational Foundation, "Mexico: End of an Era, 1982–1988."

CHAPTER 5. THE PARTISAN CONSEQUENCES OF CITIZEN ATTITUDES: VOTING INTENTIONS IN THE 1991 ELECTION

1. Roderic Ai Camp, *Politics in Mexico* (New York: Oxford University Press, 1993), 149.

2. Alberto Aziz Nassif, "1991: Las elecciones de la restauración," in *Las elecciones federales de 1991*, ed. Alberto Aziz and Jacqueline Peschard (Mexico: Centro de Investigaciones Interdisciplinarias en Humanidades, Universidad Nacional Autónoma de México, 1992), 219.

3. These paragraphs draw from José Antonio Crespo, "El contexto político de las elecciones de 1991," in *Las elecciones federales de 1991*; and Miguel Basáñez, *La lucha por la hegemonía en Mexico, 1969–1990* (Mexico: Siglo XXI, 1990), 266–68.

4. Information from the Federal Elections Institute. See also Washington Office on Latin America and Academia Mexicana de Derechos Humanos, *The 1994 Mexican Election: A Question of Credibility* (Washington, D.C., August 15, 1994), 18.

5. On the final vote on the electoral reforms, in 1990, 40 of the 101 PAN deputies left the chamber rather than vote for the bill.

6. According to the judgment of impartial U.S. government officials present in these Michoacán legislative elections, the PRD probably won those elections. Instead, the PRI claimed a majority of the seats in the state assembly. Confidential interviews conducted by Domínguez, Mexico City, July 1989.

7. See also Jorge G. Castañeda, "Las perspectivas de la transición mexicana," in *Segundo informe sobre la democracia: México el 6 de Julio de 1988*, ed. Pablo González Casanova (Mexico: Siglo XXI, 1990).

8. The most systematic recording of the repression against the political left appears in *The Other Side of Mexico*, various issues, published as one response to the protest against fraud in the 1988 election.

9. Juan Reyes del Campillo, "Candidatos y campañas en la elección federal de 1991," in *Las elecciones federales de 1991*, 144–51; Wayne A. Cornelius, "Mexico's Incomplete Democratic Transition," paper presented at the Thirty-fourth Annual Convention of the International Studies Association, Acapulco, Mexico, March 23–27, 1993, 40–42; Carlos Sirvent, "Las reformas a los estatutos del PRI," *Examen*, no. 68 (January 1995): 24; *Miami Herald*, November 7, 1994.

10. Luis Donaldo Colosio, "Why the PRI Won the 1991 Elections," in *Political and Economic Liberalization in Mexico*, ed. Riordan Roett (Boulder: Lynne Rienner, 1993), 160.

11. See the excellent description and analysis in Nora Lustig, *Mexico: The Remaking of an Economy* (Washington, D.C.: Brookings Institution, 1992).

12. These paragraphs rely on Luis H. Alvarez, "Luchar, gobernar, dialogar," *Ideas*

políticas 1 (May–June 1992): 210–23. See also his remarks cited in *Ideas políticas* 1 (September–December 1992): 224–30.

13. Luis H. Alvarez, "Political and Economic Reform in Mexico: The PAN Perspective," in *Political and Economic Liberalization in Mexico*, 144–45.

14. From "Renuncia al PAN de los miembros del Foro Doctrinario y Democrático," *Ideas políticas* 1 (September–December 1992): 244–48.

15. Jesús Galindo López, "A Conversation with Cuauhtémoc Cárdenas," *Journal of International Affairs* 43 (Winter 1990): 395.

16. Ibid., 399.

17. For a convergent view, see Adolfo Gilly, "The Mexican Regime in Its Dilemma," *Journal of International Affairs* 43 (Winter 1990): 273–90.

18. Ibid., 402–3.

19. Cuauhtémoc Cárdenas, "Encuentros euroamericanos para el redescubrimiento de los pueblos de las Américas," *Ideas políticas* 1 (May–June 1992): 225.

20. Cuauhtémoc Cárdenas Solórzano, "The False Hopes of the Economic Reform," in *Political and Economic Liberalization in Mexico*, 152–53.

21. See his remarks in *Ideas políticas* 1 (September–December 1992): 233–36.

22. Carlos Monsiváis, "Voices of the Opposition from '68 to Cardenismo: Toward a Chronicle of Social Movements," *Journal of International Affairs* 43 (Winter 1990): 393.

23. "El PRD que queremos," *Ideas políticas* 1 (September–December 1992): 249–259.

24. "Síntesis del voto razonado del Partido de la Revolución Democrática sobre el Dictamen de la Ley Reglamentaria del Artículo 130 constitucional," *Ideas políticas* 1 (July–August 1992): 215.

25. Naciones Unidas, Comisión Económica para América Latina y el Caribe, *Balance preliminar de la economía de América Latina y el Caribe, 1993*, LC/G.1794 (New York, December 1993), 46.

26. Using a different database, Charles L. Davis and Kenneth M. Coleman found that NAFTA supporters were strong supporters of the Salinas administration. See their "Neoliberal Economic Policies and the Potential for Electoral Change in Mexico," *Mexican Studies* 10 (Summer 1994): 341–70.

27. This table presents the principal categories of response within our sample. In addition to these items, about 27 percent of the respondents offered no substantive reply. About 2 percent each mentioned efforts to reduce environmental pollution, fight drug traffic, or control crime and corruption. There were also many widely scattered responses ("promote Mexico's beaches") as well as many personal comments ("has stayed close to the people," "does what he promises," etc.).

28. For a thorough analysis, see Wayne A. Cornelius, Ann L. Craig, and Jonathan Fox, eds., *Transforming State-Society Relations in Mexico: The National Solidarity Strategy* (La Jolla: Center for U.S.-Mexican Studies, University of California–San Diego, 1994).

29. Jonathan Fox, *The Politics of Food in Mexico* (Ithaca: Cornell University Press, 1992), 223–26; Denise Dresser, *Neopopulist Solutions to Neoliberal Problems: Mexico's*

National Solidarity Program, Current Issues Brief no. 3 (La Jolla: Center for U.S.-Mexican Studies, University of California–San Diego, 1991); Jane Monahan, "Rebuilding Mexico's Small Towns," *Journal of Commerce,* July 27, 1993.

30. Ciro Gómez Leyva, "Solidaridad gratuíta en todas las pantallas," *Este país,* no. 7 (October 1991).

31. Jonathan Fox, "The Difficult Transition from Clientelism to Citizenship: Lessons from Mexico," *World Politics* 46 (January 1994); María Bernadette Sandoval, "PRONASOL: Mexico's National Solidarity Program," *North America Forum,* North America Forum Working Paper no. 21 (Stanford: Stanford University, 1993), esp. 45–51.

32. In the public's perception, PRONASOL and other public works programs were nearly as likely to be considered the president's "main" achievement as were the negotiations for the free trade agreement. Referring to such programs also had about as much effect in boosting Salinas's approval ratings as did his work on behalf of free trade. Below, as evidence for this assessment, we list some of the presidential approval ratings mean scores in 1991 according to the main achievement reported by the public (F = 35.1, $p < .001$):

Believe that Salinas's Main Achievement Is:	N	Presidential Rating	
		Mean Score	Standard Deviation
None	738	7.48	2.13
PRONASOL/public works	567	8.22	1.66
Negotiating free trade	327	8.33	1.52

33. Norman H. Nie, Sidney Verba, and John R. Petrocik, *The Changing American Voter* (Cambridge: Harvard University Press, 1976), chap. 4; Russell J. Dalton, Scott C. Flanagan, and Paul Allen Beck, *Electoral Change in Advanced Industrial Societies* (Princeton: Princeton University Press, 1984), chaps. 8, 9, and 10.

34. For an argument and evidence that Mexico may have been characterized by dealignment in 1991, see Joseph L. Klesner, "Modernization, Economic Crisis, and Electoral Alignment in Mexico," *Mexican Studies* 9 (Summer 1993): 187–223; and Miguel Basáñez, "Is Mexico Headed toward Its Fifth Crisis?" in *Political and Economic Liberalization in Mexico,* 106–7. (See also our discussion of these issues in chap. 4, n. 36.) Though there may be powerful long-term dealigning forces between elections, nonetheless our data show that such tendencies are not evident on election day when voters remain very loyal to the political parties from election to election, 1991 included.

35. The functional form of our logit equations may be written as follows. If we code a preference for the PRI in 1991 as 1, PAN as 2, PRD as 3, and the other small parties as 4, then the probability of an individual voting for each of the parties is:

Prob(Vote PAN) = $\exp(x\beta_1) / [1 + \exp(x\beta_1) + \exp(x\beta_2) + \exp(x\beta_3)]$

Prob(Vote CARD) = $\exp(x\beta_2) / [1 + \exp(x\beta_1) + \exp(x\beta_2) + \exp(x\beta_3)]$

Prob(Vote OTHER) = exp($x\beta_3$) / [1 + exp($x\beta_1$) + exp($x\beta_2$) + exp($x\beta_3$)]

Prob(Vote PRI) = 1 / [1 + exp($x\beta_1$) + exp($x\beta_2$) + exp($x\beta_3$)]

In these equations, exp refers to the exponential function, x stands for a vector of all independent variables, and β_1, β_2, and β_3 correspond to the logit regression coefficients computed via maximum likelihood for each equation. Coding the dependent variable in this way allows the probability of voting for the PRI to serve as our base alternative.

36. The PMS in turn traced its origins to the old Communist Party of Mexico.

37. Aziz Nassif, "1991: Las elecciones de la restauración," 219, 230.

38. Using their different database, Davis and Coleman concur with this finding for the 1991 elections. See their "Neoliberal Economic Policies and the Potential for Electoral Change in Mexico." They also show, however, that access to PRONASOL benefits was a statistically significant predictor of vote for the PRI in the 1991 national elections, especially among low-income Mexicans; access to PRONASOL benefits was also significantly likely to create a more positive evaluation of the Salinas administration's performance.

Molinar and Weldon have also examined several political dimensions of PRONASOL using aggregate statistics. See Juan Molinar Horcasitas and Jeffrey A. Weldon, "Electoral Determinants and Consequences of National Solidarity," in *Transforming State-Society Relations in Mexico.* They find that "the allocation of federal resources to the states cannot be explained solely on the basis of the explicit goals" of PRONASOL (p. 139). More PRONASOL funds were spent where Cárdenas was strong in 1988 and less where the PAN was strong. However, after controlling for socioeconomic and regional differences, PRONASOL spending had no effect on the likelihood of voting Cardenista in various elections. Nor was there a statistically significant relationship between PRONASOL spending and voting for the PAN in gubernatorial elections when these were not held to coincide with the 1991 federal elections. Molinar and Weldon did find, nonetheless, that higher PRONASOL spending reduced the support for the PAN in local elections in 1991.

In a separate analysis (not shown here), we also included dummy variables for having mentioned "PRONASOL/public works" and "negotiating free trade" in response to the open question about the Salinas administration's main achievement. These variables do not add any statistically significant capacity to explain voter intentions once we included the summary "presidential approval" rating in the equations, which in essence took care of the important Davis-Coleman and Molinar-Weldon findings. Therefore, we dropped the PRONASOL variable from table 5-9.

39. Albert O. Hirschman, "The Changing Tolerance for Income Inequality in the Course of Economic Development," *Quarterly Journal of Economics* 87 (November 1973): 543–66.

40. For convergent conclusions, see Davis and Coleman, "Neoliberal Economic Policies and the Potential for Electoral Change in Mexico"; and Klesner, "Modernization, Economic Crisis, and Electoral Alignment in Mexico."

41. For ample evidence on many countries, see Douglas A. Hibbs, Jr., *The Political Economy of Industrial Democracies* (Cambridge: Harvard University Press, 1987).

CHAPTER 6. EVALUATION OF THE ELECTORAL PROCESS: PERCEPTIONS AND PRACTICE OF ELECTORAL FRAUD

1. *Excélsior,* July 9, 1988, 23A; *Proceso,* July 18, 1988, 26-27.

2. Cuauhtémoc Cárdenas Solórzano, *Nuestra lucha apenas comienza* (Mexico: Editorial Nuestro Tiempo, 1988), 128.

3. *Proceso,* July 18, 1988, 7.

4. For an excellent account of the problem of electoral fraud on election day 1988 and during the weeks that followed, see Silvia Gómez Tagle, "La calificación de las elecciones," in *Segundo informe sobre la democracia: México el 6 de Julio de 1988,* ed. Pablo González Casanova (Mexico: Siglo XXI, 1990). See also other chapters in this fine book.

5. Anthony DePalma, "Mexico Tracking Voters by Computer," *New York Times,* June 22, 1994; Tod Robberson, "'88 Ballot Still at Issue as Mexican Election Nears," *Washington Post,* July 27, 1994.

6. On the 1988 election, see two books edited by Pablo González Casanova: *Primer informe sobre la democracia: México 1988* (Mexico: Siglo XXI, 1988), and *Segundo informe sobre la democracia: México el 6 de Julio de 1988.* On the 1991 election, see Alberto Aziz and Jacqueline Peschard, *Las elecciones federales de 1991* (Mexico: Centro de Investigaciones Interdisciplinarias en Humanidades, Universidad Nacional Autónoma de México, 1992). More generally, see Juan Molinar, *El tiempo de la legitimidad: Elecciones, autoritarismo, y democracia en México* (Mexico: Cal y Arena, 1991).

7. Our own efforts to analyze the practice of fraud in 1988 were hampered by the same Gobernación Ministry whose computer system allegedly failed on the evening of election day. Gallup had expected to conduct an exit poll on July 6, 1988. On July 1, 1988, Gallup's Mexican affiliate, the Instituto Mexicano de Opinión Pública, received a letter from Fernando Elías Calles, the Federal Elections Commission's executive secretary. On behalf of the commission Elías Calles prohibited the exit poll because it would violate Article 41 of the Mexican Constitution, which guarantees a secret vote to every Mexican citizen. Gallup's procedures for the exit poll, of course, did no such thing. Had the exit poll been carried out, it might have been easier to assess the extent of fraud.

8. One of us, Domínguez, accompanied Carlos Salinas's presidential campaign on May 27-29, 1988. This section is taken from the field notes kept at that time.

9. Miguel Basáñez, "Is Mexico Headed toward Its Fifth Crisis?" in *Political and Economic Liberalization in Mexico,* ed. Riordan Roett (Boulder: Lynne Rienner, 1993), 104-5.

10. Council of Freely Elected Heads of Government, Carter Center of Emory University, "Electoral Reform in Mexico" (Atlanta, October 16, 1993), 29.

11. Pablo González Casanova, ed., *Las elecciones en México: Evolución y perspectivas*

(Mexico: Siglo XXI, 1985); Carlos Martínez Assad, ed., *La sucesión presidencial en México, 1928–1988* (Mexico: Nueva Imagen, 1992).

12. Statistics from Guadalupe Pacheco Méndez, "Voter Abstentionism," in *Prospects for Democracy in Mexico*, ed. George W. Grayson, rev. ed. (New Brunswick: Transaction, 1990), 71.

13. Consistency in economic preferences was measured as a simple qualitative variable, where 1 = consistently for or against neoliberal policies and 0 = inconsistent economic preferences. Neoliberal policies include favoring import liberalization, welcoming foreign investment, selling state enterprises, and servicing the foreign debt. All four questions are available for 1988; only the first two were asked in 1991. Respondents who favored all of these policies and respondents who opposed all of them were coded as consistent. Respondents who favored some such policies but opposed others were coded as inconsistent.

14. That is, we set the scale value for the "voting decides how Mexico is run" item to 4 for all respondents, which would indicate that they "strongly agreed" with the statement.

15. Of course, this imputation strategy also assumes that the choice parameters for the nonvoters whom we have "artificially activated" would be the same as those for the self-identified voters, that is, the effect of all explanatory variables included in table 4-15 would be consistent for this subgroup.

16. The results are not very different if we focus on a slightly different problem, namely, the imputed vote choice for those nonvoters who probably abstained because of apathy or because they lacked the necessary socioeconomic resources. That is, these are likely nonvoters who nonetheless believed that "voting decides how things are run in this country." Among such respondents ($N = 350$) the expected vote for Cárdenas would be 32 percent; this is higher than among self-identified likely voters but not as high as those imputed in table 6-6 (37 percent). Imputed PAN vote preferences would be no different from the tally for Clouthier among self-identified likely voters: 21 percent. This suggests that the biases in turnout caused by perceptions of fraud—the focus of the analysis in table 6-6—have stronger partisan consequences than those biases that may arise from the other sources mentioned in this note.

17. In the 1991 exit poll forty-nine voting precincts in Guanajuato were included in the survey; in figures 6-1 and 6-3 three precincts were dropped because their sample size ($N < 30$) was too small. In San Luis Potosí fifty-one voting precincts were included in the survey, but two were excluded from figures 6-2 and 6-4 because of their small size.

18. For a detailed study of Salvador Nava's long political career in San Luis Potosí before the 1991 elections, see Enrique Márquez Jaramillo, "El movimiento navista y los procesos políticos de San Luis Potosí, 1958–1985," in *La vida política mexicana en la crisis*, ed. Soledad Loaeza and Rafael Segovia (Mexico: El Colegio de México, 1987).

19. Forty-six polling places in the state of Guanajuato are represented in figure 6-1. Forty-nine voting places in the state of San Luis Potosí are represented in fig-

ure 6-2. On average, the N within each polling place is 71 in Guanajuato and 70 in San Luis Potosí. In each state the size of a community is significantly related to electoral irregularities: in Guanajuato (figure 6-1), $F_{2,43} = 5.2$; in San Luis Potosí (figure 6-2), $F_{2,46} = 6.5$ ($p < .01$ in both cases).

20. V. O. Key, *Southern Politics* (New York: Alfred Knopf, 1949), chaps. 21 and 25.

21. There are forty-nine polling places represented in figure 6-4. The least squares slope in figure 6-4 is $-.54$, with a standard error of .15 ($p < .01$) and an adjusted R^2 of .21.

22. The ordinary least squares (OLS) regression coefficient after excluding these two outliers is $-.34$, with a standard error of .15 and an adjusted R^2 of .21.

23. *New York Times,* August 22, 1991, A4. See also *Examen,* no. 29 (October 1991): 32; this magazine is published by the PRI.

24. National PRI and government officials, and probably President Salinas himself, believed that candidate Ramón Aguirre did commit substantial fraud, and that he did so contrary to Salinas's explicit instructions to him. This perception of fraud, and especially Aguirre's unwillingness to follow the president's instructions, help also to account for Salinas's subsequent decision to tell Aguirre not to accept the governorship. This information comes from confidential interviews conducted in Mexico City in August 1994.

25. *Examen,* no. 30 (November 1991): 28; *New York Times,* September 2, 1991, 3.

26. Luis Donaldo Colosio, "Pronunciamiento del Consejo Político Nacional," *Examen,* no. 29 (October 1991): 12–14.

27. Francisco Gil Villegas, "Legitimidad y consenso político," *Examen,* no. 31 (December 1991): 30.

28. *Examen,* no. 30 (November 1991): 29–31.

29. Gil Villegas, "Legitimidad y consenso político," 30.

30. *Examen,* no. 31 (December 1991): 31.

31. Amador Rodríguez Lozano, "San Luis Potosí: Consenso y organización partidaria," *Examen,* no. 49 (June 1993): 27–28; *New York Times,* April 20, 1993, A5.

32. *Examen,* no. 43 (December 1992): 28; *New York Times,* October 7, 1992. For a defense of the PRI's claim of electoral victory in Michoacán and a criticism of the PRD's behavior, see Federico Berrueto Pruneda, "Las elecciones en Michoacán y Chihuahua," *Examen,* no. 39 (August 1992): 25–29.

EPILOGUE. THE 1994 PRESIDENTIAL CAMPAIGN

1. United Nations, Economic Commission for Latin America and the Caribbean, *Preliminary Overview of the Economy of Latin America and the Caribbean, 1993,* LC/G.1794 (New York, December 1993), 35, 44; ibid., *1994,* LC/G.1846 (New York, December 1994), 39, 40, 51.

2. In contrast, in the United States all campaign contributions above $100 must be disclosed publicly. No cash donations above $100 are legal, nor are foreign contributions. Individual donations cannot exceed $1,000 to any candidate during an election. Single individuals cannot contribute more than $20,000 to a national party committee during an election year.

3. Council of Freely Elected Heads of Government, Carter Center of Emory University, "Electoral Reform in Mexico" (Atlanta, October 16, 1993), 28. For the Government of Mexico's account of these reforms, see Secretaría de Gobernación, *Democracy in Mexico: The Electoral Reform* (Mexico, 1993). For the PRI's account of the reform while it was still being debated, see José Antonio González Fernández, "Reforma electoral y consolidación democrática," *Examen*, no. 49 (June 1993): 5–7; and Salvador Rocha Díaz, "El financiamiento de los partidos políticos," *Examen*, no. 49 (June 1993): 15–16. See also U.S., Department of State, *1993 Human Rights Report: Mexico* (Washington, D.C., 1994).

4. *The Elections in Yucatan, Mexico: Summary and Conclusions of Citizen Observers* (Merida, Yucatan, November 28, 1993); *Miami Herald*, December 5, 1993; *New York Times*, December 26, 1993, 6; U.S., Department of State, *1993 Human Rights Report: Mexico*, 13–14.

5. For Colosio's nomination acceptance speech, see Luis Donaldo Colosio Murieta, "Estamos preparados para competir y estamos preparados para ganar," *Examen*, no. 56 (January 1994): 14–15; *New York Times*, December 9, 1993; and *Financial Times*, December 9, 1993.

6. For background on Chiapas, see George Collier, "The Rebellion in Chiapas and the Legacy of Energy Development," *Mexican Studies* 10 (Summer 1994): 371–82.

7. For an example of the self-satisfied approach to Chiapas' numerous problems on the part of the Mexican and of the Chiapas state governments on the eve of the insurrection, see "Chiapas: Una nueva sociedad," *Examen*, no. 56 (January 1994). This is the PRI's official magazine.

8. Comisión Nacional de Derechos Humanos, "Palabras del Lic. Jorge Madrazo Cuéllar, Presidente de la Comisión Nacional de Derechos Humanos, durante el Informe especial a la opinión pública sobre las actividades y consideraciones de la Comisión Nacional de Derechos Humanos en el caso del los altos y la selva de Chiapas" (Mexico, February 22, 1994). For the Mexican Air Force's defense against the charge that it used force inappropriately, see Secretaría de Defensa, *Press Release*, no. 28 (Mexico, February 2, 1994). Both of these texts are courtesy of the Embassy of Mexico to the United States. The Air Force denied that it ever used bombs in the Chiapas military campaign, but it admitted that it engaged in "strafing to provide cover for ground troops, whenever they were surrounded or ambushed." The Mexican government–sponsored human rights commission found evidence of aerial strafing in the municipal market and in the church in the town of Ocosingo, however, as well as evidence of the aerial destruction of granaries and other facilities located quite close to other towns and villages. See also David Clark Scott, "Mexican Army Presents Its Case on Chiapas," *Christian Science Monitor*, February 2, 1994; and, especially, Americas Watch, "The New Year's Rebellion: Violations of Human Rights and Humanitarian Law during the Armed Revolt in Chiapas, Mexico," *Mexico* 6 (March 1, 1994).

9. "Versión estenográfica del comunicado dado a conocer esta tarde por el Presidente Carlos Salinas de Gortari, en el salón 'Carranza' de la residencia oficial de Los

Pinos" (Los Pinos, Mexico, January 10, 1994), courtesy of the Embassy of Mexico to the United States.

10. Testimony of Alexander F. Watson, U.S. assistant secretary of state for inter-American affairs, before the U.S. House of Representatives, Committee on Foreign Affairs, Subcommittee on Western Hemisphere Affairs, February 2, 1994.

11. For an extensive interview with Subcomandante Marcos, see Vicente Leñero, "El Subcomandante se abre," *Proceso,* no. 903 (February 21, 1994): 7–15. In that interview Marcos acknowledged that some Zapatista forces violated human rights (p. 15). For an example of Marcos's effective political prose, see his letter to the Mexico City newspaper *La Jornada* published January 21, 1994. See also hagiographic reporting in *New York Times,* February 8, 1994; *Washington Post,* February 9, 1994; and *Financial Times,* February 9, 1994.

12. "Compromisos para una paz digna en Chiapas," March 2, 1994, courtesy of the Embassy of Mexico to the United States.

13. *New York Times,* June 13, 1994; *Epoca,* August 22, 1994, 20; *Enfoque,* August 21, 1994, 12.

14. "Resolutivos aprobados por la Convención Nacional Democrática," *Perfil de la Jornada,* August 20, 1994, 1–3; *El Financiero* (international edition), August 15–21, 1994, 14; *La Jornada,* August 21, 1994, 20.

15. The commentary on and transcription of the interview in Mexico was all the more important. See, for example, Carlos Puig, "Ante el 'Wall Street Journal,' Camacho no niega que continúa compitiendo por la presidencia," *Proceso,* no. 903 (February 21, 1994): 16–17.

16. *Washington Post,* March 23, 1994; *New York Times,* March 23, 1994.

17. Tim Golden, "Mexico Now Says Assassin Acted Alone," *New York Times,* June 5, 1994; Tim Golden, "Mexican Candidate's Assassin Is Sentenced to 42 Years," ibid., November 1, 1994.

18. *New York Times,* February 26, 1995, 1, 8.

19. Andrés Oppenheimer, "In Mexico, Anatomy of a Done Deal," *Miami Herald,* April 5, 1994.

20. Ernesto Zedillo, "La reivindicación democrática del PRI," *Vuelta,* no. 213 (August 1994): 33.

21. Federico Reyes Heroles, ed., *50 preguntas a los candidatos* (México: Fondo de Cultura Económica, 1994), 98. See also Sergio Muñoz, "Ernesto Zedillo," *Los Angeles Times* (Washington edition), April 27, 1994, A12.

22. Ernesto Zedillo, "Vamos por un nuevo triunfo," *Examen,* no. 62 (July 1994): 16. This speech was delivered before the PRI's national candidates on May 29, 1994.

23. For some of his views as party president, see Ignacio Pichardo Pagaza, "Ernesto Zedillo: Un futuro con certidumbre," *Examen,* no. 63 (August 1994): 5–6.

24. *New York Times,* April 18, 1994, A2; *Christian Science Monitor,* May 10, 1994; *Financial Times,* May 16, 1994; *Enfoque,* August 21, 1994, 11; Gerardo Albarrán de Alba, "A Hank le bastaron unos cuantos minutos para que la PGR lo exonerara," *Proceso,* no. 914 (May 9, 1994): 36–38. For a typically vague statement on the pros-

pects for distancing the government from the PRI, see Abraham Zabludovsky's interview with Zedillo in *Epoca*, August 15, 1994, 18.

25. Reyes Heroles, *50 preguntas a los candidatos*, 91–92.

26. *Ernesto Zedillo: Architect of a Modern Mexico* (Mexico City: Partido Revolucionario Institucional, April 1994).

27. Cuauhtémoc Cárdenas Solórzano, *Democratic Transition and Economic Strategy: My Proposal for Mexico* (Los Angeles: World Affairs Council, April 27, 1994), 4–5.

28. Ibid., 3–4; also Cuauhtémoc Cárdenas, "Mexico's Left Is Committed to Market Reform," *Wall Street Journal*, August 12, 1994, A11.

29. Anthony DePalma, "Mexico's Battling Presidential Contenders Converge on Economic Matters," *New York Times*, August 13, 1994.

30. Bernardo Bátiz V., "¿Por qué con Cuauhtémoc?" *La Jornada*, November 10, 1993, 5.

31. See the fine survey of the views of a wide spectrum of Mexican intellectuals in *Reforma*, August 20, 1994, 10A–11A.

32. *New York Times*, July 27, 1994.

33. *Enfoque*, August 21, 1994, 5. For slightly different numbers, see *La Jornada*, August 18, 1994, 16.

34. PAN governments in the states of Baja California Norte, Chihuahua, and Guanajuato also emphasized socially conservative policies with regard to public morals. See critique by Carlos Monsiváis, "Nadie lo dijo primero: Temas y lugares comunes del 94," *Vuelta*, no. 213 (August 1994): 38.

35. Alejandro Aura, "Entrevista con Diego Fernández de Cevallos," *ViceVersa* 14 (July 1994): 15–18; *Perfil de La Jornada*, August 21, 1994, 2; Reyes Heroles, *50 preguntas a los candidatos*, 28–29 (Fernández de Cevallos), 77–79 (Zedillo), 168–70 (Cárdenas). On Cárdenas's religious agnosticism, see also Javier Solórzano, "Cuauhtémoc Cárdenas Solórzano," *ViceVersa* 14 (July 1994): 12.

36. Cited in José A. García Hernández, "Perfil de todo un carácter: Fernández de Cevallos con Dios, la familia . . . y la política," *Revista de revistas*, no. 4411 (August 15, 1994): 39.

37. All of the citations from the debate come from the transcript published in the special edition of *Novedades*, May 13, 1994, 2.

38. Domínguez was in Mexico City at the time of the debate and watched it on television. A videotape of this exchange (as recorded by the U.S. cable television company C-Span) is available at Purdue University's Public Affairs Video Archive, West Lafayette, Indiana.

39. Miguel Basáñez, "Sondeo semanal," *MORI de México/Este país*, June 22, 1994. The sample size of most of these polls was slightly larger than three hundred; interviews were conducted on the street. For a thoughtful analysis, see also *Wall Street Journal*, May 14, 1994, A12.

40. *Financial Times*, May 20, 1994.

41. *Reforma*, June 15, 1994, 1. $N = 2,200$; three-quarters of the respondents came from urban areas and one-quarter from rural areas.

42. INDEMERC Louis Harris, "Executive Summary of a Poll Taken to Assess Electoral Preference in Different Cities of the Mexican Republic (Third Sample)," April 1994. The April poll was taken between April 7 and 11. Unlike the Gallup surveys analyzed in previous chapters, this study sampled citizens in only twelve cities, with a sample size of 5,898 (unfortunately, the Gallup Organization did not replicate its 1988 and 1991 design in 1994). No other information is available on the number of respondents for the other polls discussed in this section.

43. *Enfoque*, August 21, 1994, 5; *New York Times*, July 27, 1994.

44. Text of the agreement courtesy of the Embassy of Mexico to the United States, dated January 24, 1994.

45. Instituto Federal Electoral, *Mexico's Political and Electoral Reform* (Mexico, 1994), 4; *Washington Post*, January 29, 1994, A16.

46. Texts of Colosio's speech and of the February 28 agreements courtesy of the Embassy of Mexico to the United States.

47. Sergio Aguayo Quesada, "Réquiem para otro principio," *La Jornada*, March 16, 1994.

48. These paragraphs are based on Instituto Federal Electoral, *Address of Dr. Jorge Carpizo, President of the General Council of the IFE* (Mexico, June 3, 1994).

49. For an impartial assessment of this controversial point, see Council of Freely Elected Heads of Government, *Elections in Mexico: Third Report* (Atlanta: Carter Center of Emory University, Latin American and Caribbean Program, August 1, 1994), 12.

50. Misión Técnica de la O.N.U., *Análisis del sistema electoral mexicano* (Mexico: Instituto Federal Electoral, 1994).

51. The following paragraphs are based on Alianza Cívica/Observación 94, "La elección presidencial: Entre el escepticismo y la esperanza," *Perfil de la Jornada*, August 21, 1994, 1–3. See also Sergio Aguayo, *The Recent Presidential Elections in Mexico* (Washington, D.C.: National Endowment for Democracy, October 7, 1994).

52. *El Financiero*, August 21, 1994, 23.

53. The Council of Freely Elected Heads of Government reached a similar conclusion: "Our preliminary conclusion is that the *Padrón* [electoral registry] provides a good basis for a fair election, and is a real achievement in light of the challenges faced by the Federal Electoral Registry in compiling a list in a country as large and diverse as Mexico." They added, "The coverage of the voter list (the percentage of eligible voters actually registered) is thus comparable to most Western democracies." See their *Elections in Mexico: Third Report*, 22, 35.

54. The Council of Freely Elected Heads of Government reached a similar conclusion. In the early summer of 1994, "less than ten percent of the combined Citizen Councilors and electoral officials at state and district levels have been removed." See ibid., 14.

55. *The News* (Mexico), August 18, 1994, 4.

56. The 1988 Gallup poll found that 92 percent of Mexicans reported getting news about "current events" from television (multiple answers were permitted). The 1994 Mitofsky International–BIMSA exit poll found that 59 percent of Mexicans reported

that television was the source of the "most important" information that shaped their vote (only one answer could be given).

57. As we report in appendix 2, the three Gallup polls for 1988 and 1991 on which the bulk of this study is based were financed by TELEVISA, which did not, however, interfere at all in the design, implementation, or analysis of the survey. In 1994 Domínguez was a consultant to Televisión Azteca, which provided us with the results of the 1994 exit poll. Domínguez has appeared on various Televisión Azteca programs, including the evening news program *Hechos*, the late-night program on political commentary *Nexos*, and the 1994 election night special programming.

58. For detail, see Mexican Academy of Human Rights and Civic Alliance/Observation 94, *The Media and the 1994 Federal Elections in Mexico: A Content Analysis of Television News Coverage of the Political Parties and Presidential Candidates* (Washington, D.C.: Washington Office on Latin America, May 19, 1994); Academia Mexicana de Derechos Humanos y Alianza Cívica/Observación 94, *Las elecciones federales en México según los noticieros "24 Horas" de TELEVISA y "Hechos" de Televisión Azteca, 30 de Mayo a 30 de Junio de 1994* (Mexico, 1994); and Academia Mexicana de Derechos Humanos y Alianza Cívica/Observación 94, *Las elecciones federales en México según los noticieros "24 Horas" de TELEVISA, "Hechos" de Azteca, y "Enlace" de Canal 11* (Mexico, July 1994).

59. *New York Times*, March 21, 1994.

60. Gerardo Albarrán de Alba, "Análisis con cifras de las auditorías: El padrón, inflado, inconsistente, tramposo," *Proceso*, no. 924 (July 18, 1994): 18–25.

61. See discussion in Washington Office on Latin America and Academia Mexicana de Derechos Humanos, *The 1994 Mexican Election: A Question of Credibility* (Washington, D.C., August 15, 1994). See also *Epoca*, July 18, 1994, 12.

62. Secretaría de Gobernación, Comunicación Social, *Información de prensa*, no. 153/94 (Mexico, July 18, 1994). See also Demetrio Sodi de la Tijera's well-reasoned argument about the importance of taking the PRD's complaints seriously, in "Un último jalón," *La Jornada*, July 22, 1994, 12.

63. Luis Javier Garrido, "El fraude perfecto," *La Jornada*, July 22, 1994, 17.

64. For convergent conclusions, see Council of Freely Elected Heads of Government, *The August 21, 1994 Mexican National Elections: Fourth Report* (Atlanta: Carter Center of Emory University, Latin American and Caribbean Program, January 1995); and Washington Office on Latin America, *Peace and Democratization in Mexico: Challenges Facing the Zedillo Government* (Washington, D.C., January 12, 1995). For thoughtful assessments of the state of Mexican democracy in 1994, see Wayne A. Cornelius, "Mexico's Delayed Democratization," *Foreign Policy* 95 (Summer 1994): 53–71; and Jorge Alcocer V., *El contexto de la elección mexicana del 21 de Agosto* (Mexico: Centro de Estudios para un Proyecto Nacional, June 1994).

65. Belden and Russonello, *Press Release: Results of a National Poll of Mexican Voters* (Washington, D.C., August 11, 1994), tables 7, 15, 16. This survey among a probability sample of the Mexican electorate was conducted nationwide in households in urban and rural Mexico, July 23 through August 1, 1994. It was designed and carried out by Belden and Russonello and Ciencia Aplicada for a group of U.S. and Euro-

pean banks and financial institutions. $N = 1,526$, with a statistical margin of error of plus or minus 2.5 percent at the 95 percent level of confidence.

66. We have used the official results reported to us by the Embassy of Mexico to the United States. See also Council of Freely Elected Heads of Government, *The August 21, 1994 Mexican National Elections: Fourth Report,* 18–19.

67. The electoral court overturned the preliminary results of two single-member district seats, from Michoacán and Jalisco, that had gone to the PRI in the preliminary count; nonetheless, this made the PRI eligible to pick up two more seats allocated through proportional representation. The final count remained unchanged. *New York Times,* September 27, 1994.

68. Federico Berrueto, "Entre el PRI y el Presidente: Las relaciones del partido mayoritario y el gobernante," *Examen,* no. 66 (November 1994): 8–11.

69. Instituto Federal Electoral, Comunicación Social, *Comunicado de prensa,* no. 375 (Mexico, August 29, 1994).

70. *Excélsior,* August 25, 1994, 39A.

71. Alianza Cívica/Observación 94, "La calidad de la jornada electoral del 21 de agosto de 1994," *Perfil de La Jornada,* September 20, 1994. We are grateful to Jonathan Fox for making this document available to us.

72. Council of Freely Elected Heads of Government, *The August 21, 1994 Mexican National Elections: Fourth Report,* 12.

73. National Democratic Institute for International Affairs and International Republican Institute, *Preliminary Statement by the IRI/NDI International Delegation to the August 21 Mexican Elections* (Washington, D.C., August 23, 1994), 4–5.

74. Andrés Oppenheimer, "Most Call Election Basically Fair; Zedillo Has Big Lead," *Miami Herald,* August 24, 1994, 3A.

75. *La Jornada,* August 22, 1994, 13.

76. *Reforma,* August 25, 1994, 1A, 4A.

77. *La Jornada,* August 23, 1994, 10; ibid., August 24, 1994, 6.

78. Carlos Monsiváis, "Aproximaciones y reintegros: Los cierres de campaña," *El Financiero,* August 21, 1994, 38.

79. *La Jornada,* August 23, 1994, 18; *Reforma,* August 22, 1994, 3A, 11A; ibid., August 23, 1994, 8A.

80. *El Financiero,* August 22, 1994, 21; ibid., August 23, 1994, 45; Secretaría de Gobernación, Comunicación Social, *Comunicado de prensa,* no. 43/95 (Mexico, February 14, 1995), 2.

81. *Reforma,* September 17, 1994, 6A.

82. *New York Times,* September 27, 1994.

83. Council of Freely Elected Heads of Government, *The August 21, 1994 Mexican National Elections: Fourth Report,* 18; *Lagniappe Letter,* November 11, 1994, 6.

84. See, among others, Jorge Castañeda (professor at the National University, UNAM, who has advised Cárdenas on international affairs), "Los vicios del proceso," *El nuevo herald,* August 31, 1994, 9A; Lorenzo Meyer (professor at El Colegio de México), "Y al despertar, el dinosaurio seguía allí," *Reforma,* August 25, 1994, 7A; Federico Reyes Heroles (publisher of *Este país*), "Acatar," *Reforma,* August 23, 1994,

10A; Sergio Aguayo (professor at El Colegio de México and coordinator of the Civic Alliance), "Un balance ciudadano de la elección," *La Jornada*, August 24, 1994, 12; Adolfo Aguilar Zinser (manager of Cárdenas's campaign), "Dividir y vencer," *Reforma*, August 26, 1994, 9A; and Miguel Angel Granados Chapa (journalist and citizen member of the IFE General Council who voted for Cárdenas in 1988 and 1994), "Ganar y perder," *Reforma*, August 26, 1994, 7A. See also remarks by PAN candidate Diego Fernández de Cevallos, *La Jornada*, August 22, 1994, 13. For the views of other responsible authors who agree with Cárdenas that massive fraud was committed, see Adolfo Gilly, "Ahora es tiempo, yerbabuena," *La Jornada*, August 20, 1994, 12; and Luis Javier Garrido, "El fraude imperfecto," *La Jornada*, August 26, 1994, 14.

85. Guadalupe Loaeza, "¿Será?" *Reforma*, August 23, 1994, 11A.

86. *Reforma*, August 26, 1994, 1.

87. Felipe Chao, "El posible resultado," *Este país*, no. 41 (August 1994): 42; Raúl Rodríguez Pineda, "Provoca confusión la encuestitis electoral," *Epoca*, July 18, 1994, 16–17; David Clark Scott, "Wide Variations in Mexican Polls Add to Doubts about Election," *Christian Science Monitor*, May 18, 1994; *Wall Street Journal*, July 18, 1994; *La Jornada*, August 18, 1994, 9; *El Financiero* (international edition), August 15–21, 1994, 3; Horacio Bernal and Gustavo Cano Hernández, "Encuestas electorales: Tendencias confirmadas," *Examen*, no. 94 (September 1994): 32–34; and Luis Medina Peña, "El proceso electoral a través de las encuestas," *Examen*, no. 64 (September 1994): 35–36.

88. For technical details, see n. 65.

89. Belden and Russonello, *Press Release: Results of a National Poll of Mexican Voters* (1994), table 2.

90. Ibid., tables 5, 8, 14, and 19.

91. Ibid., table 7.

92. Unfortunately, none of the surveys conducted in 1994 replicated the key questions on which our analysis rested for the 1988 and 1991 elections. We cannot be certain, therefore, whether retrospective voting would turn out to be markedly more significant in 1994, holding other factors constant.

93. Julio Madrazo and Diana Owen, "¿Qué nos motivó, el pasado o el futuro?" *Examen*, no. 67 (December 1994): 31–33.

94. WGBH-TV Educational Foundation, "Mexico: End of An Era, 1982–1988," first broadcast on November 30, 1988, U.S. Public Broadcasting System.

95. Ernesto Zedillo Ponce de León, "Inaugural Address before Congress," December 1, 1994, 10. Courtesy of the Embassy of Mexico to the United States.

96. "Compromisos para un Acuerdo Político Nacional" (Mexico, January 17, 1995). Courtesy of the Embassy of Mexico to the United States.

APPENDIX 2. THE PUBLIC-OPINION SURVEYS

1. Jean Converse, *Survey Research in the United States* (Berkeley: University of California Press, 1987), 383.

2. Gabriel Almond and Sidney Verba, *The Civic Culture: Political Attitudes and Democracy in Five Nations* (Princeton: Princeton University Press, 1963). These data

were made available to us by the Inter-University Consortium for Political and Social Research. Neither the collector of the original data nor the consortium bears any responsibility for the analyses or interpretations presented here. We are grateful to Almond and Verba and to the consortium for the use of these data.

3. See ibid., 514–16, for these and additional details. The *Civic Culture* survey in Mexico had a number of limitations. About two-thirds of the respondents were women. Moreover, the survey focused on respondents over the age of twenty-one in towns and cities of over ten thousand people. Because rural dwellers constituted 63 percent of the population in the 1960 census, however, this is an important limitation. Ann Craig and Wayne Cornelius have noted also that a significant portion of the urban low-income population was also probably excluded from the sample because of methodological difficulties. See their "Political Culture in Mexico: Continuities and Revisionist Interpretations," in *The Civic Culture Revisited*, ed. Gabriel Almond and Sidney Verba (Boston: Little, Brown, 1980), 328. In spite of its shortcomings, this survey was the first nationwide survey conducted in Mexico that met prevailing international professional standards for public-opinion polling. It captures a significant era in Mexican politics, when the PRI reigned supreme.

4. The occupational categories are government official, business leader, political leader, farm producer or cattle rancher, industrialist, merchant, business executive in service sector, professional or expert technician, white-collar worker, government worker, housewife, student, blue-collar worker, peasant, no regular employment. In order to be able to perform subanalyses on each of these categories, Basáñez had to draw a very large sample.

5. Miguel Basáñez, *El pulso de los sexenios: 20 años de crisis en México* (Mexico: Siglo XXI, 1990), 360–61. The data were made available by the Roper Center for Public Opinion Research (University of Connecticut, Storrs). Neither Dr. Basáñez nor the Roper Center bears any responsibility for the analyses or interpretations presented here. We are grateful to Dr. Basáñez and to the Roper Center for making the data available to us.

6. These data were made available by the Inter-University Consortium for Political and Social Research (ICPSR 8666) (University of Michigan, Ann Arbor). The data for the *New York Times* Mexico survey, 1986, were originally collected by the *New York Times*. Neither the collector of the original data nor the consortium bears any responsibility for the analyses or interpretations presented here. An overview of the survey appeared in the *New York Times* on November 14 and 15, 1986; the journalists were concerned principally with the perceptions Mexicans had of the United States.

7. We are grateful to Richard W. Burkholder, vice president, the Gallup Organization, and to Ian M. Reider, president, IMOP/Gallup México, for allowing us to use the poll's data for this research. The first poll was financed by ECO, Inc., a Los Angeles television station that is a subsidiary of Mexico's large privately owned network, TELEVISA. The 1991 polls were financed by TELEVISA directly.

8. Originally, three thousand interviews were planned. Gallup México concluded, however, that forty of those interviews were unreliable; they were discarded.

9. Warren Mitofsky, "Technical Statement of Methodology," August 17, 1994, and personal communication from Mitofsky International, Inc., for which we are thankful. We are grateful to Mary Klette, director for elections and polling of NBC News, and to Mexico's Televisión Azteca, for making the results of this poll available to us.

10. "El sondeo de la Gallup intenta preparar el fraude electoral: Cuauhtémoc Cárdenas" and "Manipulación total en las encuestas de los resultados de comicios: Clouthier," both in *El Día*, June 22, 1988, 6.

11. See, for example, Jorge Castañeda, "Las encuestas, un juego de maquillaje de verdades, para adecuarlas al gusto del cliente," *Proceso*, no. 608 (June 27, 1988, 10–11); and Homero Campa, "Las encuestas favorecen a . . . todos los candidatos," ibid., 10–15.

12. The best description, critique, and comparison of various polls appeared in *Mexico Service*, July 7, 1988, 12–27.

13. This point was best articulated by Jorge Castañeda, a Cárdenas supporter, whom we cited earlier as a critic of the Gallup poll. *Washington Post*, July 10, 1988, A27.

14. For a similar argument, see Miguel Basáñez, "Encuestas de opinión en México," in *México: Auge, crisis, y ajuste*, ed. Carlos Bazdresch, Nisso Bucay, Soledad Loaeza, and Nora Lustig (Mexico: Fondo de Cultura Económica, 1992), 185–88.

15. See Gallup-TELEVISA, "Encuesta electoral nacional: Manual de procedimientos," August 18, 1991, 2.

16. This and the next several paragraphs on Basáñez polling experiments are based on the same source: MORI de México / *Este país, Sondeo semanal*, June 1, 1994. See also Miguel Basáñez, "Las encuestas experimentales y la elección presidencial," *Este país*, no. 40 (July 1994): 14–15.

17. David Clark Scott, "Wide Variations in Mexican Polls Add to Doubts about Election," *Christian Science Monitor*, May 18, 1994. See also Tod Robberson, "Mexican Voters Who Don't Tell the Truth Make Election Tough to Call," *Washington Post*, July 21, 1994; Anthony DePalma, "Mexicans Bring Fear to the Ballot Box," *New York Times*, June 12, 1994, section 4, p. 3; and Ulises Beltrán, "Mexican Polls Reliable If Properly Understood," *Wall Street Journal*, July 18, 1994.

18. Belden and Russonello, *Survey of Electoral Preference in Mexico, 1994: Executive Summary* (Washington, D.C., August 11, 1994), 5–6.

19. Otherwise, on-street interviews may undersample housewives and the elderly.

20. For a thoughtful discussion of many of these issues, see Nancy Belden, *Considerations of the Mexican Electoral Polls of 1994: Political and Methodological Concerns* (Washington, D.C.: Belden and Russonello, December 1994).

21. The tapes remain at WGBH-TV, Western Ave., Boston, Mass., 02134.

INDEX